THE
EXCELLENT
EXPERIENCE

THE EXCELLENT EXPERIENCE

A BLUEPRINT FOR ORGANIZATIONAL, TEAM, AND INDIVIDUAL SUCCESS

Foreword by
Stephen M. R. Covey
The New York Times and #1 *Wall Street Journal*
bestselling author of *The Speed of Trust* and
coauthor of *Smart Trust*

C. David Crouch

iUniverse LLC
Bloomington

THE EXCELLENT EXPERIENCE
A Blueprint for Organizational, Team, and Individual Success

Copyright © 2013 C. DAVID CROUCH.

All rights reserved. No part of this book may be used or reproduced by any means, graphic, electronic, or mechanical, including photocopying, recording, taping or by any information storage retrieval system without the written permission of the publisher except in the case of brief quotations embodied in critical articles and reviews.

iUniverse books may be ordered through booksellers or by contacting:

*iUniverse LLC
1663 Liberty Drive
Bloomington, IN 47403
www.iuniverse.com
1-800-Authors (1-800-288-4677)*

Because of the dynamic nature of the Internet, any web addresses or links contained in this book may have changed since publication and may no longer be valid. The views expressed in this work are solely those of the author and do not necessarily reflect the views of the publisher, and the publisher hereby disclaims any responsibility for them.

*Any people depicted in stock imagery provided by Thinkstock are models, and such images are being used for illustrative purposes only.
Certain stock imagery © Thinkstock.*

ISBN: 978-1-4917-0932-0 (sc)
ISBN: 978-1-4917-0933-7 (hc)
ISBN: 978-1-4917-0934-4 (e)

Library of Congress Control Number: 2013917958

Printed in the United States of America.

iUniverse rev. date: 11/07/2013

TABLE OF CONTENTS

Foreword 9
Acknowledgments 11
Introduction 15

Section 1
Design a Blueprint
Chapter 1: Excellentology 21
Chapter 2: Design a Blueprint 28

Section 2
Lay a Solid Foundation
Chapter 3: Build on Rock! 49
Chapter 4: The Mission 64
Chapter 5: The Vision 82
Chapter 6: The Principles 97
Chapter 7: The Standards 111

Section 3
Erect the Structure
Chapter 8: The Quality Pillar 137
Chapter 9: The Service Pillar... 153
Chapter 10: The People Pillar 175
Chapter 11: The Growth Pillar 194
Chapter 12: The Finance Pillar 212

Section 4
Assemble the Roof
Chapter 13: The Organization Scorecard 241
Chapter 14: The Team Scorecard 248
Chapter 15: The Individual Scorecard 269

Section 5
Top It Out!
Chapter 16: The Blueprint for Excellence! 312
Chapter 17: Leading Excellence 336
Chapter 18: America the Excellent! 378

Appendices 433
Bibliography 465
Index 473

In memory of

Clarence Crouch Jr.,
my father and my hero,
a man of honor and excellence,

and

Mr. Ed Grady,
my high school drama coach
and leader of my first transcendent
excellent experience

FOREWORD

Stephen M. R. Covey

Aristotle once observed, "We are what we repeatedly do. Excellence, then, is not an act, but a habit." How true this is! Not only is excellence a habit, it is also a discipline. Because it is a discipline, it can be learned. And nobody understands the *science of excellence*—and how to teach it—better than David Crouch.

David is a friend whose character and work I sincerely admire, and I am grateful for this opportunity to share my thoughts and feelings about his remarkable book. As I read it, I was thrilled to discover that his approach to the pursuit of excellence rang resonant chords of truth for me time and time again.

First and foremost, I immediately recognized David's focus on self-evident, universal principles. By definition, principles withstand the test of time. They are like a lighthouse that provides solid, consistent, accurate direction in the rough seas of today's tumultuous environment or tomorrow's next new crisis. Unlike so many of the approaches today that espouse "fly-by-your-pants" techniques that promise to magically morph your business, your family, or even you into the ideal you desire, David's approach sticks with the tried and tested. He shows that the real search for excellence is a work in progress—and that there are no short-lived bullets to success, no quick-fix agendas, and no magic strategies to achievement.

I was impressed by the simple yet powerful metaphor that David employs as he frames his book's message; that is, that we build excellence in our lives in the same way we build a quality home—from the foundation up. As with any structure, a blueprint is vital to success. Only with a clear blueprint can we see the way ahead or begin with the end in mind. No organization, church, family, or individual can achieve true excellence without it. In addition, a strong framework is essential to the integrity of the whole. David points to the value of mission, vision, principles, and standards in creating a foundation for excellence. Building on this foundation, he adds five pillars—quality, service, people, growth, and finance—that define the critical elements of excellence in any organization, whether in business or the social sector. He shows how each of these pillars is vital to the completion and success of the whole and how true excellence requires vigilant attention to the details—the little things that enable the big things to work effectively together.

For me, the book really took off in its application chapters because they show the "guts" of David's model and how it works in differing environments and circumstances. He gives superb examples from business, sports, the Christian Church, and even the federal government to illustrate the effectiveness of his approach. He discusses key components, such as building relationships of trust, learning how to effectively communicate, creating an individual mission, forming a shared vision, and promoting effective leadership on every level. Yet as he points out, it all comes back to one thing: it is adherence to the standards and principles of the model that makes excellence achievable.

Again, back to Aristotle, excellence is not an act but a habit. In his warm and eloquent style, David shows us how to make excellence a habit in our lives and organizations. He gives us the framework, language, and process so that we not only have knowledge and understanding of the standards required for excellence—we also have the tools to actually achieve it. In sharing an abundance of insightful anecdotes, thoughtful quotes, and practical steps to follow, David takes us by the hand and warmly invites us to undertake the quest for excellence. After reading the book, and knowing the genuine goodness of its author, I am personally excited by the promise—and the achievability of the quest.

Stephen M. R. Covey
The New York Times and #1 *Wall Street Journal* bestselling author of *The Speed of Trust* and coauthor of *Smart Trust*

ACKNOWLEDGMENTS

Writing a book has been a goal on my bucket list since I was twenty years old. I started writing in the summer of 2007 while pursuing my master's degree. Dedicating a lot of time to writing was difficult while working full time. I wrote early in the mornings before going to work, on Saturdays, and during holidays. When I volunteered to be downsized out of my job in October of 2010, I found myself with plenty of time to write and made great progress over the next four months. It wasn't long before I landed another job, and making time to write became challenging again. As fate would have it, I was downsized out from that company too, and I found myself once again with plenty of time to write. It was during this time, in the fall of 2011, that I was able to complete the initial manuscript.

This project has been one of the most fulfilling experiences of my life, and I have many people to thank for their support and encouragement.

My wife, Debbie, who has stuck by me through it all—both downsizings, two periods of unemployment, and long days, weeks, and months enduring my extreme focus, which I'm sure felt at many times like I was ignoring her. She always made sure the details of food and shelter were taken care of in addition to her own job so I could focus on my writing. She remained positive and supportive through it all. She is my strength, my partner, my lover, and my friend. Thank you so much, sweetheart. You complete me!

My parents, Clarence and Jane Crouch, have always stood behind me and encouraged me through even the stupid things. They have provided me with an example of excellence in parenting and family life for which I am forever grateful. Dad transitioned to his eternal home in May of 2012 and left a legacy of excellence for us all.

My kids, Isaac, Samuel, and Callie, who have taught me how to love and who allowed me to practice many of the excellence concepts in the book as a parent.

My brother, Ron, who talked with me nearly every day during the project and allowed me to bounce ideas off him to gain understanding.

My sister, Beverly Lyons, who celebrated the milestones with me and shared her own authoring experiences to help me grow.

My brother-in-law, Dr. David Lyons, who challenged my thinking and encouraged me to consider all sides of the issue. Dr. Dave, a published author himself, also provided valuable insight and balance for chapter 18.

My colleagues Kathy Laing, Jackie Lawrence, and Carrie Mull, who helped shape my strategies and thought processes as their team leader. They invested time in many conversations with me about excellence as I searched for its truth.

My best friend since the seventh grade, Rick McGimsey, who continually encouraged me and supported me through all the good times and the bad. Rick has demonstrated excellence in friendship to me for more than forty years.

Stephen M. R. Covey coached me on the writing process and so graciously wrote the foreword. Zig Ziglar planted the seed in my heart to write at an early age (circa 1980).

All those I consider fellow excellentologists from whom I have learned so much—Ken Blanchard, Marcus Buckingham, Oswald Chambers, Jim Collins, Daryl Conner, Stephen R. Covey, Patrick Lencioni, Napoleon Hill, John Maxwell, Joyce Meyer, and Rick Warren.

Most importantly, I want to acknowledge the role of God in the project and in my life. Many of my understandings have come from the book of knowledge itself, and I've learned of its truth through the application of its principles. I thank God every day for saving me, forgiving me, giving me strength to overcome, and providing me with a source of eternal hope, joy, and fulfillment.

Countless other friends and colleagues have contributed to my understanding as well. If there's one thing I've learned for sure about excellence, it's that it doesn't occur in a vacuum—it always involves others. Thank you to all those who have impacted my quest for excellence and have helped shape me into a dedicated *excellentologist*.

C. David Crouch

INTRODUCTION

Everyone can be excellent at something! Each of us has been placed on this planet for a specific purpose. The secret to a fulfilling life lies in our discovery of that purpose and our passionate pursuit of it. Writing this book has enabled me to clarify my own purpose in life—*to encourage excellence in others*. My sincere hope is that excellence will be encouraged in you as you read and study this material and that, if you haven't already, you'll gain greater clarity about your own passion and purpose in life.

The past thirty years of study has taught me that building a life of excellence is a lot like building a house. It requires a blueprint to guide you along the way, a strong foundation upon which to build, a structure that will provide balance and strength, and a sturdy roof to keep it aligned and hold it together. My experience has also taught me that most of us don't invest the time it takes to consider such things of life. Many of us aren't even aware that we should. We plan our projects. We plan our vacations. We plan our parties. We passionately plan our weddings. We may even plan every detail for tomorrow. But too many of us don't plan for excellence. We should. A life that strives for excellence becomes a life that matters.

I don't presume to know everything there is to know about excellence. I am a perpetual student of the topic. I consider myself an *excellentologist*, one who studies and strives to practice excellence. What I do know is that when we pursue excellence with passion, life gets better. Others become inspired by our pursuit; and we do too. We become energized by a positive strength that propels us forward, in spite of the obstacles, in spite of the challenges, and in spite of the failures, all of which will inevitably come. We learn that excellence is a journey, not a destination. When we encounter failures and setbacks, we learn to rejoice in them because they bring us new insight into the quest. Imagine reaching a point in your own life's journey in which you're able to rejoice in your failures. The mountaintops are for celebration and visioning, but the valleys are where we learn and grow. Since life is full of both, we might as well learn to enjoy them both.

As we journey through this discussion together, we'll take the elements of my model one at a time, discuss the concept, and then apply it to five environments—an organization, a team, a church, a family, and an individual. My hope is that when you see how this model can be applied across five diverse environments, you'll be convinced that you can apply it in your life as well.

A word about the church, family, and individual environments: I've used many examples from my own experiences to illustrate key points in each chapter. Consequently, you'll readily identify my perspective on life, religion, and other social issues. My hope is that you will view my perspective not as an attempt to persuade you to it, but simply as an attempt to help you better understand the concepts of excellence. When I mention the church, I'll be using examples from a Christian church, because that's where I've applied the model. These concepts can be applied in any church environment—just as they can in the Christian church.

Similarly, in chapter 18 where I apply the model to America, some of my political bias may come through in spite of my sincere attempt to avoid it. Again, my hope is that you will not view those comments as an attempt to persuade you to my political point of view; rather, you will view them as my attempt to demonstrate how the model can be applied to a country as well. Chapter 18 was one of my most enjoyable chapters to write, and I hope you enjoy its journey as much as I did.

I encourage you to view this book as a field manual to help you experience excellence in whatever pursuits you undertake. As you read each chapter, consider the things you're trying to accomplish now and compare them to the suggestions in the book. Make notes as things come to mind that make sense to you. Remember that excellence is a journey, not a destination. Our conversations throughout this book are intended to help move you in the right direction on your journey toward excellence.

My prayer is that, after reading and studying this book, you'll be closer to your life's pursuits than you are now; that you'll be reminded that excellence is a noble and worthy pursuit, one that brings joy and fulfillment to everyone it touches; and that it will change your life, and all those around you, for the better if you let it.

God bless you in your quest. May the wind be at your back. Enjoy the journey!

C. David Crouch

SECTION 1

Design a Blueprint

CHAPTER 1

Excellentology

> Far better it is to dare mighty things to win glorious triumphs even though checkered with failure than to take rank with those poor souls who neither suffer much nor accomplish much because they live in the gray twilight that knows neither victory nor defeat.
> —Theodore Roosevelt

> Life is either a daring adventure, or nothing!
> —Helen Keller

We all want to be a part of something special—to feel swept away in an adventure that transcends us—to feel like we matter to the world around us in some significant way.

It was the spring of 1975, and I had been selected to play the part of Jesus in our high school production of the Broadway musical *Godspell*. Our director, Mr. Grady, had a true love for drama and an exceptional ability to get kids to perform at their best. He worked us hard every day after school and built a passion in us to be the best we could be. He required persistent discipline from us as we learned our lines, worked on the dance steps, and stumbled through the scenes. He had to start from scratch with many of us, including me. After all, we were just high school kids, not seasoned actors.

Perhaps the most challenging and frustrating skill I had to learn was tap dancing. There was a scene in the play where Judas and Jesus performed a vaudeville tap dance. I've never been much of a dancer. I can slow dance, I can half-step disco, and I can shag. But I can't tap dance. Mr. Grady had a heck of a time getting me to learn to tap. He brought in the school's best dancer, Sherri, who worked with me for weeks after school, trying to help me learn to tap dance. Finally, almost ready to give up on me, she figured out how to simplify it in a way that looked like tap, but was much easier for me to do. I realized that when you're on a journey to excellence, sometimes you have to figure out ways to compensate for your weaknesses. Since no one is good at everything, learning what you're good at and what you're not is critical. I also learned that any personal quest for excellence is not really so personal at all. It always involves others. I needed Sherri's help to do that dance.

The unique talents and capabilities of the kids in the play, shaped by Mr. Grady's talented and unique style of leadership and encouragement, combined to create one of those remarkable adventures that transcended each of us. As it was happening, I felt I was a part of something really special. Following the opening night of the play, every performance was sold out with standing-room-only crowds. The public responded so positively that we extended its run a full week. Mr. Grady, in his infinite wisdom, had us stop right there, believing you should always leave your audience wanting more.

Godspell was an experience of excellence in my early life. It made a difference in the lives of those it touched, both in the production itself and in the audiences for whom we played. It left a mark on my heart and in my life that I'll never forget. To this day, it's still one of the most positive memorable experiences I've had in my fifty-plus years. Even as I write about it now, I feel warmth in my heart and a sense of accomplishment at having made a difference in some small way in the lives of others. Each of us gave our best, and it was undoubtedly an excellent experience. Excellence makes a difference in the lives of others.

Principles of excellentology revealed in the *Godspell* story

1. *Excellence requires hard work, persistence, and discipline.*
   - We practiced every day for three months.
2. *Excellence demands that you learn how to compensate for your own weaknesses.*
   - We had to find a way to make the dance look like tap.
3. *Excellence always involves others.*
   - It was a team approach that came together with synergy.
4. *Excellence requires effective leadership.*
   - Mr. Grady inspired us to give our best.
5. *Excellence produces distinguishable results.*
   - We played to sellout crowds every night and ended with them wanting more.
6. *Excellence makes a difference in the lives of others.*
   - Cast members and people in the audience alike were deeply impacted.
7. *Excellence creates a positive memorable experience for everyone involved.*
   - All of us involved remember the experience as a powerful one in our lives.
8. *Excellence provides a tremendous sense of accomplishment.*
   - We felt like we had done something really special and great.

Since that spring of 1975, I've had many other excellent experiences. Those are the times of my life I remember most. They stand out. They made a difference to me—and others—and gave me a tremendous, wonderful sense of accomplishment about doing something that really mattered.

Building Excellence

Throughout my career, I've invested countless hours with many people, teams, and organizations in dozens of different industries, researching the concepts of excellence and practicing how to build it. I've also pursued the keys of excellence as they apply to my marriage, family, and life. You could say I've become an *excellentologist*, one who studies excellence and then puts it into practice.

As my journey progressed, I wondered if there was a framework for excellence that, if followed, would yield the greatest opportunity for success. Whether it's a for-profit business, a charity, a marriage, a family, a civic club, a sports team, a church group, or any other organization where two or more people come together to accomplish something really special, is there a blueprint we can apply that really works?

- How can we create an environment that leads to excellence?
- What needs to happen to enable every individual in an organization or team to perform at his or her best?
- Are there principles we can follow that will produce excellence every time?
- Is there a framework for excellence that will guide us in the right direction and give us the best opportunity for success in everything we set out to do?
- Is it possible to create a blueprint for excellence that, when applied, will generate the best possible outcome?
- Can anyone learn how to apply this blueprint to his or her own life, work, or team?

These are not necessarily new questions, but in my research, I failed to find a specific blueprint to guide the way. However, I did find numerous resources on the subject that explored the questions of excellence from many different angles. I'll introduce you to most of them as we journey through this book together.

As I searched for excellence in theory, I also searched for it in practice. I studied some of the great organizations that exist today, including Disney, Ritz-Carlton, Southwest Airlines, and Toyota. I searched for examples of excellence in their cultures, respecting what they had accomplished and learning from their experiences.

The answers to these questions are the focus of this book. My objective is to provide you with a framework for building excellence that you can apply to any aspect of your life. I'll show you how these timeless principles and tested practices will work in any environment. It's my sincere hope that applying this framework for excellence in your life will do as much for you as it has done for me. I believe it will.

Building a House of Excellence

In my recent work and personal life, I've had several transcending experiences where many elements have come together to create an outcome of excellence. Many of the results I've experienced are nothing short of remarkable. Working with others, we have built our *house of excellence.* You can too!

The blueprint is not just a way to get great results in business, personal, or group endeavors. It's much more than that. I've approached this work from the standpoint of creating a blueprint that truly drives excellence—not "good enough," mediocrity, or minimum standards. This work is only intended for those who earnestly strive for an experience of excellence in their lives. If you want to improve the results you're getting in any area of your life—at work, home, school, church, or in the community—then read on.

Albert Einstein said, "Insanity is doing the same thing you've always done but expecting a different result." If you want to change your results, you must change how you got those results. It's as simple as that.

Furthermore, this blueprint will help you create an experience of excellence you will always remember and cherish. Your effort will make a difference in your life and in the lives of others. You'll get excellent results, you'll produce higher-quality products and services, you'll deliver better service to your customers and guests, you'll create positive, memorable experiences for everyone involved, you'll grow, and you'll earn financial rewards.

You'll also realize that life is more than results, profits, or personal gain. You will discover that it's an opportunity to matter in the world around you, to have a lasting impact on those you serve, and to leave a legacy of hope and encouragement for others to follow. Excellence creates a life of significance—a life that matters. It's a noble and worthy pursuit. I hope you'll make the commitment right now to begin anew in your pursuit of excellence in everything you do, whether personal or professional. If you do, I guarantee that you, and all those around you, will never be the same again. And if you so desire, you too can become an *excellentologist*.

Welcome to your journey toward excellence. Welcome to the science of *excellentology*.

Summary of Chapter 1: Excellentology

1. Excellentology is the study and practice of excellence.
2. Excellence requires hard work, persistent discipline, a plan, and the commitment to see it through.
3. There is a blueprint for creating and sustaining excellence that anyone can learn and apply.
4. Applying the blueprint will create a life of purpose, meaning, and worth for you and all those around you.

Take Action

1. Analyze your current situation.
    - Are you satisfied with the results you're getting?
    - If not, what are you going to do differently to get different results?
    - Do you want your effort to be one of excellence—or are you willing to settle for mediocrity, complacency, good, or good enough?
2. Make a decision.
    - Decide right now to commit to creating excellence in whatever it is you're doing.
    - Share your decision with one or two other people you trust who will encourage you along the way.
3. Commit to a new direction.
    - Commit to the decision you have just made.
    - Document your commitment, sign it, and date it. Let this be the first entry in your new journal of excellence.
    - Document your thoughts, actions, revelations, and results along the way. We can learn much from our experiences if we just pay attention.

CHAPTER 2

Design a Blueprint

> I know of no more encouraging fact than the unquestionable ability of man to elevate his life by conscious endeavor.
> —Henry David Thoreau

Can you imagine trying to build a house without first designing a blueprint for the builders to follow? Similarly, what makes us think we could experience any level of excellence without a blueprint, a plan to guide us toward our destination? Does such a blueprint for excellence exist—or do we have to figure it out for ourselves? That was my question thirty years ago as I began the search for such a plan.

As a result, I've learned that the blueprint for excellence does exist. When diligently pursued, it can produce remarkable results in any environment. Using this blueprint, my organization soared rapidly to national attention as rookie of the year with a national healthcare consulting firm. We achieved dramatic improvements in quality, customer perception of service, turnover, employee engagement, and growth. Using this blueprint at the team level, my team gained national recognition for three best practices in organizational development interventions, taking us to the national conference platform every year from 2004 to 2009. Using this blueprint at the individual level, my teammates soared to new performance levels and were recognized internally as some of the highest performers in the organization. Additionally, I, as their leader, experienced significant personal growth and achieved a higher level of excellence in my own career and personal life—a level of personal value and fulfillment I had never before achieved. My team members also say the same about themselves.

Using this blueprint at church, we discerned balanced clarity of focus in our activities and rallied the members to new levels of Christian action. Using the blueprint at home, we have found peace and joy in an environment of love and service. Using it in my own life, I have found joy, fulfillment, and purpose that brings worth and value to others and me. This Blueprint for Excellence can be applied to any endeavor.

> *9. Excellence produces a life of joy and fulfillment.*

So where do we start? What is this blueprint I keep referring to? Building a culture of excellence is like building a house—and the beginning of any home-building project requires a blueprint. We need a plan to show us how to gather the raw materials, lay a solid foundation, frame it up, attach the roof, and apply all the finishing touches.

The Raw Materials

Before we begin laying the foundation, we should assemble the appropriate raw materials. As I talk with other organizations, teams, and individuals around the country, I'm often asked these questions:

- What two or three things have had the most impact on your organization's success?
- What is the secret to your success?

The answers to these questions are the raw materials for our own house of excellence.

1. **Leadership excellence.** Organizations of excellence have excellent leadership. As the leader goes, so goes the team. As described by Jim Collins in *Good to Great*, it starts at the top with a level-five leader. Without a dedicated level-five leader, everything will be a challenge—and many things will be impossible. Collins defines a level-five leader as one who "builds enduring greatness through a paradoxical blend of personal humility and professional will." A level-five leader is humble and determined and represents the highest level of executive capability. Level-five leaders are self-effacing individuals who display fierce resolve to do whatever needs to be done to make the organization great. They are incredibly ambitious, but their ambition is first and foremost for the institution, not themselves (Collins, *Good to Great*, pp. 20-21).
2. **The right people in the right roles.** The right person in the right role at the right time with trust and accountability at all levels. First who, then what. Sub-standard, low performance cannot be tolerated. Attitudes that derail the team must be eliminated. As Collins puts it, you must have the right people in the right seats on the bus.
3. **A proven and tested method.** A framework that guides and promotes excellence. Left up to chance, most efforts will fail. The framework is the road map—the blueprint. Tactics, processes, and all activities must be targeted toward achievement of the mission and vision. The framework must require consideration of all important aspects that drive organizational success. The house of excellence blueprint provides such a framework.

In chapter 17, we'll explore the first two of our raw materials—leadership excellence and the right people on the bus. The third raw material, a framework, is the focus of chapters 3-16.

The Roof

Let's begin with a discussion about the roof. Stephen Covey, in *The 7 Habits of Highly Effective People*, points out that we should "begin with the end in mind." The roof represents the end objective, the desired ultimate destination, and is divided into three sections.

The first, or top, section is *organizational excellence*. Your overall objective is to create an organization of excellence. Using a tool many refer to as an organizational scorecard, we'll create specific measurable objectives that will enable you to measure your progress. The top management team is responsible for this level of outcome. In business, this would include the top leader and his or her direct reports. The leader's compensation, future, and well-being in the organization should rest on the progress achieved at this level. If a pay raise is awarded to this team in any performance period, it should be based on the progress of the organization as measured by these goals. In chapter 13, we'll describe these goals in detail and introduce you to some tools to make this happen.

The second, or middle, level of the roof represents *team excellence*. Most organizations are comprised of a subset of teams or departments. For the organization to perform at a consistently high level of excellence, each team within the organization must perform at a consistently high level of excellence. Excellent teams build excellent organizations. Team goals must align with organization goals. This may appear obvious and elementary, but have you ever worked in an organization or been part of a team effort where striving for excellence was never even mentioned? Most of us talk a good game about creating high-performing teams—but only in the well-structured teams and organizations is there an intentional plan for making it happen. In chapter 14, we'll describe the specific plan and strategy for ensuring team excellence.

The middle manager or team leader is responsible for execution at this level. As with the senior team, advancement in the organization by the team leader should directly depend upon performance of the team he/she oversees. Far too often, we fall victim to the Peter Principle, promoting leaders too rapidly beyond their capability to perform. This is a dangerous practice.

Leaders who find themselves in this position can become extremely frustrated and unproductive, realizing the role is requiring more of them than they are capable of delivering. Leaders are hired to get results. Any pay increases, promotions, and rewards must be directly related to the results they achieve, and they must be held accountable for getting results in the right way. We'll talk more about the right way in chapters 6 and 7 and more about the leader's goals and measurements in chapter 14.

> *10. The essence of excellence lies in the quality of the individual's performance.*

The third and final section of the roof represents the most fundamental element—*individual excellence*. Every team is composed of individual team members, and excellence in the team depends on each individual performing at a consistently high level of excellence in their particular role. Consequently, the essence of organizational excellence lies in the quality of the individual's performance.

Frank Sacco, CEO of Memorial Healthcare System in Hollywood, Florida, said, "When our employees succeed, we succeed."

An individual's effort must align with—and enable—the team's objectives. This is where most organizations and teams miss the mark. Too often, we fail to effectively align each individual team member to the team and organizational goals. Your main task, therefore, is to figure out how to create an environment in which each individual can align with the team and perform at his or her best. In chapters 15, 16, and 17, we'll introduce specific tools you can use to create and sustain a highly productive environment for individual excellence.

The Foundation

A Language of Excellence, Inspiring a Culture of Trust

Building a solid foundation for any structure requires two actions: digging the footings and pouring the slab.

Digging the Footings

Digging the footings represents a concept that permeates every aspect of excellence. It provides strength, cohesiveness, and support to all levels of the structure. Very simply, we're talking about how we communicate—the language we use to describe who we are and what we do.

Disney, considered one of the best organizations in the world, contends that everything we communicate and everything we do should be intentional. We should leave nothing up to chance. Our research reveals that excellence doesn't happen by chance. It springs forth from serious purposeful intent.

This philosophy begins with how we talk about what we do and how we present ourselves to those we serve. Do we use a *language of excellence*? Do we require and encourage the use of that language with everyone on our teams? Do our language and communication behaviors inspire trust and accountability in all stakeholders? You must deliberately determine your own unique language and use it to dig the footings for your foundation of excellence.

> *11. Excellence springs forth from serious purposeful intent.*

In chapter 3, we'll discuss how to create a language of excellence, and in chapter 17, we'll discuss how to sustain that culture by inspiring trust and accountability with passion.

Pouring the Slab

A foundation of excellence contains four essential cornerstones: mission, vision, principles, and standards. Notice the acronym these four elements create. A strong foundation creates MVPs (*most valuable players*).

Mission

Cornerstone #1, the *mission*, answers these basic questions.

- Why does our organization exist?
- What is our main purpose?

It's literally impossible for anyone to achieve any level of excellence without confidently and clearly articulating the answer to these questions. I've seen a *mission statement* on the wall in just about every organization I've entered. Everyone knows we need mission statements. What everyone doesn't seem to understand is how to use those mission statements to inspire excellence.

Many leaders fail to realize that every individual on the team must believe that he or she can accomplish the personal mission while serving the team. For an individual to deliver excellence every day, in spite of all the obstacles and challenges that inevitably come, he or she must be confident about fulfilling their own personal mission in life in the process. Excellence requires connectivity to purpose by all members of the team.

> *12. Excellence requires connection to purpose by all members of the team.*

Disconnected individuals will hold the team back at best, and totally derail the team at worst. The leader's most important job is to help each individual team member align and commit to the team's mission—or get off the team. In chapter 4, we'll explore the process for discerning your mission and igniting the passion of others for its accomplishment.

Vision

Vision answers the question *where do you want to go?* Where do you see yourself at some point in the future? A compelling vision creates motivation to deliver on the mission. The vision provides a clear picture of the desired end result. For example, the mission of a healthcare organization may be stated as *to enhance life by excelling in care*. The vision may be *to become the best healthcare system in America*. The vision serves as a target—or focal point—for achievement, and everything done in that organization must serve to fulfill both the mission and the vision.

> *13. Excellence requires vision.*

Like the mission, each individual must be able to confidently align with the team and organization's vision. As an individual team member, you must be able to proclaim that by helping the organization get where it wants to go, you will also be going where you want to go. To do that, you have to know where you want to go. A sad reality is that many people have not invested the time it takes to clearly discern their own vision in life.

Someone once said that we spend countless days and weeks planning for the wedding, but we hardly invest any time at all planning for the marriage. The leader's role is to help each individual on the team answer some very basic questions about his or her own life. Why am I here? What do I hope to accomplish in my life? Once you understand the answers, you can assess whether or not this is a team or organization that will help you get there. You cannot have individuals on the team who are just there to earn a paycheck.

In chapter 5, we'll describe a method for discerning your vision, communicating it to others, and using it to inspire your team forward.

Principles

John Maxwell, in *Today Matters*, states that our [*principles*] help us make decisions today about how we'll behave tomorrow. Principles lay the foundation for daily behavior and answer the question "How do you want to get there?"

- What are the nonnegotiable values that will guide you toward your mission and vision?
- Are there lines you're not willing to cross?
- What principles will govern your daily behavior as you interact with your teammates, customers, suppliers, and other stakeholders involved in your pursuit?

The organization must determine what it values and then require each individual team member to commit to uphold those values every day. Each individual must know his or her value and be able to assess their personal connection to the team's values.

> *14. Excellence demands that the leader model the way.*

Remember that it's the leader's job to help each individual team member commit to the principles—and live them every day. The leader must behave according to the values and require each team member to do the same. Hypocrisy in leadership *will not* work. The leader cannot preach one thing and do another and expect excellence to be the outcome.

A leader who is unwilling or unable to model the way must be removed. According to Kouzes and Posner in *The Leadership Challenge,* if you're committed to excellence, leaders must model the way. In chapter 6, I provide more detail on how to discern your principles and values and use them to guide your team and organization toward excellence.

Standards

Standards are specific behaviors that demonstrate the principles. They serve to create guidelines for everyone to more specifically clarify what's expected in daily behaviors and interactions. Again, leaders must model the way. Standards create consistency of performance at all levels. In chapter 7, we'll discuss how to develop your own standards of behavior to demonstrate your culture of excellence.

The Supporting Structure

Every house needs a structure equipped to bear the weight of the roof. The structure of our house of excellence is composed of five main pillars, or areas of focus. Explained by Quint Studer in *Results That Last,* and used in various forms across the globe, this pillar approach to organizational excellence provides an outline for balanced clarity of focus. It forces the team to consider all areas that may impact the outcome and serves as a guideline for tactical action. The five core pillars are listed here in order of priority.

1. **Quality**—Deliver consistent high-quality products and services to those you serve. Excellence in quality is the focus of chapter 8.

2. **Service**—Develop loyalty by creating a positive, memorable experience for everyone you serve. Excellence in service is the focus of chapter 9.
3. **People**—Inspire commitment and full engagement with every stakeholder on your team. Making it a great place for people to work and live is the focus of chapter 10.
4. **Growth**—Promote, encourage, and maintain positive, continuous improvement in products, services, processes, and people. Excellence in growth is the focus of chapter 11.
5. **Finance**—Demonstrate exemplary stewardship over all resources entrusted to your care. Excellent stewardship is the focus of chapter 12.

The House of Excellence Blueprint

These five pillars of performance serve as a framework for developing specific, relevant, and meaningful actions to accomplish a mission or vision. The organization should develop key objectives under each pillar. Each team leader can then develop actions and objectives that support those of the organization. This produces alignment between the organization and team levels and ensures that everyone is focused in the same direction. At both the organization and team levels, these goals are objective, measurable outcomes—things that can be measured by counting, rating, or ranking. At the individual level, it's a combination of objective and subjective measures. In chapters 13, 14, and 15, we'll discuss how to set goals under each pillar at organizational, team, and individual levels.

Remember that it's the responsibility of the leader to get results. The pillar framework provides an objective goal-setting method through which the leader's performance can be assessed. While it's important for the leader to get the results in the right way, it's the results that determine the leader's effectiveness. What's the right way? The right way is determined by the principles and standards you identify in your foundation.

In *The Speed of Trust*, Stephen M. R. Covey points out that excellence in leadership is measured in two ways. A leader must be *competent* (get good results), and a leader must behave with *character* (get the results in the right way). When it comes to measurement, we focus on the results. If the leader achieved those results but did not demonstrate strong character by modeling the principles and standards, he or she should be required to find another role to play or another team to join. Character must become a nonnegotiable aspect of leadership. Character must be evidenced in the heart and habits of the leader or excellence will not be sustained over time. We'll explore this further in chapter 17.

> *15. Excellence needs a framework for planning and measurement.*

The pillar structure also provides a framework for setting goals and measuring performance at the individual level. These measurements are a combination of specific measurable outcomes and subjective behavioral descriptions. Identifying objective outcomes of behavior that can be counted, rated, or ranked is a bit more difficult at the individual level, especially in roles that require a high degree of personal interaction with others.

In chapter 15, we'll present a framework for individual measurement that will guide you in developing the right combination of measurable outcomes and behavioral descriptions to inspire, encourage, and recognize individual excellence. Our framework of eight behavior outcomes has earned national recognition as a best practice. Once you learn it, you'll be able to apply it to any job or role performed by any person in any team or organization at any time.

In chapter 16, we'll take the house of excellence model from concept to application. You'll learn a basic seven-step process to transform your blueprint into actual application, and I'll provide you with several examples in the five environments. In chapter 17, we'll explore our discussion of leadership excellence and introduce you to several tools to help you sustain excellence in your team every day. In chapter 18, we'll surprise you with a unique application of the model that's sure to get your mental cogs turning.

Lastly, I'm sure you've noticed that I'm identifying principles of excellence as we discover them in the writing. By the end of the book, I will have introduced you to eighty-three principles of excellentology that you can take to the bank. I encourage you to adopt these principles into your philosophy for living and to use them to propel you toward excellence.

Summary

There you have the Blueprint for Excellence. The remainder of this book will help you understand and apply these timeless principles of excellence in your organizations and teams. Your mastery of these principles and techniques will elevate your impact on the world around you. You'll become a leader who gets excellent results in the right way—and inspires the same in others. You'll become a catalyst for excellence, making a dramatic, positive difference in the world around you. You'll become someone who others will want to have on their teams.

Your marketability and income will likely increase. Your team will prosper because of your leadership example—and so will your family. You'll learn how to make every experience in your life an experience of excellence. You'll be inspired to do it every day with everyone every time. You will grow to become a true *excellentologist*.

In the chapters that follow, I'll explain each element of the house of excellence and provide examples of application in various environments from businesses, teams, churches, families, and individuals. At the end, I'll show you how you can assemble your own house in a document called your *Blueprint for Excellence*. With these tools at your disposal, you'll have what you need to create excellence in any endeavor you pursue.

Summary of Chapter 2

The Blueprint of Excellence

1. Our metaphor for creating and maintaining a culture of excellence is a house. The building of any house begins with a blueprint—or model—from which to build.
2. The three most important raw materials for a house of excellence are
    a. Leadership excellence,

     b. Having and keeping the right people in the right place, and

     c. Using a proven and tested strategic framework.

3. The roof represents your ultimate end objective—to create excellence at the organization, team, and individual levels.
4. The essence of excellence lies in the quality of each individual's performance. The key is to create a culture in which each individual is inspired to voluntarily and passionately perform at his or her best every day.
5. Undergirding the foundation of a house of excellence is meaningful communication—a language of excellence that inspires a culture of trust.
6. The foundation is comprised of a meaningful mission, inspiring vision, nonnegotiable principles, and standards that demonstrate them. These enable all team members to become MVPs.
7. The supporting structure represents the strategic framework that serves to provide a balanced approach to excellence. The framework is comprised of five pillars of performance—quality, service, people, growth, and finance.
8. This framework enables goal setting at three levels of measurement—organizational, team, and individual.
9. The Blueprint for Excellence can be applied to any environment where two or more people come together to make something special happen. Whether it's a business, a team, a church, a club, a family or an individual, this blueprint will help you build a life of excellence in anything you strive to do.

Take Action

1. If you have not already done so, begin the journey of discovering your personal mission, vision, principles, and standards.
2. Assess your personal commitment and connection to the teams of which you are a member.
   a. Is your passion ignited by the team's mission and vision?
   b. Do you feel that by being a part of the team, you are accomplishing your personal mission and vision in life as well?
   c. Can you confidently continue to support the mission, vision, and principles of this team?
   d. Is this a team you should continue to be a part of?
3. Recommit to your direction.
4. If, after careful consideration, you feel disconnected to your team, consider resigning from the team and finding another one with which you can connect. And do it soon.
5. If you do feel connected at this fundamental level, then recommit to delivering excellence in your role on the team. Begin studying and applying the principles in this book so you can become a leader and role model to those around you.

SECTION 2

Lay a Solid Foundation

> Core ideology defines the enduring character of an organization—its self-identity that remains consistent through time and transcends product/market life cycles, technological breakthroughs, management fads, and individual leaders. In fact, the most lasting and significant contribution of the architects of visionary companies is the core ideology.
> —Jim Collins, *Built to Last*

The Foundation

In order to withstand the test of time and the elements, your dream house must be built upon a strong, *solid foundation*. Houses built on foundations of sand are easily swept away when the storms of change, adversity, or challenge approach. Evidence the devastation and destruction along the coastline when a hurricane makes its way across the sandy shores. A well-designed *core ideology* is the foundation of a house of excellence.

In the 1970s, I worked construction one summer between college years. I was a common laborer, carrying cinderblock, shoveling dirt, providing materials and supplies to the brick masons and carpenters, and performing whatever additional odd jobs were required. One day, the backhoe operator, while digging the footings for the foundation, accidently dumped the dirt into the center of the footing perimeter instead of to the outside. Mounds of dirt were in the way of grading, leveling, and pouring the cement slab floor. We had to move it. Jim, my labor partner, and I were each handed a shovel and instructed to get to work. For two days, we shoveled dirt by hand from the inside of the footings to the outside. The mistake had cost the construction company two days' pay for two laborers and the delay of time to pour the cement flooring, but the error had to be corrected. Too much dirt under the cement floor would create an unstable foundation. We had to get the foundation right before we could go any further.

The same holds true in a culture of excellence. The foundation, or core ideology, must be strong and right. There are five core elements of the foundation—language, mission, vision, principles, and standards. In this section, we will explore each of these elements in detail and apply them to the five environments—the organization, team, church, family, and individual.

Mission   Vision   Principles   Standards

A language of excellence inspiring a culture of trust

CHAPTER 3

Build on Rock!

> The way to change a culture is to change the conversations. If we want to give birth to a workplace that [delivers excellence], we must engage people in radically different ways and invite engagement as the means of creating change. Engagement draws on the power of conversations—the common and conventional talking we do with one another. It is in our conversations that we create and disclose to those around us the future we are pursuing.
> —Joel Henning, *The Power of Conversations at Work*

In order to withstand adversity and change, you must build on rock. In a house of excellence, your *language* is the rock. The way you talk to others about what you do determines the strength of your foundation.

A Language of Excellence

Everything Communicates, Everything Is Intentional

A language of excellence is comprised of two basic elements: *what* you say and *how* you say it. While that may sound simple, only a distinguishable few invest the time to create an intentional language of excellence to infuse their cultures with life, energy, and passion. An instance of ineffective communication is always found in the root cause of every problem. It is that profound realization that has led me to position effective language and *communication* as the rock upon which to build your culture of excellence. A unique language that describes the culture you are pursuing used in regular daily conversations keeps the life force of excellence pumping. It's like the blood flowing through the body, nourishing every element. Excellent organizations, excellent leaders, and excellent individual performers have learned how to intentionally communicate with those around them to inspire trust, accountability, and passion. Let's first discuss *what* you say.

> *16. An instance of ineffective communication can be found in the root cause of every problem.*

What You Say

The Disney Company, considered by many as one of the best organizational cultures in the world, doesn't refer to their team members as employees. They call them *cast members*. They're not hired to do a job; they're *cast for a role in the show*. They do not wear uniforms at work; they put on their *costumes* every day to perform their *roles in the show*.

To apply for a job at Disney, you journey to the *Casting Center*, a structure depicting the imagery of Cinderella's Castle. The Disney orientation program is called *Disney Traditions*, an effort to communicate the organization's culture to new cast members. All cast members work together to create and maintain the *Disney Magic*, a cultural mystique that Disney has fostered so well. When asked how many people dress up like Mickey Mouse throughout the park, there is only one scripted and taught answer—there is only one Mickey Mouse! How devastating it could be to a little kid's fantasy if it were revealed that Mickey Mouse was not real, but simply a regular person dressed up in a costume. The organization goes to great lengths to preserve that fantasy. Perhaps most importantly, their customers are referred to as *guests*, thus creating the perception of a warm and welcoming environment in all the parks, restaurants, shops, and attractions.

The Ritz-Carlton, another excellent organization and winner of the 1999 Malcolm-Baldridge National Quality Award in the service sector, employs a similar strategy with respect to intentional language. *Ladies and gentlemen serving ladies and gentlemen* is their credo. Their employees are referred to as *ambassadors* of the Ritz-Carlton *mystique*. Like Disney, their customers are referred to as *guests*. Bellhops wear tuxedos and white gloves. The facilities and images are icons of class. All the language, both spoken and unspoken, is an intentional effort to communicate the first-class culture to their guests.

> *17. In a culture of excellence, everything is intentional.*

Blue Ridge HealthCare, a community-based healthcare system located in the beautiful foothills of western North Carolina, also created a unique language to communicate a desired culture of healthcare excellence. Employees, regardless of their role, are referred to as *care team members* and work together to create a *positive memorable experience* for their *guests* in every *sacred encounter* entrusted to them. Doesn't that sound better than taking care of patients who are sick or injured? The orientation program is called *Blue Ridge Connections*, attempting to *connect* each new *care team member* to the language and cultural norms of their intended culture. They don't hire new employees; they *select* new *care team members*.

Church leaders go to great lengths to use intentional language with their followers to differentiate the church culture from that of the world in general. If you hang around church members very long, you'll undoubtedly hear words such as *sanctification, justification, saved, blessed, propitiation of sin, resurrection of the body, Holy Spirit, eschatology*, and *child of God* just to name a few. It's a unique language intentionally designed to create a culture of excellence in the church environment.

In my own family environment, we've chosen to promote certain words and behaviors with one another and avoid the use of others. Words and behaviors that demonstrate *love, joy, peace, encouragement, support, listening,* and *cooperation* are welcomed, and words and behaviors that depict selfishness, hatred, destruction, abuse, and disharmony are discouraged. Likewise, in our individual quests for excellence, it's best to adopt such words and actions that are positive, productive, and encouraging rather than negative, destructive, and judgmental.

Your language is foundational to the creation and maintenance of a culture of excellence. It's not just the words you use; it's everything you do as well. As Disney so profoundly proclaims, in a culture of excellence, *everything communicates and everything is intentional.*

How You Say It

Everything communicates! Consider every instance in which you interact with any of your stakeholders. Every contact with an employee, team member, or family member should be executed with intent. Every interaction with a guest, customer, or stakeholder should be executed with intent. Every interchange with a supplier or vendor should be executed with intent. All actions, words, and images come together to communicate your intent, your strategy, and your expectations—the future you are pursuing. A deliberate, intentional approach engages every stakeholder in passionate, voluntary pursuit. Many organizations, teams, and individuals fail to give this fundamental element due consideration, building their houses on sand rather than rock. Unintentional communication is less likely to withstand inevitable obstacles and challenges, guaranteeing eventual failure—or, at best, perpetual mediocrity.

To build on rock, you can't leave the basic element of language up to chance. Carefully deliberate what you say and do. Your language must be intentional, consistent, and clear. It must be taught and reinforced with every member of your team. The signs on the highway, the security guard who greets, the area where guests park, the entrance of your facility, the greeters at the door, the way you dress, what you say and how you say it, the look and feel of your environment, the directional signs in your buildings, and the way you speak to and treat others all communicate the future you are pursuing. Consider what you're saying to others today through the people and things that represent you. Is it a message of excellence?

Communication fostered around a unique cultural language is the first foundational question in building a house of excellence. Everything else you do will be built upon this principle. Let's talk about the words, symbols, and images—the specific language—that will help you create your desired culture.

A New Way of Thinking

- When will they ever get us some more help?
- Why do they always keep changing things around here?
- When will they ever get rid of Joe? He's terrible to work with.
- Why don't they get off their duffs and come work with us a while? Then they'll see what it's really like!
- How do they expect us to do our jobs if they don't train us?
- Why do they make us go to all these meetings? I don't have time for that. I've got work to do!
- Why won't they do something about all that gossip and back-biting? No wonder no one wants to shop here!
- Who's running this place anyway? Are they nuts?
- Where did they ever come up with a cockamamie idea like that? No wonder nobody wants to work here! It's amazing they stay in business.

Does any of this sound familiar? Have you ever heard anyone say things like this? Or worse, have you ever said things like this yourself? Over the past twenty-five years, I've heard people utter destructive comments like these in every organization I've worked. It's the destructive cancer of *blaming attitudes* and *managing others down*. It's the negative gossip that permeates around the water cooler and spreads like wildfire through the organization and the community.

Human beings are negative by nature, and many love to spread that negativity to others. Absent effective leadership and accountability, these cancerous behaviors tear down others and prevent everyone from experiencing excellence.

> *18. To maintain a culture of excellence, you must remove the cancer caused by negative behaviors.*

This destructive negativity must be removed and never tolerated again. It must be replaced with positivity and the art of managing others up. *Managing up* is a concept that simply means speaking about others in a way that creates a positive perception. Combating the natural negativity of the human state requires an intentional positive alternative. The more you encourage the good in others, the less you have to deal with the bad. *Encouragement* and managing up create a desirable environment that feels good when you're in it. You create an atmosphere of positivity with the words you use and the behaviors you encourage and tolerate. Destructive behaviors must not be tolerated. Once identified, you must remove the cancer before it spreads.

In a recent visit to another organization, I was tasked with the responsibility of training leaders in a new way of measuring individual performance. During the presentation, the CEO pointed out that this new way was causing frustration with many leaders. The system used a one-to-five rating scale with the middle of the scale—level three—representing the first level of high performance. The CEO proclaimed that since we had all been raised with the understanding that the middle of a rating scale represented average, or a C grade, leaders were struggling. He persisted in his explanation of leader resistance, claiming it could be a stumbling block for success with the new system. In other words, this new system required a new way of thinking.

> *19. Excellence requires a new way of thinking.*

My response was simple. "Stop thinking that way!" I said. "Level three is not average or a C. Level three is *fully successful*—an A. This *is* different! And the sooner we start thinking, speaking, and behaving differently, the sooner we'll be able to build a new culture of excellence."

Creating an organization of excellence requires a new way of thinking. If we keep on thinking the way we've been thinking, we'll keep on doing the things we've been doing. And if we keep on doing the things we've been doing, we'll keep on getting the things we've been getting. If we want to change the results we're getting, we must change the way we think.

Stephen Covey reminds us that we're perfectly aligned to get the results we're experiencing. If we want to change our results, we have to change what we've been doing to get those results. What this group of leaders needed was a new way of thinking. We had to create a paradigm shift in their minds that would lead to a behavioral shift in their words and actions. We had to create and use a new language for excellence—and the CEO had to lead the way.

A New Language

Joel Henning reminds us that we reveal the future we are pursuing to those around us in our daily conversations. We must pay attention to our language—the words we use in our everyday conversations. For example, when we talk about our performance, do we talk about minimum standards (words of mediocrity) or becoming *fully successful in our roles* (words of excellence)? Do we refer to ourselves as employees like everyone else—or do we use a more inspiring cultural term such as *ambassadors, cast members, or caregivers*? Do we hire new employees or do *we select new team members*? When someone asks us how we're doing, do we give them the same old response of "fine, how are you?" or do we respond in a distinguishable fashion with something like "excellent," "fantastic," or "if I were any better, I couldn't stand it"?

When someone thanks you for your service, do you respond by saying "you're welcome" or do you say something like "it was my pleasure"? People who generate distinguishable results speak a different language. If you want to create a culture of excellence and trust, you must use a language of excellence that *inspires* a culture of trust. Here are some keywords for you to consider adopting into your daily vocabulary of excellence. Let's begin with the word *excellence* and its cousins.

Excellence, *n.* excelling, surpassing; outstanding, of exceptional merit and virtue. If you want to build a culture of excellence, use the word excellence when you talk about it. If you do not like the word excellence, find one of its cousins that you do like. Here a few cousins of excellence for you to choose from. Any of them are better than the typical language of mediocrity we normally hear and use.

Synonyms of excellence—first-class, outstanding, exceptional, superb, superior, great, mighty, premium, best, top, prime, select, exquisite, fine, admirable, magnificent, wonderful, extraordinary, memorable, remarkable, distinctive, highest, world-class, champion, prized, accomplished, supreme, estimable, distinguished (set apart, differentiated, characterized, conspicuous, illustrious, renowned, memorable, noteworthy, celebrated, reputable, striking, unforgettable, salient, foremost, legendary), enticing, unique, custom-made, incomparable, transcendent, priceless, rare, matchless, invaluable, skillful, superlative, worthy, sterling, refined, exemplary, praiseworthy, brilliant (gifted, profound, ingenious, eminent, meteoric, noble, venerable, grand, esteemed), classic, commendable (laudable), masterful, competent, paramount (supreme, dominant, principal, top), notable, terrific, sensational, marvelous, phenomenal (exceptional, unique, rare, unparalleled), splendid, divine, heavenly, sublime, super, cool, crackerjack, sharp, keen, groovy, A-one, grade-A, classy, top-notch, tiptop, top-flight, blue-chip, frontline, out of this world, out of sight, in a class by itself, as good as they get, to die for, dynamite, hot, bad, at the peak, or as my northern colleague Phil would say—wicked good.

I like to make up synonyms for excellence too. Some of my favorite made-up excellence words include fantabulous, superbalicious, greatational, magnifacious, incrediblacious, wondiferous, and even superbafantabulacious! I encourage you to find words of excellence that resonate with you and use them in place of the typical words of mediocrity.

Here are a few more words of excellence that help to build a culture of trust for you to consider adding to your daily vocabulary.

Key Words and Phrases in a Culture of Excellence
(a partial list)

accountability	affirm
accuracy	alignment
admirable	ambassador

appreciate
availability
balance
belief
Can I help?
Can we talk?
challenge
commitment
communication
compassion
competence
compliment
complaint
conflict
congratulations
connection
continuous improvement
crucial conversations
customer
dependable
determination
distinguished performance
doer
dragger
driver
durability
duty
eager
edify
efficient
empathy
enthusiasm
excellence
faith

fervent
focus
fully present, fully aware
fully successful
Great job!
growth
guest
high performer
honor
hope
How can I . . . ?
humility
key words
knowledge
I (we) can
I made a mistake.
I understand.
improvement
I'm listening.
I'm sorry.
innovation
integrity
It's my fault.
It's my pleasure.
joy
justice
lean
liberty
loyalty
make a difference
manage up
May I be of service?
measurement
mining for conflict

mission	risks
Mr., Mrs., or Miss	sacred
mutual benefit	security
my bad	service
Never give up!	standards of performance
noble	strategy
opportunity	superior performance
organizational impact	talent
our	team
partner	team member
passion	teamwork
performance	tenacity
perseverance	thank you
personal accountability	transparency
please	trust
Please forgive me.	truth
poor performer	unacceptable performance
positive	unity
principles	value added
productivity	values
progress	virtue
pure	vision
purpose	volunteer
quality	we
recognize	What can I . . . ?
relationship	wisdom
resilience	worthwhile work
respect	Yes, ma'am (or sir).
results	zeal
reward	

Just as we should use words of excellence in our conversation, we must also avoid words of mediocrity. Here are some words not to use when referring to our new culture of excellence— good or pretty good, fine, mediocre, good enough, average, okay, so-so, all right, terrible, poor, inferior, and minimum standard are all words of mediocrity. Below are others. They should only be used when calling them out as unacceptable and coaching to improve.

Key Words and Phrases in a Culture of Mediocrity
(also a partial list)

anger	good enough
annoy	gossip
anxiety	guilt
apathy	I (we) can't.
arrogance	idle
average	illegal
blame	immoral
bored	impatience
cheat	indifferent
common	inferior
complacency	lazy
complain	lying
conceit	me
condemnation	meager
criticism	mediocre
customary	meets expectations
department	minimum standard
disrespect	mundane
dread	negative talk
dull	normal
ego	okay
employee	It's not my fault.
fear	It's not my job.
fine	poor
fury	pretty good
frenzy	pride
good	problem

rage	typical
regular	unethical
routine	unnoticeable
satisfaction	unsafe
self	usual
selfishness	vanity
silo thinking	victim thinking
steal	When are they …?
slothful	Why are they …?
terrible	worry
they	

How a typical conversation might go . . .

At a table in a restaurant in a culture of mediocrity.
    Guest: "Excuse me, but this isn't what I ordered."
    Server: "I don't know why they did that. I wrote it down like you told me. They never get anything right in the kitchen. It's hard to find good cooks anymore."

How a typical conversation might go . . .

At a table in a restaurant in a culture of excellence.
    Guest: "Excuse me, but this isn't what I ordered."
    Server: "I'm very sorry, sir. Our goal is to exceed your expectations. What exactly isn't right? (*response*) I apologize for the inconvenience. I'll get the correct item for you right away. Our cooks are the best in town, and I know they'll be eager to help make this right. Again, please accept our apology."

In the statement above, the phrase "*Our cooks are the best in town, and I know they'll be eager to help make this right*" is a way of *managing up* the cook staff to the guests. It's important for everyone to position others in the most positive way possible. Never speak negatively about other members of your team, leadership, or organization to those outside of the team.

> *20. Excellence is demonstrated when we manage others up.*

Keep problems and concerns inside the team and present a positive approach to others. There's nothing more destructive to excellence than backstabbing and negative gossip. If *you* don't speak positively about your teammates, why should the guests? Furthermore, if this is the team where you earn your living, does it really make sense to bite the hand that feeds you? Don't misunderstand me. It's important to deal with problems in your environment, but take them to someone who can do something about them, not the guests. Don't ever violate the principle of *managing up*. It can ignite the cancer of failure and poison a culture of excellence.

Begin thinking about how you talk about what you do and what your behavior communicates to others. Your language helps create the future you are pursuing. What does your current language say about you and your future? Are you satisfied with it—or should it change?

Summary of Chapter 3—Build on Rock

1. A rock-solid foundation for excellence begins with a language of excellence that inspires a culture of trust.
2. Everything communicates, and everything must be *intentional*.
3. There are many words and phrases you can use to communicate your culture of excellence. Choose the ones that connect with you and the others you lead.
4. A language of excellence must intentionally be created and reinforced in the culture. Begin developing your unique

language to describe the future you are pursuing in your team or organization.
5. The concept of *managing up* is critical in a culture of excellence. Always speak positively about other team members and position everyone on the team in a positive way to guests at all times.

Take Action

1. Evaluate your language and behavior. Consider every time and place where your guests, employees, or other stakeholders come into contact with you, your employees, or your facilities. Does the language and behavior communicate what you want? Do those who represent you speak for you the way you want them to? If not, what needs to change? Make a list and start making every element of communication intentional. This is not a one-time activity; it is a way of life in a culture of excellence. Things constantly change, and you must constantly evaluate your message to keep it intentional.
2. Document this foundational information. This will become part of your Blueprint for Excellence. You'll add more to it later as you continue to build. Keep a good record of your language of excellence. You'll use it to do the following:
    - guide your own conversations
    - teach it to others
    - create your description of fully successful performance in your measurement system

CHAPTER 4

The Mission

> The man without a purpose is like a ship without a rudder—a waif, a nothing, a no man.
> —Thomas Carlyle

> I know in my heart that man is good—that doing what is right will always eventually triumph, and that there's purpose and worth to each and every life.
> —Ronald Reagan

Every person and everything needs a clearly defined purpose. Without it, we're like a ship adrift at sea, wandering to and fro aimlessly. There's nothing to energize the spirit or inspire the passion.

The first cornerstone of your foundation for excellence is the *mission*. Everything of worth has behind it a fundamental purpose that can inspire the passion of others to actively participate. It must be more than making money or it will fail to capture the inspiration of the people. The challenge of the leader is to effectively articulate the purpose so it will inspire others to voluntarily and passionately pursue it. Its intention is to arouse the personal best from each member of the team or organization. The key question is "Why do we exist?"

Have you ever been to a Disney theme part? Whether you have or haven't, you can probably finish this sentence:

At Disney, we exist to make people _____.

What was your first thought? Every time I've asked this question with a group, most people complete the sentence with the word *happy*.

They're right. The Disney mission statement is literally *to make people happy*. It goes on to say *by providing the finest entertainment for people of all ages everywhere*. Disney has determined that they exist to make people happy. Wow! Even more incredible is this observation. When I ask anyone who has ever been to a Disney park if the company has succeeded in delivering on their mission, it's always a resounding yes. Disney does such a fantastic job of living their mission every day that people intuitively know what it is. I find that profound—especially when you consider that they accomplish that feat in the midst of long waits, scorching heat, and exorbitant prices. Perhaps this is the real Disney magic.

There's a lesson for us about mission in the Disney story.

> *We should live out our mission every day in such a way that when we come in contact with others, they can discern it intuitively without us having to tell them.*

- Does your team or organization have a mission that's intuitively discernable?
- Do you even know your team or organization's mission?
- How is it stated?
- What does it mean to you?

An effective mission should inspire excellence every day, be lived out by all who join the team, and create a personal connection in the heart of every team member. The team's mission must align with the individual team member's personal mission. An individual must believe that by living out this team's mission, they are simultaneously living out their own personal missions. For you to be able to assess this alignment, you must clearly understand your personal mission in life. Do you?

We've just uncovered the first stumbling block to excellence—the lack of a clearly communicated purpose that inspires team members and connects to their personal missions. Most organizations and teams have some type of mission statement posted on the walls or hidden in an orientation book. People may even carry it around in their pockets. However, rarely do organizations use the mission statement effectively as a foundational cornerstone of excellence. I would rather you have a mission consistently communicated through the behavior of your team members than one posted on every wall that no one pays any attention to. You must find a way to integrate your team mission into your everyday life so everyone on the team can live it out with passion every day.

The Mission Exercise

To clearly discern your mission, you need a team of no more than twelve people. They should be team members who fervently share your passion for the endeavor. Assemble blank 3x5 cards, a flip chart, markers, and a meeting room. Bring everyone together, preferably in a neutral, off-site location free from the daily interruptions of the regular routine.

It's best to start a synergistic meeting of this type with a connective activity designed to help build trust. Helping others relax and connect fosters interactivity and creativity. Patrick Lencioni, in *The Five Dysfunctions of a Team*, positions lack of trust as the first dysfunction of struggling teams. Whenever you have your team together is an opportunity to build trust, and it's wise to take advantage of it. Remember, as we dug our footings in chapter 3, we learned how to use a language of excellence to build a culture of *trust*. We'll explore this concept in more detail later.

If this is the first time you've met like this with your team, or if you have not intentionally led the team through trust-building exercises before, start with a tool like the Myers-Briggs Personality Profile. An activity of this type will take about two hours to complete. If you don't have that amount of time to invest, consider simply asking each team member to respond to a statement like "*Tell us about the best day of your life*" or "*Tell us what you're most proud of in your life*" or "*Tell us about your favorite place on earth to visit and why.*" The idea is to get members of the team to share something about themselves that others will not know. Be creative, and come up with your own questions that may relate better to your team. You'll probably need about thirty minutes for this type of activity. You'll be surprised and impressed by how it will help you build trust and cohesion in the team. It builds bridges of connectivity between team members that deepen trust over time.

After you finish the trust-building activity, pose these mission questions to the team:

1. Why does this team exist?
2. What is our main purpose?
3. What is the main thing we're here to do?

Have everyone on the team write down on a blank 3x5 card what they think are the answers to these questions. Next, take up the cards and read them back to the group. They're usually very different, demonstrating to the team that the mission is not clearly communicated or understood. The task is to discern the *main* purpose of the team. Use the statements on the 3x5 cards to pull out common elements mentioned and write them on a flip chart. Begin discussing the elements identified. Engage every team member in the discussion so everyone feels like they have a part in the decision process.

Remember that people are much more apt to support what they help create. Stay with it until clarity emerges. Your goal is to identify a short statement that captures the essence of the team's purpose. When you reach consensus, end the meeting and ask everyone to ponder what you have created. In about two weeks, hold a second meeting to revisit the mission statement and confirm or revise it as needed. It's okay if this is not yet the final product. The quest for excellence is a journey, not a destination, and your goal at this point is to begin gaining clarity on your purpose.

From this simple exercise, you should have greater clarity about your mission than you've ever had before. It may not be perfect yet, but you'll be on the right path toward excellence.

> *21. Excellence requires clarity of purpose.*

The Leader's Responsibility

While involving your team members in developing your team's mission is the right approach, it's important to note that the leader of the team is ultimately responsible for this process. Ken Blanchard, Bill Hybels, and Phil Hodges, in *Leadership by the Book* put it this way:

> People look to their leaders for [mission], vision, and direction. While you want to involve your experienced people in shaping the direction, as a leader you can't delegate this function. The responsibility for establishing vision and direction falls on you.

Implementation, however, is a different story. Once the direction is clear, the organizational chart must be turned on its head. The most effective method for implementation is for the leader to take on a servant's heart, providing all the tools, equipment, support, and encouragement to the troops to enable them to implement with excellence. We'll discuss this more later on. You can also learn more about the *servant heart* concept from Blanchard and Hodges in *The Servant Leader*.

Mission in the Five Environments

The Organization's Mission

If you lead a large organization or a team larger than twelve, you'll need to assemble what Napoleon Hill refers to in *Think and Grow Rich* as your *mastermind* group. This may be your senior team, board of directors, a subset of the two, or key team members. Keep the group size to twelve or less to maintain intimacy and order. Follow the mission exercise noted earlier.

Once discerned, it will be your responsibility as the leader to begin communicating the mission throughout the larger team and organization with the goal of inspiring everyone to voluntarily live it every day. Since all foundational elements will need to be communicated, it is best to wait until you have your complete foundation established before you move forward with your communication strategy.

Let's apply this exercise to our healthcare example. Try to finish this sentence like we did with Disney.

In healthcare, we exist to make people _____.

What comes to mind? Healthy? Well? Cured? Healed? In a room of healthcare professionals, I hear them all. An effective mission is one that team members can achieve every day. Do any of the above adjectives fit that description? Many times in healthcare, the patient dies, so making them healthy, well, cured, or healed is not always possible. Perhaps healing or curing is not the right purpose in healthcare. It's interesting that many well-educated, highly degreed healthcare team members do not have the same clarity of mission that teenage cast members at Disney do. What does that say about healthcare? I'll leave that to you to ponder.

I would suggest the mission of healthcare is to make people *feel better*. Think about it. The profession of healthcare began with the intent to make people feel better. Technological advances and modern medicines have only existed for a short time. The best a healthcare professional could do before the last one hundred years was throw some whiskey on the wound (and perhaps in the mouth) and go to work digging out the bullet or the infection. The whiskey served as both an anesthetic and infection control as the doctor began to dig for the bullet. He was trying to make his patient feel better. Any time a nurse, doctor, nursing assistant, food service worker, or housekeeper takes care of a patient, they are trying to make them feel better. Whether the patient lives or dies, the healthcare professional has accomplished his or her mission if he or she has made them feel better while in their care.

What a wonderful purpose it is to help people feel better. I highly respect the work of healthcare, having had the privilege of serving in that environment for many years. There are countless wonderful people striving very hard to do great work, to make a difference in the lives of those they serve. No doubt, the profession is experiencing undaunted challenge. A clearly discerned and communicated mission is the first step toward inspiring everyone on the healthcare team to engage in the solutions.

Blue Ridge HealthCare stated their mission very simply: *To enhance life by excelling in care.*

Enhancing life is another way to say *make people feel better*. The phrase *excelling in care* begins to describe how they intend to do it. It's simple, easy to communicate and understand, and can be achieved with every patient every day by everyone in the organization. It was developed by the senior team and is communicated to all new care team members during orientation. It's the responsibility of leaders at all levels to demonstrate their commitment to the mission daily in their interactions with others and to reinforce it with other team members at every opportunity. Well done, Blue Ridge HealthCare.

> 22. Excellence requires alignment of purpose at the
> organizational, team, and individual levels.

The Team's Mission

How do you make sure each smaller team unit or department creates the right mission to support the organizational mission? Since each team needs a clear understanding of its main purpose to be successful, this question has to be addressed by middle managers as well. Using the Blue Ridge mission statement, let's explore ways it can cascade into the departmental teams to make sense, align to the organization's mission, and inspire excellence at the team level.

One required rule of thumb is that a sub-group's mission must help achieve the overall purpose of the organization. It must support and enable the organization's mission. For example, the nursing teams within a healthcare organization could simply adopt the organization's mission as their team's mission if they so choose. It could certainly make sense for them and provide inspiration for nurses, nursing assistants, and unit secretaries to give their best.

At Blue Ridge, however, nursing leadership wanted to take it a step further. They added a few extra words that were very important to them. The nursing team mission statement reads *to enhance life by excelling in competent, confident, compassionate care*. Not a huge variation from the organization's mission—but it is an important one to them. As you can clearly see, it supports and helps enable the organization's mission.

> 23. Excellence becomes easier when
> everyone is involved.

Other support groups in the organization may need to create variations of the organization's mission as well to make it meaningful, specific, and relevant to their team members. For example, my learning team decided to use the organization's mission structure and customize it to our service. It reads *to enhance care by excelling in learning services*. The bio-medical team at Blue Ridge led by Director of Bio-Medical Engineering, Tim Johnson, connected their team's mission to the organization's mission very simply in a similar manner. *To enhance life by excelling in service* works to inspire Tim's team to excellence. His bio-med team has earned the well-deserved reputation as one of the best teams within the organization when it comes to the understanding and delivery of support service to the other departments. Tim's example teaches us a good lesson. The team mission doesn't have to be elaborate at all. Perhaps simpler is better.

Many other support teams in the healthcare system use the same approach. Most importantly, the team's mission must support the organization's mission. It must be relevant to the individual members of the team to inspire them to achieve it. You can use the same exercise noted earlier to discern your team's mission.

Remember that *people are much more apt to support what they help create*. Getting the team members involved in the creation of the mission will make it much easier to gain their support and full commitment. Excellence becomes easier when everyone is involved.

The Church Mission

Working with my church to discern its unique mission was one of the most fulfilling experiences of my life. Seeking clarity on God's purpose for the church can take a group to new spiritual heights. In the spring of 2005, Pastor Dave decided he wanted to identify a clear mission for the church. I'm not sure he realized exactly what he was asking—and neither did I.

To help prepare the mastermind group, we assigned prework. It included readings from several sources on church mission, including Rick Warren's *Purpose Driven Church*, John MacArthur's *The Master's Plan for the Church*, Robert Lewis's *The Church of Irresistible*

Influence, and Charles Schwartz' *Natural Church Development.* We also included readings from Daryl Conner's material on change from *Managing at the Speed of Change* with instructions to complete Conner's resilience assessment. Our intent was two-fold:

1. To encourage participants to begin thinking about what change would mean to the church
2. To present them with several expert perspectives on church mission to help prepare their hearts and minds for a productive experience at the retreat

We gathered the administrative council together for a two-day retreat. We met off-site at a neutral location to create an environment that would hopefully spur new creative thought. Of course, we provided food. The first session was on a Friday night. The majority of our leadership council attended. We began with a time of praise and worship, hoping it would prepare us to discern the mission for our church. It was a good move.

Next, we helped the group understand the concepts of change. Many in our mastermind group were not familiar with change concepts, and we expected resilience challenges. It was time well invested. It helped us lay important groundwork for discussions the next day. It also provided common ground as everyone realized we are all challenged by change to some degree. We finished the evening with prayer, praise, and worship and requested that each participant come back prepared to share their thoughts about our church's main purpose.

On Saturday morning, we began brainstorming the mission. Everyone shared his or her personal perspectives. We captured all the ideas on flip chart pages and taped them to the walls around the room. It was difficult to make sense of it all. We decided to break the room into smaller groups and gave them each a subset of the material to review. Next, each team shared what they thought about their material, and it spurred lively discussion. It was so lively, in fact, that

I lost control as a facilitator. We had descended into minor chaos; everyone was walking around, looking at the walls, and talking at once. I called a break to calm things down.

Following the break, we joined together in prayer, asking God to help us gain clarity amidst the confusion. Immediately after the prayer, Carl, a wise elderly member of the group, offered a suggestion for the church's mission statement.

> To be an instrument, empowered by the Holy Spirit, representing the Lord Jesus Christ, fulfilling the Great Commandment (Matthew 22:36-40), and the Great Commission (Matthew 28:18-20).

It was as if a violent calm had settled over us all. One of the members of Carl's group wrote the statement on a flip chart page in the front of the room. We all just sat there and stared at it. After what seemed like an eon, someone said, "I think that's it! That's our mission!" And so it was. We invested another couple of hours seeking to better understand what we had done, and then we reached a consensus.

This example demonstrates one way the process of discerning a mission statement can transpire. Sometimes it may seem like chaos is ensuing and you're losing control of the discussion. However, if you persevere, clarity will come. Confusion precedes revelation. Don't give up! Sometimes you just have to persevere until the revelation comes. Many times we give up in the face of chaos or confusion right before we're about to embark upon the revelation. Hang in there. Rejoice in the confusion. The revelation will emerge.

> *24. Confusion precedes revelation. Don't give up! Persevere until the revelation emerges.*

If you'd like more information about church mission, I recommend Rick Warren's *Purpose Driven Church*. In the book, Warren discerns five main purposes for the church—worship, discipleship, fellowship, ministry, and evangelism. He describes each one in depth and presents a structure to fulfill them.

The Family Mission

One of the most important and fulfilling journeys in life can be the adventure of discovering your family mission. It's a journey I fear too many families never undertake.

I want to share my personal family mission with you. I have one of those modern blended families formed from the ruins of two previous failed marriages. I learned that excellence in family and marriage is possible even in the midst of such personal failure and despair. So much depends on there being joy in the home that it behooves us to do everything we can to get it right in the family and the marriage.

Following first failed marriages for both of us, Debbie and I had independently invested many years on our own personal journeys of rediscovery and adjustment. The end of my first marriage had been very painful for me. I lost everything in my life that I considered important—my wife, custody of my children, my home, my church, my business, my material possessions, and my friends. I felt like an utter failure. I was alone, hurt, angry, confused, and bankrupt. Had it not been for my faith, I may not have found reason to continue. This was the lowest point in my life. I was mad at women and didn't want anything to do with them. I had determined that I would simply strive to be as good a father as I could to my three small children and not consider a serious relationship with another woman at all—at least until the kids were all in college. Then I met Debbie.

After seven years of being single again, and ten years for Debbie, we met on November 4, 2002. My new boss introduced her to me during the interview process. Phil had a knack for match-making. I think he also wanted to keep me from getting in trouble as a single-again forty-something male in this mostly female healthcare environment.

Finally, after much encouragement from Phil, I decided to ask her out. It was November 24—a nice autumn evening—a Sunday. We enjoyed a nice dinner at the Olive Garden. We were so enthralled with one another that, being the partiers we were, we closed the place down. Time was of no significance. I was mesmerized! Something special had happened, and I couldn't wait to see her again. The next month, we saw each other practically every day. One thing quickly led to another, and we were married on March 2.

My brother-in-law, Dr. Dave, works for a healthcare system too. When he learned I had taken a job in healthcare as a single-again male, he prophesied I would be married within a year. You see, the ratio of women to men in healthcare is about four to one, and he had evidently seen it happen many times before. Obviously, I proved him wrong. It only took four months.

Excellence becomes possible when opportunity and preparedness meet. Debbie and I had both been prepared by our previous failures, and the opportunity for excellence in marriage presented itself. We simply went along for the ride.

> *25. Excellence becomes possible when opportunity and preparedness meet.*

Debbie and I discovered our family mission by observing what we both demonstrated that we value. We were so well connected at that deep spiritual level that it didn't take long for us to agree on our mission statement:

> Maintain an environment in our family and home that brings glory to God and is characterized by love, joy, peace, self-control, gentleness, goodness, and faith (Galatians 5:22-23).

You'll notice this mission statement is a bit longer than the ones we've looked at so far, but it's one that inspires *us* to strive for excellence in our home. It guides our daily behavior with one another. Plus, it's a mission we're able to achieve every day with every member of our family. It works for us, and that's what's important. A journey to excellence is both personal and unique. Your mission must work for you and your team—nothing else is as important.

Sometimes the discovery of the mission can come easy, like this one. Sometimes it comes hard, like with the church. It's a dynamic and unique process that cannot be rushed or predicted. You have to be willing to go with the flow of the journey and let the mission emerge in its own time.

In 2011, my twenty-year-old son moved in with us. Samuel's mother and I divorced when he was seven, and aside from short visitation periods, he had not lived with me since. This was a significant event in my life—and in his. I wanted to make sure we began on the right foot together, realizing we didn't really know one another on that living-together level that family members usually do. The first night, we talked on the sofa for two hours. I shared our family mission with him and explained how Debbie and I were committed to it in our home. I told him that for us to have a successful experience together, I would need him to understand our family mission and commit to live by it every day while he was with us. I also told him I would discuss it with him as much as we needed for him to gain clarity and be willing to commit.

It didn't take much. Samuel told us he had witnessed the evidence of this mission in our lives when he visited us—and that he had often talked about it with his brother and sister. This was one of the main reasons he wanted to live with us. He connected personally with the way we lived and wanted to be a part of our family team. It was this experience, more than any other in business or life, that taught me the value of a clearly discerned, communicated, and demonstrated mission. We had lived our mission every day, and my son had seen it.

Samuel joining our family team was one of the most fulfilling experiences of my life. He made the commitment to join us in our mission, and he made a significant, positive impact on our home. Through the experience, he and I reached a new level of understanding and respect for one another, and our love and commitment to each other deepened tremendously. What could be more powerful or meaningful in life for any parent than that?

A clear, inspiring mission is pivotal for any team to have a chance at excellence. If you haven't already done so, take the time now to discern your family mission and use it to create a home full of love, joy, and peace. Is anything in life more worth doing?

> *26. A journey to excellence is both personal and unique. You must be willing to go with the flow.*

The Individual Mission

It seems rare to find individuals who have seriously considered their personal missions in life. I was one of those until I was thirty-seven years old. In a seminar, the speaker asked, "Do you know your personal mission for your life?"

It bothered me that I had no answer. I invested the next eight months in intense personal study and reflection, searching the scriptures and seeking advice from my respected mentors Zig Ziglar, Ken Blanchard, and Stephen Covey. I struggled with key questions of life like *why am I here* and *does God have a specific and unique purpose for me? If so, what is it?* That was 1994. It was a personal journey of discovery that left me a changed person. If you have not already done so, I highly recommend you consider such a journey for yourself. Here is the result of that effort.

> My personal mission in life is to *do the right thing in love to glorify God and patiently trust him for the results.*

Every word in that statement means something important to me. Every word is intentional, and every word is personal. This is a mission that I can strive to live out every day in every way with everyone, and it has served me well. Today, when I consider joining a new team of any kind, I ask myself a few questions. If the answers to these questions are yes, this becomes a team I can consider joining.

- Will I be able to do the right thing in love in my role on this team?
- Will I glorify God when I fulfill my role on this team?
- Will I be able to trust him for the results?

As you have most likely discerned, I consider myself a spiritual man. I hope that doesn't offend you. I share that with you to help you understand my basis for personal purpose.

Rick Warren in *Purpose Driven Life* said, "If you want to know why you were placed on this planet, you must begin with God. You were born by his purpose and for his purpose."

Oswald Chambers, in his daily devotional guide *My Utmost for His Highest*, helped me see that my purpose in life is not my own, but God's. I must lose any idea of myself and let God take me into his purpose for the world if I am to truly experience a life of significance. That's the way it is for a Christian. For me, living this way has provided more than I ever thought possible. I must admit, however, that it was difficult for me to give up control over my own life.

I have always been a type-A overachiever, setting goals for everything. To give that up and give it to God was a real challenge that has taken me a long time to overcome. Sometimes I still struggle. Yet since I decided to put him in the driver's seat, I've experienced a much richer and fuller life of joy, peace, and meaning. Maybe you can now better understand why the words of my personal mission statement mean so much to me—*to trust God for the results* rather than myself.

I'm sure you've also noticed that a very explicit purpose for my life has emerged over time as well—*to encourage excellence in others.* This is my specific mission, and *doing the right thing* is my general daily mission. I use them both to guide me in my life's pursuits.

I realize your foundation may be different, and you may need to tap into your own perspective for personal strength. However, if you're interested, the scriptures that undergird my mission statement are Matthew 6:33, Matthew 22:39, Ephesians 1:12, Romans 8:25, and Proverbs 3:5-6. These scriptures, and my personal mission statement, have become the core of my foundation for an excellent life.

Mission Summary

The house of excellence we're building can be applied to any aspect of life—work, personal, community, education—anywhere where two or more people come together to make something happen. There is literally no way for a team to achieve excellence if the team members involved do not connect to the team's purpose. To connect, you must have a strong understanding of your personal mission in life.

You'll enrich your life to a new level of meaning you perhaps never imagined possible. If you lead a team, you'll need to lead your team members in their own personal mission discovery quests. It's the only way they can proclaim with confidence that they personally connect to the team's mission and will commit to fulfill it every day in every way. It's the secret to excellence with the first cornerstone of our foundation. Individual, team, and organizational excellence depend upon it.

Summary of Chapter 4—The Mission

1. The first cornerstone of the foundation is the *mission*. Why does the team exist? What is its main purpose? Each

individual's personal mission must align with the team and organization's mission. Team members must believe they are accomplishing their personal missions and goals by being a part of the team.
2. Discerning your mission will require the participation of your *mastermind* group, a group of twelve or less that you select, and with whom you hold in high regard.
3. A clear, inspiring mission at all three levels of performance — organizational, team, and individual—is required for excellence.

Take Action

1. Discern your organization's mission. Why does your organization exist? What is your organization's purpose? Use the mission exercise in this chapter to help you get started with your mastermind team.
2. Discern your team's mission. Why does your team exist? What is your team's purpose? Use the mission exercise in this chapter to help you get started with your team. If you haven't done so already, begin using trust-building exercises with your team at every opportunity. It will make a huge difference in your team's effectiveness and will help you all mature through the journey together.
3. Discern your family's mission. Why does your family exist? What is your family's purpose? Use the mission exercise in this chapter to help you get started with your family.
4. Discern your personal mission. Why do you exist? What is your purpose in life? Invest whatever time it takes to gain clarity of personal purpose.
5. Document this foundational information. This will form the first section of your Team Blueprint for Excellence.

CHAPTER 5

The Vision

> Where there is no vision, the people perish.
> —Proverbs 29:18

> Vision without action is just a dream. Action without vision just passes the time. But vision with action can change the world.
> —Joel Barker

> If you don't know where you're going, you might not like where you wind up.
> —Zig Ziglar

My favorite bird is the majestic North American bald eagle. There's so much I admire about it. They are specialists at soaring, and they're strong enough to carry the equivalent of their own weight in flight. Like leaders, they don't flock. You find them one at a time. Yet during the tough times of winter, they watch out for one another. When in conflict with another over food, they pay close attention to the behavioral cues of their opponents. They mate for life. They live life on the edge, preferring to nest on high cliffs or at dizzying heights in the trees. They tend to their offspring with great gentleness. They are magnificent creatures of grace and strength.

My most favorite attribute of all is their keen vision. A bald eagle can spot a rabbit on the ground from a mile in the sky and swoop down with skillful precision to snatch its prey. Their keen vision enables them to see precisely where they want to go and then to pursue their objective with fervor and strength.

> *27. Excellence requires a clear vision that inspires others.*

The next question to ask yourself is "Where do you want to go?" Cornerstone #2 in your foundation of excellence is discerning a clear and inspiring *vision*. What type of future do you envision for your team? Just as it's the team leader's responsibility to discover and articulate a clear mission, it's also the leader's responsibility to capture an inspiring vision. Again, the best way to do this is to involve your mastermind group.

The Vision Exercise

Set aside at least half a day and gather your mastermind group in a casual, off-site environment that will encourage open thought and brainstorming. Begin with a short trust-building activity like you did with the mission exercise to relax everyone, create connectivity, and get the creative juices flowing. Keep it positive and uplifting. Next, review the mission you have already articulated and ask for any reflections about it. This can provide a good place to start the vision exercise. When it feels right, pose the following question to the group.

> *If there were no restrictions or limitations on what we could do, what would we like our team to look like ten to twenty years from now?*

Your goal is to remove all barriers of thought and let people dream. A follow up question to help clarify your intent might be:

> *How would we describe our team and environment in the future if everything happened as we would dream it to be?*

Your vision should be a specific *bhag goal* (big, hairy, audacious goal) that can be achieved in a specific time frame (*Built to Last,* chapter 11, Collins and Porras). Have everyone in the team write down everything that comes to mind on a blank piece of paper. Allow enough time for everyone to individually exhaust his or her thinking. Then, one at a time, ask each team member to share one item from his or her list. Write it on a flip chart and continue around the table as long as it takes for everyone to exhaust all ideas. Capture them all on the flip chart.

At this point, your objective is to inspire open thought and exorbitant dreaming. You can review and wordsmith later to make better sense of it all. As you fill a flip chart page, tear it from the chart and tape it to the wall so everyone can continue to see all the ideas as you develop them. It's always a joy to observe the team members' growing excitement about the possibilities for the future. This exercise is an inspiring one for the team. The beginning of the belief that you can accomplish something great and special together begins to emerge here. From this dreaming exercise, your vision statement will emerge.

Vision in the Five Environments

The Organizational Vision

When I joined healthcare in 2002, my new organization, Blue Ridge HealthCare, had already discerned its vision statement.

> The Blue Ridge HealthCare Vision is to be the best community healthcare system in America; to become
>
> - a great place for people to work,
> - a great place for physicians to practice, and
> - a great place for patients, residents, members and guests to receive care

To be honest, I thought this was an unrealistic, unachievable goal. I'm usually not the one questioning a *bhag* goal like this. I had grown up in this small community and couldn't remember it ever being described as the best in America in anything. Don't misunderstand me. It's a wonderful and beautiful small town—a lot like Mayberry (Andy Griffith's town in the TV show) or Bedford Falls (from the classic movie *It's a Wonderful Life*). But for a small-town community like this one, the *best healthcare system in America* seemed a bit over-the-top.

Over time, we proved to ourselves by our performance that it *was* possible. We proved it not only by our own measures of excellence, but by the community's measure as well. There's nothing more motivating to team members than success. *Excellence breeds excellence.*

When we began to make huge strides toward that vision, our beliefs began to grow. That perpetual strengthening of our beliefs propelled us toward our goals. It helped create the *flywheel effect.* Another term coined by Jim Collins in *Good to Great*, the flywheel effect occurs when the collective energy of the team begins to build, causing greater and greater things to happen with less and less effort exerted. Progress toward the vision accelerated exponentially as a result.

> 28. *Excellence breeds excellence.*

Part of my role was to communicate the mission and vision to new team members as they joined our organization and to inspire their acceptance and belief. Our continually improving performance made that task easier and easier to accomplish. The evidence was in the results.

While I cannot say that we achieved that level of performance in every area we measured, I can honestly proclaim that we achieved most of them. That was enough to inspire the belief that if we can achieve it in some, we can achieve it in others. It inspired us to keep striving to *enhance life by excelling in care*. That's what a good vision should do—inspire members of the team to keep striving for excellence, regardless of the tremendous adversity and challenges.

The Team Vision

The organization's vision must also align at the team and individual levels. Use the same vision exercise mentioned earlier to develop the team vision. The best approach is to involve the team or the mastermind group as we did before. Here's an example from a nursing team:

> *Our vision for nursing is to become the best community model of nursing practice in America.*

They believed this vision motivated them to deliver on their mission *to enhance life by excelling in competent, confident, compassionate care* every day. As you can see, it connects to their mission and to the mission and vision of the organization of which they are a part. That's what alignment looks like. They also chose to write a descriptive paragraph using all the ideas generated in the brainstorming session to create a clear word picture of their envisioned future.

> In the future of nursing, we see a culture that enables us to lead the best community model of nursing practice in America. There is a strong culture of pride in nursing as we have attracted and retained the best of the best in the communities we serve. We have a true speak-up culture without retribution characterized by real teamwork and collaboration. Nurses are true nurses. They are all BSN certified and are literally managing care, not just following orders. They are highly adaptive and resilient, handling stress

well while avoiding negative behaviors in the workplace. Nurses truly enjoy caring for people and deliver excellent service with every patient and guest at every appropriate time. The definition of what it takes to be considered an excellent nurse includes more than just being clinically competent. It certainly includes that, but they must also be considered strong positive members of the team by their teammates. Our selection practices are world-class, enabling us to select the right people to join our team followed by a thorough, individualized on-boarding program for each new nurse and team player. Nursing leadership is unified and talks the language of business with their words matching the data. We are highly responsive to staff concerns, which are second only to patient concerns. We have earned respect from all other areas of the organization for our sharp business acumen, enabling finance to support us effectively. We have also earned physician respect. Physicians believe in us and practice a standardized, collaborative approach to care. There is meaningful collaboration among all members of the care team, creating a strong, unified, synergistic effort. Everyone takes accountability for his or her work and voluntarily does his or her best each day to meet the needs of the patient, the team, and the business. Evidence-based practice drives decision-making.

This culture of excellence has become evident in all result areas. We have become the employer and provider of choice in the communities we serve. The hospitals are growing, and the census remains high. There are no patient injuries, and patient loyalty is strong. Patient perception data bears witness that every patient receives exceptional nursing care every time. We have achieved Magnet status and other healthcare systems around the country visit us often to learn from us. Team members are highly motivated and fully engaged in the journey. Turnover is very low, and retention of high performers is very high. We enjoy a strong, positive reputation in the community, supporting a growing market share. Patients and guests see us as a great place to receive care, physicians see us as a great place to practice medicine, and team members see us as a great place to work. We have become the best community model of nursing practice in America, and it feels great to be a part of this world-class team!

A descriptive paragraph like this can help everyone on the team understand more clearly what leadership sees for the future. It can also serve to more effectively inspire passion for the journey. It's like a self-fulfilling prophecy. In *Think and Grow Rich,* Napoleon Hill states, "Whatever the mind of man can conceive and believe, it can achieve."

Your journey toward excellence begins with conceiving a clear vision of the future and then doing whatever it takes to gain the belief in its realistic possibility by every member of the team. Describe it however you must in order to gain that belief.

Here's another example from my learning team:

Our vision in Learning Services is to become a true learning organization.

This vision actually came from words spoken by our CEO and served to inspire us *to enhance care by excelling in learning* every day (our mission). Do you see the connection? In this case, it was important for us to define what a true learning organization looks like. To help accomplish that, we added a descriptive paragraph:

> We believe that becoming a true learning organization will play a large role in making our organization the best community healthcare organization in the country. We will create an environment and culture that promotes, encourages, provides, supports, and rewards continuous improvement through knowledge enhancement. In this culture, every employee will want to continually learn and grow. And with this culture, our organization will produce dramatically improved results.

Tim Johnson's bio-medical engineering team provides another example:

> *Our vision in Bio-Medical Engineering is to be the best community healthcare system medical equipment service department in America.*

Obviously, his team chose to piggyback off the organization's vision and tie directly to it. That's certainly an acceptable approach and is a simple way to ensure alignment. Remember that the team vision supports the organization's vision and inspires team members to excellence. Do what works best for your team.

The Church Vision

Our church vision didn't actually come to us until five years after we discovered the mission. We had a change of pastors during that time, and the leadership council lost interest in moving the project forward. In 2010, under the leadership of a new pastor, we reaffirmed the mission developed in 2005 and used the exercise described in this chapter to create a vision statement and paragraph of description.

A Vision for the Future of the Church

The strategic planning team members all agreed that we see growth for our church in the future. We're not sure if the majority of our membership is willing to embrace what it will take to realize that growth, but we do believe we have enough members who are willing to move in that direction to make a difference. We express strong faith that it is what God would have us to do and that he will enable us to do it.

A growing church, serving and sharing Christ as God has uniquely designed us to do

Within ten years, we see a future for our church in which 95 percent of the members clearly understand how God has uniquely designed them for his service, are active in some type of ministry, and are sharing Christ with others through evangelism in the way he has designed them to love to do—or they are on a path of discipleship and personal Christian growth toward that end. That dramatic change in the personal development of the members of the church will yield many benefits for the church community, the community at large, the body of Christ, and the world we impact.

Among those benefits, we see more Sunday school classes in existence. We see full utilization of all our facilities with expanded services on Sunday and Wednesday nights, and perhaps other nights as well. Younger leaders have been mentored and developed such that they are actively leading the church in a period of dramatic growth, characterized by growing membership, attendance at services, ministries in action, testimonies being shared, and non-Christian conversions to belief in Christ being witnessed on a regular basis. The growing membership has created the need for a correlated growth in clergy to support it. The growth in ministries has enabled us to reach out to greater areas of our county, state, and perhaps even to the country and the world. Our thriving, active, meaningful, and energetic fellowship is inviting to others and creates a synergy of action and excitement that is contagious to anyone exposed to it. There is a full contemporary worship service in the all-purpose building with a full complement of musicians and singers ministering to people of all ages several times per week. We have created a vibrant outdoor sanctuary in nature on the property where members and visitors can gather individually or in small groups to pray, study scripture, worship, and fellowship together as they grow in Christ. Members seek out ways to serve and volunteer for service and ministry opportunities on committees and ministry groups.

Our church leaders are committed heart and soul to church growth. Nearly every Christian is using his or her spiritual gifts to edify the church. Most members are living out their faith with power and contagious enthusiasm. Church structures are evaluated on whether they serve the growth of the church or not. Worship services are a high point of the week for the majority of members, and the loving and healing power of Christian fellowship can be experienced in small groups of many kinds. Nearly all members help fulfill the Great Commission and the love of Christ permeates all church activities. God has created an environment in our church in which members and nonmembers, Christians and non-

Christians, are drawn to on a regular basis. Non-Christians are accepting Jesus Christ as their Lord and Savior on a regular basis.

The vision brainstorm can provide valuable information to create a clear picture of the future you want to pursue. Be sure to capture all ideas during the exercise so you can create a paragraph like this for your vision if you so desire.

The Family Vision

> *Every member of the family is living out God's unique purpose for their life with joy, passion, and enthusiasm, adding value to the world around them.*

This is the Crouch family *team* vision. It inspires us to maintain an environment in our home that brings glory to God, which as you recall, is our family mission. Again, notice the connection. Our family vision came to us quickly due to our deep spiritual connection with one another. It taught me that the stronger your relationships with the members of your team, the easier it is to gain clarity on your foundational cornerstones. That's the main reason it's so important to initiate action at every opportunity to strengthen the relationships with your team members. Since families typically live in close proximity with one another for so long, we learn much about one another by default. In the work or church environment, however, relationship building must be more intentional.

> *29. The stronger your relationship with the members of your team, the easier it is to gain clarity on your foundational cornerstones of excellence.*

We also chose to include some description to clarify:

> Our goal is to maintain a family and home environment based on the Judeo-Christian ethic as revealed in the Bible. In the Crouch home, the husband/father is the head of the household, and the wife/mother is his right hand and helpmate, an equal partner in decisions and ways. The husband commits to love his wife as Christ loved the church, willing to give his life for her and the family if required. The wife commits to love her husband and submit to his authority as a Christian does to the Lord. Other family members actively participate in family matters and submit willingly to the parental authority. It is this wonderful and mysterious mix of love and respect for God and one another that enables our family to build and maintain a harmonious and joyous living experience.

The Individual Vision

As with mission, it is rare to find people who have invested the time to discern their personal visions as well. I hope I've already persuaded you of the importance of these foundational cornerstones. Even if you don't yet have a clear personal vision, I suspect you have some intuitive sense of whether or not the team you are a part of is helping you get where you want to go in life. Tap in to that intuitive sense until you have your vision clearly identified—but allocate the time soon to gain clarity on your personal vision for your life.

It took me the better part of a year to arrive at my personal vision statement below. It has served me well for several decades and inspires me every day. I'm sure by now that you're not surprised to see that it also portrays a spiritual perspective.

My personal vision is to hear the words "well done, thou good and faithful servant" after I take my last breath.

I've added the following descriptive paragraph for clarity:

In the future, I am living a life of humility that glorifies God and serves others. My focus is not on myself but on what I can do every day to help someone else. My life is a living example as a follower of Jesus Christ. I am salt and light to the world around me. I have discerned God's unique and specific purpose for my life and am living it out every day with passion. My wife and children respect me as a man of honor. Many others will be joining me in eternity as a result of my faithful living witness.

This vision of my final destination inspires me to try *to do the right thing every day, in love, to glorify God,* which as you recall, is my personal mission statement. Again, notice the connection.

Vision Summary

Together, the mission and vision provide a compass for excellence—clarity for direction. They also act as a rudder to steer you toward your goals. Zig Ziglar was fond of saying we need to *keep the main thing the main thing.* Your mission and vision are the main things.

Spencer Johnson reminds us in *The Present* that we must guard against living too much in the future state the vision describes for us. Living in the future can cause us to miss the opportunities of the present. I know this all too well from my own experiences.

> *30. Excellence requires that you live life in the present, always keeping the end result in mind.*

I've learned to keep the end result in mind, but I live for today, keeping my mind, heart, and eyes open to whatever and whoever crosses my path. Life—and therefore excellence—happens in the present. It's too short to miss by living in the future. Live in the present, keep the end result in mind, and always strive to make forward progress toward the vision. Like my former and favorite CEO, Kenneth W. Wood always said, "It's all about progress, not perfection."

> *31. Excellence is about progress, not perfection.*

Remember to remain flexible about changing your plans if current circumstances dictate. A vision is only as good as you can see today. Perhaps you will be able to see better tomorrow. Be ready and willing to adjust when your vision improves. Developed with these warnings in mind, the mission and vision provide the first two cornerstones in a strong foundation for excellence.

Summary of Chapter 5—The Vision

1. The second element of the foundation is the *vision*. The vision exercise can help you guide your team to the discovery of a powerful, inspiring vision.
2. Each individual team member's personal vision must *align* with the team's vision, and teams must align their visions with the larger organization's vision. Team members must believe that by being a part of this team, they are getting where they want to go in life. The vision must be compelling enough to inspire active involvement.

3. It may be a good idea to capture all the specifics that emerged from the vision brainstorm in a descriptive paragraph to create clarity and inspire others to help make it happen.
4. A strong vision will inspire members of the team to keep striving for excellence in the pursuit of their mission, regardless of the obstacles, challenges, and setbacks that will inevitably come.

Take Action

1. Discern your organization's vision. Use the vision exercise in this chapter to help you get started with your mastermind group.
2. Discern your team's vision. Use the vision exercise in this chapter to help you and your team. Use trust-building exercises at every opportunity.
3. Discern your family's vision. Use the vision exercise in this chapter to help you and your family. Use trust-building exercises at every opportunity.
4. Discern your personal vision. Where do you personally want to go in your life? What do you personally want to become at some point in the future?
5. Document this foundational information. This will form the second section of your Blueprint for Excellence.

CHAPTER 6

The Principles

> Principles help you decide today how you're going to behave tomorrow. They form guidelines for daily behavior to ensure that you don't compromise on the things that are most important to you.
> —John Maxwell

Author Hal Lindsey shares a story about one of his trips to the Holy Lands. He was visiting Mount Sinai when he noticed a beautiful eagle soaring high in the heavens. He also noticed a severe storm in the distance in the eagle's path. A member of his group expressed concern for the eagle heading toward the storm. The guide informed them that the eagle has the ability to rise above the storm and fly over it to the other side. To do this, they lock their wings as they approach the heat thermals created by the storm, which allows them to effortlessly rise above and over it. For human beings, *principles* are like the heat thermals in the storm. They allow us to rise above adversity, hardship, and trial by locking our wings on them until we arrive safely on the other side. Principles help form the foundation for excellence.

Once you've developed your mission and vision, your next task is to consider what principles are important to you. What are the nonnegotiable values upon which you will not compromise during your journey toward excellence? As the writer of Proverbs said, "What does it profit a man if he gains the whole world and loses his soul?" To keep you on course and to attract, retain, engage, and inspire your team to excellence, you must clearly understand the parameters of principle that are important to you and the team.

> *32. Excellence is not possible without a clear understanding of your guiding principles.*

Principles help you determine today how you will behave tomorrow. What exactly does that mean? Imagine one of your nonnegotiable principles is integrity. You decide today that you want to behave with integrity while pursuing your goals. As you're going about your work, a customer offers you a bribe of one hundred dollars if you will give them special treatment over others. What do you do? Absent a predetermined value of integrity, you may take the bribe and give them what they want. After all, you could certainly use the money. However, if you have predetermined integrity as one of your core principles, you'll behave differently.

Integrity is defined as adherence to moral and ethical principles, soundness of moral character, and honesty. It's *doing the right thing*. If integrity is a principle you value, what would you do in this case? Most would agree that taking a bribe and giving special treatment in return is not demonstrating integrity. Your team may even have an ethics policy that specifically prohibits the acceptance of bribes. The right thing to do would be to respectfully decline the bribe.

The great thing about determining your principles in advance is that you don't have to think about what to do when a situation like this presents itself. You simply and quickly act with integrity. That's how predetermined principles help you decide today how you will behave tomorrow. *What do you value? What are the nonnegotiable principles that will guide your behavior on a daily basis?*

The Principles Exercise

Assemble your mastermind team in an offsite location. To begin, give everyone the principles exercise handout (see Appendix A). Have them discern their personal principles first and then transition to your team and organizational principles. I've found that most people have not invested time in discerning their personal principles, and they really appreciate this exercise.

Follow the directions on the principles exercise until each team member has a list of his or her twelve most important principles, six most important principles, and top two principles. Collect everyone's top two principles on a flip chart. This represents what's most important to your team from a personal perspective and is an important first step. Each team member's personal principles must align with the rest of the team. To accurately assess alignment, each team member must have first identified his or her personal principles.

At this point, I like to give the participants a chance to talk a little about what they've just experienced. *How did it make them feel? Did they find the exercise valuable? Did it bring the team closer together in the process?* Usually, they will find strong value in what they've done.

Now repeat the exercise, this time making sure everyone has the team in mind instead of themselves. This will produce healthy discussion about desired team behaviors. Make sure someone takes good notes. Using a flip chart is helpful. Remain persistent until you gain consensus on a set of four to six principles the team values most. These will become your team's core principles. It's also wise to have a dictionary on hand. Words and their meanings are important. Assign the dictionary to one participant and have them accept responsibility for defining words when necessary. For more information on how to discern your principles, read *Built to Last* by Collins and Porras.

The Leader's Role

I must now issue a critical warning. All this work on principles will prove counterproductive if leadership, at every level, does *not* model the way. Remember that your culture of excellence is determined foremost by what you do—not by what you say or write into official policy.

Communication and language undergird your house of excellence, but if actions do not match the words, your house of excellence comes crumbling down. Zig says, "What you do speaks so loudly that I can't hear what you say." Avoid this destructive path by following through in behavior that which you proclaim in words.

> *33. Excellence can be achieved only when leaders, at every level, model the way. Actions must match words.*

When leader hypocrisy is allowed, excellence is severely compromised. In one organization, *respect* for one another was identified as a core principle. An executive consistently demonstrated the behavior of yelling at employees in front of others, often embarrassing and degrading them in the process. The behavior appeared to go unchecked by her boss. Over time, the executive became known throughout the organization as a hypocritical leader. Eventually, the principle of respect became laughable, thwarting the excellence journey.

Following are several examples of the results of this exercise in the five environments. There are no right or wrong answers—only agreed-upon ones. Gain consensus with your team on your principles and commit to demonstrate them every day in every way.

Principles In The Five Environments

The Organization's Principles

Assemble your mastermind group. It's best to consider surveying your larger team or workgroup to ask what they consider their core principles to be. It will communicate that you care and that you want to consider their opinions. Your hope is to find strong alignment between what team members say they value and what the leadership mastermind group values. Lead your mastermind team through the principles exercise described above to determine your top four to six core principles. Clearly define each one—and keep it simple enough to easily communicate to others in the organization.

Blue Ridge HealthCare's mastermind group conducted this exercise for their eighteen-hundred-member organization. Their list of five core principles form the acronym **CRIES**, which seemed appropriate for a highly personalized healthcare service during which many people become very emotional.

Blue Ridge HealthCare Principles—guiding us in our quest to be the best!

- *Commitment*—personal dedication to fulfilling the mission and achieving the vision of BRHC.
- *Respect*—polite consideration and courtesy toward the cultures, roles, interests, opinions, and wishes of patients, physicians, care team members, and others.
- *Integrity*—steadfastly adhering to high moral principles and professional conduct that models the standards of the organization and builds trust.
- *Excellence*—an uncompromising drive to deliver outstanding performance in every aspect of responsibility.
- *Service*—putting others above self by meeting and exceeding expectations and creating superior experiences at every opportunity.

The Disney Company states its principles on its website:

> The Walt Disney Company has come a long way from the days of Steamboat Willie in 1928. But it is still true to its core mission of providing quality entertainment for people around the world. This is what we do. And we continue to do it better than anyone else does. So what does it mean to be part of the Disney team?
> Values Make Our Brands Stand Out

- *Innovation*
    - o We follow a strong tradition of innovation.
- *Quality*
    - o We strive to follow a high standard of excellence.
    - o We maintain high-quality standards across all product categories.
- *Community*
    - o We create positive and inclusive ideas about families.
    - o We provide entertainment experiences for all generations to share.
- *Storytelling*
    - o Every product tells a story.
    - o Timeless and engaging stories delight and inspire.
- *Optimism*
    - o At The Walt Disney Company, entertainment is about hope, aspiration, and positive resolutions.
- *Decency*
    - o We honor and respect the trust people place in us.
    - o Our fun is about laughing at our experiences and ourselves.

(Retrieved November 4, 2010, from www.corporate.disney.go.com)

The Ritz-Carlton states its principles in complete sentences.

Service Values: I Am Proud To Be Ritz-Carlton (emphasis mine).

1. I build strong *relationships* and create Ritz-Carlton guests for life.
2. I am always *responsive* to the expressed and unexpressed wishes and needs of our guests.
3. I am *empowered* to create unique, memorable, and personal experiences for our guests.
4. I understand my role in achieving the Key Success Factors, embracing Community Footprints, and creating the *Ritz-Carlton Mystique*.
5. I continuously seek opportunities to *innovate* and improve the Ritz-Carlton experience.
6. I own and immediately resolve *guest* problems.
7. I create a work environment of *teamwork* and lateral service so that the needs of our guests and each other are met.
8. I have the opportunity to *continuously learn and grow*.
9. I am *involved* in the planning of the work that affects me.
10. I am proud of my *professional* appearance, language, and behavior.
11. I protect the privacy and *security* of our guests, my fellow employees, and the company's confidential information and assets.
12. I am responsible for uncompromising levels of *cleanliness* and creating a *safe* and accident-free environment.

(Retrieved November 4, 2010,
from www.corporate.ritzcarlton.com)

The Team's Principles

Perhaps the most important element for the team is to ensure it adopts, supports, and emulates the principles of the parent organization. Alignment is the starting point for team principles. The team should then use the exercise in this chapter to determine its principles. Here are some examples of actual team principles that have been put into practice:

The Learning Team

In addition to the organization's values of commitment, respect, integrity, excellence, and service, we value innovation, trust, passion, fun, communication, and continuous improvement.

- *Innovation*—Regularly implement new ideas and methods to improve our work.
- *Trust*—Demonstrate dependability and trustworthiness to build strong, high-trust relationships. Practice what you preach and maintain consistency of behavior to build credibility and expectancy.
- *Passion*—Demonstrate intense, sincere enthusiasm for your work and your team's work.
- *Fun*—Smile, laugh, and joke tactfully along the way.
- *Communication*—Accept responsibility to ensure that others understand your message.
- *Continuous Improvement*—Actively seek personal growth and improvement. Aggressively work to improve the service you deliver and the work you do.

Value Statements

1. We will always strive to do the right thing in everything we attempt and everyone with whom we come in contact.
2. We will expect and encourage excellence in all educational activities and in all services we provide to our customers.
3. We will interact with *integrity*, respecting all individuals with whom we come in contact.
4. We will seek to develop and maintain relationships of high *trust* with each other and each of our customers.
5. We will constantly *innovate* and strive to *continuously improve* the value and quality of our products and services.
6. We will strive to *communicate* effectively with all those with whom we come in contact and create *fun* and joy in all we do.

Nursing Team Principles

Nursing is "AT BAT"

I. *Accountability*—the ability and willingness to assume responsibility for one's actions and accepting the consequences.

II. *Teamwork*—sharing common values and goals and exercising concerted effort to ensure that all patients receive competent, confident, compassionate care seamlessly.

III. *Balance*—a state in which opposing forces cancel each other out; dynamic ebb and flow of key components of faith, family, friends, and finance (work), producing harmony and equilibrium in life.

IV. *Achievement*—measurement of effort set forth in sound judgment.
V. *Trust*—relying on the integrity, strength, and ability of others.

The Church's Principles (an example)

We commit ourselves by God's grace to strive to uphold the Judeo-Christian principles outlined in God's Word, the Holy Bible. God's principles are numerous; however, we view love, faith, and hope as the core.

> And now these three remain: faith, hope, and love.
> But the greatest of these is love.
> —1 Corinthians 13:13 (NIV)

1. *Love*—an act of worship demonstrating adoration, devotion, and service to God and others.
    - "Love the Lord your God with all your heart, and love your neighbor as yourself" (Matthew 22:39).
2. *Faith*—complete trust, confidence, and reliance on God and his promises in the Word.
    - "The righteous will live by faith" (Romans 1:17).
3. *Hope*—an optimistic expectation in God's promises for the future as clearly communicated in his Word, the Holy Bible.
    - "May the God of hope fill you with all joy and peace, as you trust in him, so that you may overflow with hope by the power of the Holy Spirit" (Romans 15:13).

The Family's Principles

Notice that with the family principles, we have quite a few more than four to six as I stated earlier, but we have identified three as core (love, faith, and hope). Since we're a Christian family and choose to live our lives according the Word of God, we chose the same three as the church. We also decided to list all the things we value in our home and family and use them as a framework for discussion in our conversations and daily encounters. It has worked quite well. I encourage you to use these guidelines to customize and develop what works best for you and your family team.

Intent

Our principles and standards are not rules we have to live by, but we have agreed upon these guidelines for daily behavior and strive to demonstrate them with one another, realizing that doing so enables us to accomplish our family mission and vision and maintain a better experience for everyone. Our goal is to maintain a family and home environment based on the Judeo-Christian ethic as outlined in detail in the Bible. Our first priority is to ensure that each family member is also in the family of God, having accepted Jesus Christ as Lord and Savior.

Other principles we value highly:

- *joy*—deep, inner happiness; fun
- *peace*—a general state of order and calm
- *temperance*—self-control, restraint, frugality
- *goodness*—kindness, fairness, and generosity toward one another
- *integrity*—honesty; striving to do the right thing
- *teamwork*—putting the needs of the family above one's own needs

- *respect*—courteous and tactful consideration for one another
- *cooperation*—behaving in harmony and solidarity with one another
- *personal accountability*—responsible and answerable for one's own behavior; owning up to mistakes and accepting the consequences
- *good stewardship*—moral responsibility for the careful use of the resources of time, money, materials, and methods
- *cleanliness*—keeping things neat, tidy, and fresh
- *order*—a place for everything, and everything in its place
- *health*—maintaining fitness of mind and body
- *adventure*—positively attacking each day with boldness and excitement
- *commitment*—promising to do one's best to demonstrate our family's values and standards

The Individual's Principles

This exercise is highly personal. Conduct the principles exercise on yourself. Here are mine. I reexamine them every year around the holidays and renew my commitment to them for the next year. I hope this example may help you determine yours.

My Personal Principles

I pledge to uphold my family's principles and everything they stand for, and I add these to my personal list as well.

- *marriage*—always put my wife first; work to improve and deepen our relationship
- *family*—strive to be a good parent, son, brother, and friend
- *service*—seek to fulfill God's purpose in ministry

- *humility*—stay away from the world's lure if it takes me away from God
- *learning*—maintain an attitude of personal growth and improvement
- *excellence*—always striving to do my best in every endeavor
- *fun*—make laughter a way of life

I also like this acronym someone once shared with me for personal values—LIFE.

L: love, **I**: integrity, **F**: faith, **E**: excellence

Personal principles enable you to live life to the fullest while staying true to what's fundamentally important to you. They're your compass and your guide, especially when the going gets tough. Without them, the pressures of life and relationships may cause you to detour from your quest for excellence. Invest time now to determine what's truly important to you.

Summary of Chapter 6—The Principles

1. The third cornerstone of the foundation is the *principles.* Principles serve to guide daily behavior to ensure team members strive to accomplish the mission and realize the vision without compromising on what's most important to the team. Every member of the team must commit to add these team principles to his or her list of personal principles and strive to demonstrate them every day in actions and interactions.
2. Team leaders at every level must demonstrate *commitment* to upholding the principles of the team by demonstrating them every day. Remember that what you do speaks so loudly that people can't hear what you say. Culture is determined by

behavior first, followed by communication that aligns with action.

Take Action

1. Discover your organizational principles. Assemble your mastermind team and explore these questions. What are you not willing to compromise? What principles will guide your behavior no matter what? Use the principles exercise to help you get started.
2. Discover your team principles. Assemble your team or a mastermind subset of it and explore the questions noted above. Use the principles exercise to help you get started.
3. Discover your family principles. Assemble your family or a mastermind subset of it and explore the questions above. Use the principles exercise to help you get started.
4. Discover your personal principles. Use the information in this chapter and explore the questions above. You must gain clarity on what matters to you most if you're going to build a life of excellence. Remember that excellence starts with you.
5. Document this foundational information. This will form the third section of your Blueprint for Excellence.

CHAPTER 7

The Standards

> Once values are agreed upon and behaviorally defined, [team members] within the organization must be expected to behave in a manner consistent with these definitions. Without this set of operating values [and behaviors], you're at the mercy of people's good intentions. Great leaders don't create optional cultures.
> —Ken Blanchard, Bill Hybels, and Phil Hodges,
> *Leadership by the Book*

The fourth and final cornerstone in your house of excellence—the standards—are behavioral guidelines your team has determined are critical to its success. When modeled by leadership and demonstrated by team members, standards reveal your team's values and principles. The standards represent critical behaviors team members agree to demonstrate as they perform their duties.

Standards must be agreed upon, not mandated. Standards must be modeled by leadership and demonstrated by every team member—without exception! Clearly identified standards of behavior must be built into the team's performance-measurement process. Sometimes, they're included in the values statements. Other times, they're listed separately in more detail. Perhaps most importantly, there must be commitment from top leadership to behave according to the standards with evidence of that commitment in daily behavior. Otherwise, standards will have an adverse impact on the team's performance. Let me explain further with an example.

> *34. Sustained excellence depends upon clearly defined standards of behavior consistently demonstrated by all members of the team.*

Disney has a standard of behavior called the *Disney Scoop*. The Disney Scoop requires anyone who passes by a piece of trash to *scoop* it up and throw it into a trash can. No exceptions. It's one reason you rarely see a piece of trash on a Disney property. Quality is one of their values, cleanliness communicates quality, and the Disney Scoop is one of their standards of behavior to ensure cleanliness. Disney is very successful in gaining buy-in from their cast members to demonstrate this behavioral standard.

What would happen if the president of the Disney Company walked right by trash on the ground without scooping it up—and a Disney cast member saw him do it? What would it do to cast member commitment? They just witnessed the top leader of the organization behave contrary to their stated standards of behavior. I believe that's called *hypocrisy*, which is the opposite of a *leaders-model-the-way* culture. Hypocritical leader behavior destroys team member commitment. You're better off not having standards at all if leaders are not required to demonstrate them. Leaders *must* model the way.

The Role of the Leader

John Maxwell says leaders must know the way, go the way, show the way, and grow the way. *Know the way* connotes having a clear mission and vision for the organization. *Go the way* speaks to being a role model—walking the talk. *Show the way* is referring to the leader as a teacher and mentor. *Grow the way* means listening and paying attention, recognizing and rewarding right behaviors, and dealing swiftly and fairly with wrong behaviors. It's here that many cultures break down. People will not continue to voluntarily and passionately give their best every day if they observe their leaders demonstrating hypocritical behavior.

In *I Quit but Forgot to Tell You,* Terri Kabachnick refers to a team member who has become disengaged with the team's work but is still working there. They stop giving their best and do just enough to operate under the radar. A disengaged team member is an infectious cancer cell to a culture of excellence. If the leaders don't walk the cultural talk, the cancer will emerge and spread. Hypocritical leaders breed cancerous team members. Both will derail an effort of excellence.

> *35. Hypocritical leaders breed cancerous team members, derailing any effort of excellence.*

Principles and standards only work if leaders model them and reinforce them in others. Otherwise, the best you can hope to achieve is a culture of mediocrity. What you'll most likely achieve is unadulterated failure.

The Standards Exercise

Remember that people are much more apt to support what they help create. It's best to use your mastermind team to develop your standards, but all team members should have an opportunity to provide input. For a large organization, this can be done through surveying. Smaller workgroups might want to consider personal touch focus groups in which the leader interfaces directly with team members.

You may also want to find examples of standards in like teams or organizations. Work your contacts, check with consultants in your profession, access the Internet, study great organizations you admire, or check the Malcolm-Baldridge Quality Award winners. Share what you learn with your mastermind group before meeting with them.

Here are some areas that might help you get started. Assess each area to ascertain if there are specific behaviors important to the team that need to be considered. You'll want to organize them under your principles, but use this generic list to get you started. To ensure alignment, the standards team will need to consider the principles you've already established and ask this question:

Under each of our principles, what specific behaviors do we think are critically important to creating and sustaining excellence in our team?

Areas Where Standards May Be Needed

1. Customer impact
    a. Complaints from guests or teammates
    b. Use of service standards
    c. Connecting with guests
    d. Following-up with guests
    e. General conduct in the presence of customers and guests
    f. Use of a service recovery process to rectify service failures
    g. Answering the phone
    h. Responding to e-mail communications from guests
2. Team impact
    a. Mentoring others
    b. Dress codes
    c. Attendance expectations
    d. What is an unexcused absence?
    e. How many absences allowed and still fully successful?
    f. On-the-clock behavior
    g. Attendance at team and company meetings and events
    h. Who to communicate with in case of late arrivals

  i. How to approach one another with crucial conversations
  j. Resolving conflicts and mining for conflict
  k. What to do if you recognize a problem
  l. Electronic devices used in the presence of others
  m. How to reward and recognize each other
  n. Providing one another feedback, good or bad
  o. Representing (managing up) the team to others outside of the team
  p. How to make team decisions and supporting group decisions
  q. What to do when you see another team member behaving contrary to stated and agreed-upon standards of behavior
  r. On-the-clock breaks
3. Personal growth
  a. Continuing-education expectations
  b. Completion of certifications (when, who's responsible)
4. Critical processes
  a. Unsafe acts
  b. Repetitive errors
  c. Work schedule expectations (arrival, departure, handoffs)
  d. How to handle changes
  e. Contributing ideas for improvement
  f. Implementing positive changes
  g. Recycling and reuse of equipment, materials, and supplies

Now let the brainstorming begin. Take one principle at a time and ask the key question. Give everyone a copy of the list above to help generate ideas. If ideas are not flowing, you may need to ask each team member to write down one specific behavior standard they think is important to demonstrate for a particular principle. After everyone has done this, collect the ideas on a flip chart. You may need to repeat this for each principle as you move through the exercise.

Continue the process until you have a list of specific standards that are important to your team. This will eventually become a document that you will ask each team member to sign, indicating their commitment to uphold the standards every day. If you're in a larger team or organization, you may choose to conduct a public *standards of behavior* signing by the senior leaders. Such an event can send a powerful message to the organization. Remember that once you take that step, there's no turning back. You're now committed to behave this way. Be prepared to make that commitment yourself before you ask anyone else to do it. Leaders *must* model the way!

36. Excellence demands humility.

When it comes to modeling the principles and standards, your long-term pattern of behavior will be your witness. It's nearly impossible to hide a pattern of hypocrisy. Excellence demands you set aside your pride and practice humility.

Standards in the Five Environments

Organizational Standards of Behavior

Using the tips in this chapter, Blue Ridge HealthCare created the *Blue Ridge HealthCare Standards for Excellence*. At a meeting with all leaders in attendance, the executive team signed a large *statement of commitment* document with the standards team standing behind them. Copies of the document were given to each leader to post in his or her work area and to communicate to his or her team members. Thus, the *standards of behavior* were launched. Human resources built the standards into the orientation and performance management processes so that all team members would be held accountable for demonstrating them. The actual standards document is too long to include here, but here are a few excerpts shared with permission.

Blue Ridge HealthCare Standards of Behavior
A Word from the Standards Team

We are committed to improving the behaviors of Blue Ridge HealthCare team members to assist us all in creating "a great place for employees to work, a great place for physicians to practice, and a great place for patients and residents to receive care."

We believe that our team members are a caring force. Ensuring that behavior means incorporating these Standards of Service Excellence into our daily work lives.

Everyone is expected to hold each other accountable to these standards and help create an environment founded on positive **A**ttitudes, **C**ommitment, and **T**rust. How we **ACT** as employees will ultimately determine our success on our Journey to Excellence at Blue Ridge HealthCare.

Commitment: Personal dedication to fulfilling the mission and achieving the vision of Blue Ridge HealthCare.

> Your personal mission as a care team member of Blue Ridge HealthCare is the same as the mission of our organization as a whole: To enhance life by excelling in care. Fulfilling this mission requires a personal commitment on your part. All Blue Ridge HealthCare team members are expected to work together to create a "team spirit." Our common mission, vision, and values link us to one another. "That's not my job" is not in our vocabulary.

- Develop a sense of personal ownership in Blue Ridge HealthCare.
- Work to create a positive environment. Negativity affects everyone with whom you come into contact and will not be tolerated.
- Be responsible, take pride in your work, and create successes that we can all enjoy. Strive to do the job right the first time.

Integrity: Steadfastly adhering to high moral principles and professional conduct that models the standards of the organization and builds trust.

> Building trust involves supporting a Blue Ridge HealthCare belief system that is founded in truth, integrity, and consistency. As members of the team, we are expected to do the following:

- Be supportive of each other.
- Treat each other with courtesy and respect.
- Help coworkers feel comfortable enough to ask for your help.
- Have regard for each other's areas of expertise.
- Be honest with each other and respond truthfully—with the best interest of the organization at heart.
- React professionally in all situations.

The Disney Company

Here is an excerpt from Disney's Standards of Business Conduct from their public website. The document contains sections A-N with a welcome letter at the beginning followed by instructions and amendments. As you might expect, it's quite comprehensive.

I. Ethical Standards
A. Responsibility to Guests and Customers
Our guests and customers expect and deserve the best.

Quality

The Walt Disney Company and its subsidiary and affiliated companies (collectively the "Company") are recognized around the world as providers of high-quality entertainment of all kinds, including films, television shows, attractions, consumer products, stores, and resorts.

It is the responsibility of all Cast Members and employees who come in contact with our guests and customers to be courteous, to be knowledgeable about our products and services, and to help our guests and customers enjoy the highest quality experience we can provide. Further, all Cast Members and employees who create the products and services that we sell must always strive to do the best they can to create things we are proud to identify with the Company.

Guest Safety

The health, safety, and welfare of our guests and customers are of paramount importance to the Company. These cannot be sacrificed to financial goals, inattention, or anything else. We are committed to designing, building, operating, and maintaining attractions, products, and facilities that meet the high standards we have set for ourselves. All of us share the responsibility for making guests feel safe and secure.

(Retrieved November 5, 2010 from http://corporate.disney.go.com/corporate/conduct_standards2.html)

The Ritz-Carlton

The Ritz has developed its *Gold Standards,* which include a credo, motto, the Three Steps of Service, Service Values, the Sixth Diamond, and the Employee Promise. The Gold Standards can be viewed on their public website at www.corporate.ritzcarlton.com.

Gold Standards

Our Gold Standards are the foundation of the Ritz-Carlton Hotel Company, LLC. They encompass the values and philosophy by which we operate and include:

The Credo

- The Ritz-Carlton Hotel is a place where the genuine care and comfort of our guests is our highest mission.
- We pledge to provide the finest personal service and facilities for our guests who will always enjoy a warm, relaxed, yet refined ambience.
- The Ritz-Carlton experience enlivens the senses, instills well-being, and fulfills even the unexpressed wishes and needs of our guests.

Motto

At the Ritz-Carlton Hotel Company, LLC, "We are Ladies and Gentlemen serving Ladies and Gentlemen." This motto exemplifies the anticipatory service provided by all staff members.

Three Steps of Service

1. A warm and sincere greeting. Using the guest's name.
2. Anticipation and fulfillment of each guest's needs.

3. Fond farewell. Give a warm good-bye and use the guest's name.

(Retrieved November 5, 2010 from http://corporate.ritzcarlton.com/en/About/GoldStandards.htm)

Team Standards

My learning team standards are more specific to the work of learning and education and apply only to that team. The team standards must not conflict with the organization's standards. Here is a sample from the team document.

Learning Services Standards of Excellence

1. Service Standards:
    a. Answering the phone: "Thank you for calling Blue Ridge Learning Services. This is (state your name). How may I be of service?"
    b. Dress
        i. Directors:
            1. Nonclinical: coat and tie
            2. Clinical: business casual with lab coat, or navy and white of the nurse uniform.
        ii. Learning staff:
            1. Nonclinical: (men) coat and tie, (women) business casual.
            2. Clinical: same as director
        iii. Administrative staff: business casual, professional look.
        iv. Everyone: adjust up to the audience when needed, dress a notch above the audience, and follow company policy at all times.

    c. Class conduct
        i. Have the classroom completely set up thirty minutes before class start.
        ii. Ensure you, or a member of our team, is in the classroom at least thirty minutes prior to start time to meet and greet guests as they enter.
        iii. Meet and greet using CARE and AIDET standards.
        iv. Ensure a member of our team opens the class, coordinates participant introductions, and introduces the main speaker/teacher.
        v. Gain the speaker's permission/assurance that all is well before leaving the classroom.
        vi. Ensure a member of our team is present at the close of class. Thank the presenter. Collect the sign-in roster and evaluations.

Church Standards

Our church team chose to acknowledge our commitment to model the behavior of Jesus Christ. Some of the behaviors noted in the Bible are listed below. There are many, and it takes a lifetime of commitment and the enabling of the Holy Spirit to learn and model them. The key in this case is to realize that in our own power, there is no way we can live this way every day. But by the power of the Holy Spirit who lives within all those who have accepted Christ, all things are possible. In this manner, a life modeled after Christ becomes a believable reality. According to the Bible, no one is perfect except Christ. Any attempt to be perfect will be met with failure. A member of a Christian team must realize this and draw on the power of the Holy Spirit. That's what makes the church team effort different—the mysterious participation of the Holy Spirit.

Christian Standards of Behavior *(partial list)*

Love God

1. Do the right thing (be righteous).
2. Serve him.
3. Sacrifice.
4. Don't conform to the world.
5. Abhor evil.
6. Cling to good.
7. Treat others well.
8. Honor others.

Trust God

9. Learn his precepts.
10. Read and study the Word.
11. Memorize scripture.
12. Fellowship with believers.
13. Hear the gospel preached.
14. Pray without ceasing.
15. Surrender to his will.
16. Apply his principles and obey him.
17. Watch him; he is trustworthy.
18. Be patient.

Love Your Neighbor

19. Give to him.
20. Honor him.
21. Speak the truth in love.
22. Show mercy to him.
23. Show him grace.
24. Humble yourself.

25. Confess your wrongs to him.
26. Forgive him.
27. Encourage him.
28. Do what you say (be trustworthy).

Love Yourself

29. Experience salvation.
30. Get to know God.

Witness of His Glory in You

31. Practice righteousness.
32. Share with others.

Perhaps you would appreciate a simpler look at a list of ten standards of behavior that Dr. Tom Cocklereece shares as biblical expectations of believers in *Simple Discipleship*.

Worship (Connect—Matthew 22:37-38)
1. Attend a daily private worship time with God (Luke 5:15—16).
2. Attend weekly worship on the Lord's day with other Christians (Hebrews 10:23-25).
3. Give God his tithes and offerings (Matthew 6:24; Luke 11:42; Malachi 3:8).

Word (Develop—Matthew 22:39)
4. Study the Word of God with other Christians (Acts 2:42—47).
5. Love people (John 13:34-35).
6. Obey the word of God (John 14:23-24; Luke 6:46).

Ministry (Engage—Ephesians 4:11-13)
  7. Every Christian is a minister for the church (1 Cor. 12:4-13:13; Eph. 4:11-13). This section assumes one trains for ministry, serves in ministry, and equips others for ministry.

Missions (Deploy—Matthew 28:18-20)
  8. Be a witness for Christ (Acts 1:8).
  9. Invest in others' lives (Matt 5:13-16).
  10. Invite others to worship (John 4).

Church standards could very well be summed up in one word—love. When the man asked Jesus what was the greatest commandment of them all, Jesus replied, "You shall love the Lord your God with all your heart, mind, soul, and strength; and you shall love your neighbor as yourself." When a church team member learns the truth about love, he or she is equipped to fulfill the rest of the church standards.

Family Standards

As a family of faith, we adopt and adhere to the Christian standards described in the Bible. We have also chosen to add some very specific and practical standards for our family team that help us more clearly demonstrate our principles to our children and maintain an orderly and peaceful household. They also help us take accountability for behaving according to our intentions and set a better example for our children to follow.

Crouch Family Standards of Behavior

Each member of the family pledges to strive to behave according to these standards, realizing that perfection is not possible, therefore relying on the forgiveness afforded us by faith, and making it a priority to ask for forgiveness from God and one another when we fall short.

1. **Love**—for God, each other, and others
    a. Treat others the way you would appreciate being treated.
    b. Consider family needs first, before friends, work, church, or school.
2. **Joy**—deep, inner happiness; fun
    a. Laugh often.
    b. Make sure fun, sarcasm, and joking do not offend others.
3. **Peace**—a general state of order and calm
    a. Clean up after yourself.
    b. Keep the home clean and orderly.
    c. Communicate with one another peacefully. If you can't converse peacefully in the moment, wait until you can.
4. **Temperance**—self-control, restraint, frugality
    a. Keep the home free from illegal activity and substances.
    b. Avoid behaviors that have negative impacts on self or others.
5. **Goodness**—kindness, fairness, and generosity toward one another
    a. Be kind and fair to one another.
    b. If a family member has wronged you and asked for your forgiveness, offer it freely.
    c. Give cheerfully of your time and resources to others.
6. **Faith**—complete trust, confidence, and reliance on God and each other
    a. Accept Christ for who he says he is in the Bible.
    b. Before acting or responding, ask, "What would Jesus do?"
    c. Be dependable and reliable; your word is your bond.

d. Strive to build relationships of high trust by being trustworthy. Choose to trust one another unless one's behavior makes you do otherwise. If trust is lost, work together until it's regained.
7. **Integrity**—honesty; striving to do the right thing
   a. Tell the truth with respect and tact.
   b. Do the right thing in love.
8. **Teamwork**—putting the needs of the family above one's own needs
   a. If you see dishes in the sink, items on the floor, dirt, or any other thing that needs to be done, take care of it without worrying about whose fault it is. If there's doubt, ask other family members before proceeding.
   b. Do your fair share of the work required to maintain the home.
9. **Respect**—courteous and tactful consideration for one another
   a. Communicate in a peaceful, loving manner with courtesy and tact.
   b. Own up to your behavior, apologizing when necessary and seeking one another's forgiveness for wrongs.
10. **Cooperation**—behaving in harmony and solidarity with one another
    a. Seek first to understand before being understood.
    b. When communicating, consider the other person's point of view.
    c. Interact with one another in a spirit of harmony and mutual benefit.
11. **Personal accountability**—responsible and answerable for one's own behavior; owning up to mistakes and accepting the consequences
    a. Rather than blaming others for problems, ask, "What can I do to make a positive difference?"

b. If you wrong someone, acknowledge your error, apologize for the act, and ask for forgiveness.
   c. Accept the consequences of your actions.
12. **Good stewardship**—moral responsibility for the careful use of the resources of time, money, materials, and methods
    a. If you find yourself with more than a few hours per day of idle time, find ways to be productive and add value:
        i. Work outside the home and contribute financially to the family needs.
        ii. Volunteer to serve in the community.
        iii. Find ways to improve the living conditions for other family members.
        iv. Note: idle time is defined as time spent that is purely for selfish, personal reasons and adds no value to the family experience overall. Everyone needs some idle time to refresh and revitalize, but too much is not fair to others or good for the soul. Time invested *playing* together is not idle time because it adds value to the family experience.
    b. Keep your financial commitments to the family and its members
        i. If you borrow money, pay it back as agreed.
        ii. If you commit to contribute, do so timely as agreed.
    c. Consider family needs first in financial matters, before spending on self.
    d. Take care of material possessions in the home, regardless of whose they are, making them last as long as possible. If you break something, it's your responsibility to fix it or have it fixed.
    e. If you see a better way to do things, suggest it to other family members for consideration.

13. **Cleanliness**—keeping things neat, tidy, and fresh
    a. If you've got time to lean, you've got time to clean. If something's dirty or messy, take the initiative to clean it up rather than waiting for someone else to do it, regardless of how it got that way.
    b. Before enjoying rest time, ask, "Is there anything that needs cleaning up first?"
14. **Order**—a place for everything, and everything in its place
    a. Work to understand the system of order in the home and always put things back where you got them.
15. **Health**—maintaining fitness of mind and body
    a. Control quality and quantity of food you eat to maintain a healthy body.
    b. Exercise regularly to keep fit.
    c. Feed your mind daily with the good, the clean, the powerful, and the positive.
16. **Adventure**—positively attacking each day with boldness and excitement
    a. Strive each day to have a positive impact on the world and the people around you.
17. **Commitment**—promising to do one's best to demonstrate the family values and standards
    a. Strive to behave each day according to these values and standards.

Individual Standards

As a Christian, I have chosen not to develop additional standards of behavior; I acknowledge and affirm my commitment to strive to live a life modeled after Jesus Christ. He is my role model of behavior, and I strive to emulate his standards of behavior, which are clearly communicated in the Bible. I study it daily. I'm thankful two of his principles are mercy and grace because I screw up a lot. Just ask my wife. Ken Blanchard and Phil Hodges have done a great job describing how to live a life modeled after Christ in *Lead Like Jesus*. If you're interested in learning more about the Christian path, the Bible and Blanchard's book are great places to start.

Standards of behavior form the fourth and final cornerstone of the foundation of our house of excellence. Taking time now to work with your team to develop your own will serve you and the team for years to come. Don't make the mistake of neglecting this critical cornerstone of excellence as so many others do.

Ken Blanchard said, "Great leaders don't create optional cultures."

Summary of Chapter 7—The Standards

1. The fourth and final cornerstone of the foundation is standards of behavior. Standards provide specific behavior guidelines to demonstrate the team's principles.
2. Everyone on the team must make a *commitment* to behave according to the standards every day.
3. When (not if) you mess up, you must initiate action *immediately* to make it right.
4. Leaders must model the way.
5. Standards of behavior should be integrated into the language and the performance measurement process used by the team.

Take Action

1. Develop key standards of behavior for your organization. Start simple. You can always build upon what you have as you go along.
2. Develop key standards of behavior for your team in like manner.
3. Develop key standards of behavior for your family in like manner.

4. Develop key standards of behavior for yourself. Using the standards exercise, identify specific behaviors that demonstrate your commitment to your values and plan to demonstrate them on a daily basis.
5. Document this foundational information. This will form the fourth section of your team or personal Blueprint for Excellence.

Summary Of Section 2: The Foundation

This completes your foundation for excellence—a solid mission and vision supported by reasonable and sound principles and standards, clearly communicated to everyone on the team using a language of excellence and modeled daily by leadership and required of every team member. This is a foundation built upon a rock that will withstand any storm, adversity, or challenge that is inevitably coming your way. Invest the time now to build your own foundation for excellence. You'll be glad you did—and so will everyone else on your team.

Next, let's look at the supporting structure—the pillars of performance excellence.

SECTION 3

Erect the Structure

*To reach a port, we must sail—sail, not tie an anchor—
sail, not drift.*
—Franklin D. Roosevelt

A Framework for Execution

When Debbie and I take a trip, I love logging on to Google Maps to check out the route. Geography has always intrigued me. I identify the routes, study the terrain between where we are and where we want to go, and plot the best course. If you're going somewhere you've never been before, it's best to have a map.

The structure is the map in our house of excellence. It helps you develop a plan for deployment to get you where you want to go. The foundation is your compass. The structure is your map.

The framework for execution is called the five pillars of performance. Some have come to refer to this as the balanced scorecard approach. Many organizations use these areas of focus, or similar ones, to guide them in planning and execution. Few, however, use them to guide performance at the team and individual levels as well. This section will help you understand the methodology behind the framework in all five environments.

Balanced planning is the main benefit of the five-pillar framework. By considering objectives and tactics in each of the five areas, you ensure balanced clarity of focus. Have you ever worked in an organization where it seemed all they cared about was money? Did you enjoy working there? It's certainly important to pay attention to finances—if you don't, you could go out of business—but if finances are all team members perceive the leaders of the organization to care about, many will feel disenfranchised.

The path to financial stewardship is paved with people who believe you care about them as much as, if not more than, the money. You must consider the impact of your financial decisions on the other four pillars of performance—or you will likely do things that de-motivate your team and negatively impact your guests. Used effectively, the five-pillar approach will produce balanced clarity of focus, leading to daily action that matters.

The Five Pillars of Performance

The five strategic pillars of performance are quality, service, people, growth, and finance. Everything you do will fall into one of these five categories. Your task is to develop goals and tactics within each area that will drive your focus, keep you on target, and take you where you want to go. The five pillars are comprehensive in scope and will envelope all organizational, team, and individual activities in all environments.

There is also a specific order to the pillar thinking that helps you prioritize your action when faced with multiple priorities. In this section, I will discuss the pillars one at a time in priority order and ask two key questions about each:

1. What is the main objective in this pillar of focus?
2. What will happen if you do not achieve it?

I'll apply this understanding in each of the five environments—organization, team, church, family, and individual.

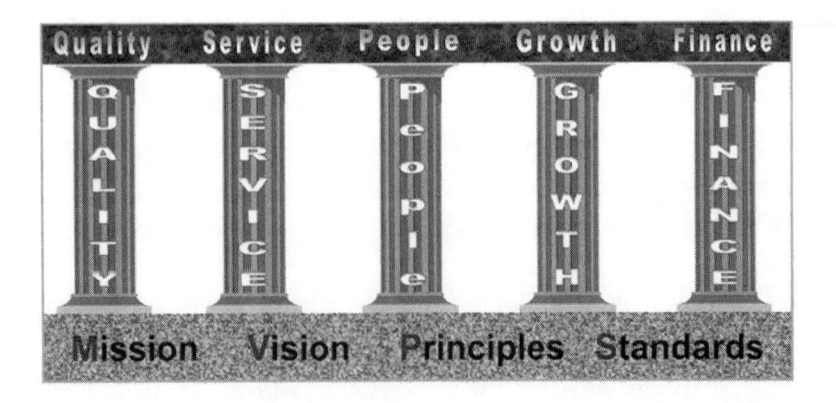

CHAPTER 8

The Quality Pillar

> The cause of the decline of Western industry is that management has walked off the job of management, striving instead for dividends and good performance of the price of the company's stock. A better way to serve stockholders would be to stay in business with constant improvement of quality of product and of service, thus to decrease costs, capture markets, provide jobs, and increase dividends.
> —W. Edwards Deming

We often hear it said that *quality* is job one. The only goal for quality is *excellence.* What's the worst thing that could happen if you fail to deliver excellent quality? In healthcare, someone could die. At a theme park like Disney, someone could be unhappy with his or her experience. On a ride or attraction, they could be seriously injured or killed. At a hotel like the Ritz-Carlton, someone could be unhappy with his or her experience, tell others about it, and cause business to decline. If the food quality in a restaurant was bad enough, someone could die from food poisoning. For a car manufacturer like Toyota, the car could malfunction and cause serious injury or death. For an airline like Southwest, the plane could crash and injure or kill the passengers. For a drug company like Pfizer, someone could die from tainted medicine. For my learning team, someone could receive bad information or knowledge that could lead to serious injury or death. For Tim's bio-medical engineering team, a piece of equipment could malfunction, causing serious injury or death to a patient. For a church, members could be misled and suffer a life of loss and pain. For a family, members could distance themselves from one another and suffer serious long-term effects from a negative family environment. For an individual, the adventure of life could be one of doom and despair, perhaps even leading to suicide.

Consider the consequences of poor quality and use that understanding to inspire your team to deliver great quality every time. Quality really is job one.

37. Quality really is job one.

If poor quality persists over time, failure is imminent. In healthcare, high quality is taken for granted by the patient. When you go to a hospital, you expect the doctors and nurses to know what they're doing and to do it well. Have you ever asked the nurse to explain what's in the drip bag hanging from the IV pole next to the bed? My guess is probably not. Most of us don't ever think to ask that question. We take it for granted that what's in the bag is what's supposed to be in the bag. However, if the hospital has a reputation for poor quality, patients will question the procedures or find somewhere else to go. Quality in healthcare is taken for granted, unless the patient has reason to believe otherwise. Perhaps that's true of any product or service in any environment.

Some might suggest that high quality is not a priority of Walmart, the largest retail company in the world. Let's think about that for a moment. What is Walmart really selling? Are they selling clothing, household supplies, toys, electronics, yard and garden supplies, or groceries? Is that their main product or service—or are they really selling something else? Is it possible that Walmart's huge success is due to the way they offer just about everything you might need at a reasonable price in a convenient manner? Aren't they really selling value and convenience? In that regard, Walmart has created and perfected a way to provide value and convenience that has become the best in the world. Their quality in the delivery of convenient products at a high value is second to none. Many would even say that the literal quality of their products is very high as well.

Is it possible that the main problem with industry in America today is the customer's perception of quality? Consumers have come to believe that America has lost the ability to compete on quality in the car business. The Big Three now refers to Honda, Toyota, and Nissan—not Chevrolet, Ford, and Chrysler. Americans have lost faith in the quality of American-made cars. Why is that? Could it be related to the number of recalls and repairs, the lower resale value over time, and the shorter life cycle of the products compared to the foreign competitors? Recently, American carmakers have taken on this challenge, and many would say that the quality of American cars is improving, even amidst tremendous economic struggles.

Excellent quality is the goal, and bad things can happen if we don't achieve it. There's no way to create and sustain a culture of excellence with poor quality. It's the first and most important pillar of focus to consider in building your framework for excellence. Next, let's consider the five environments and answer two questions.

1. What does excellence in the quality pillar look like in this environment?
2. How will you know if you're delivering excellent quality?

Quality in the Five Environments

Organizational Quality

What does excellent quality look like at the organizational level? To answer that question, we must consider two variables.

1. Do you provide a product or a service?
2. How does your customer define quality?

Products are tangible items for consumption that you can touch and use. A *service* is an act of assistance that is delivered by one person or group of people to another. Usually, the higher the quality, the higher the price. When we begin to consider price in the equation, we embark upon the *value* discussion.

A customer's perception of value is determined by the combination of quality and price. Perceived value goes up when the customer believes that he or she is receiving higher quality at a fair or low price. Typically, as quality goes up and price goes down, perceived value is improved. Most of us use the words *bargain* or *deal* when we find that magical combination. When people say, "I got a great deal on that TV," they think they received high quality at a low or very fair price. However, buyer beware. Many times you get what you pay for.

Value is an elastic feature of a product with many determining variables. A more detailed discussion of value and the other marketing aspects of products fall outside of the scope of our discussion here. Our objective is simply to understand how quality can affect value as it relates to a customer's overall perception of quality. To explore those concepts further, you may want to visit the marketing section of Amazon.com or Barnes and Noble.

If the organization produces and sells a tangible product, quality will be determined by such factors as safety, durability, strength, comfort, style, usefulness, and appearance of the product. Examples include a house, a car, a table, a computer, a pen, a book, a cup, a lamp, a phone, a television, hairspray, toothpaste, clothing, or any one of the millions of other consumable products produced and sold every day in the world. If the product is food, we add taste and smell to our quality definition.

The variations on the definition of quality can depend upon the target consumer of the product. Organizations invest millions of dollars trying to understand the customer's definition of quality and then strive to meet or exceed that expectation to remain successful. If the organization does a good job understanding and delivering on the customer's expectation of quality, the customer will continue to purchase the product and ideally tell others about its high quality.

> 38. *When the organization and the customer's definition of quality align, excellence becomes possible.*

My wife loves to drive a Honda. She loves it because she's had good experiences in the past with the quality of her Honda. It lasted her a long time (durability). It kept her safe on the road (safety). It's comfortable for her to drive (comfort). She likes the way it looks (style and appearance). It's also economical (usefulness). That's how she defines the quality of her Honda, and she likes to tell others about it whenever she has the chance. Honda defines quality the same way. Consequently, Honda has been very successful over time as an organization. When the organization and the customer's definitions of quality align, excellence becomes possible.

For my morning coffee, I love a fresh-brewed cup of Colombian supreme mixed with French vanilla bean. I enjoy the entire experience at the supermarket of filling my bag with fresh coffee beans, pouring them in the mixer, and hitting the on button to watch and listen as they're churned into fine granules. It smells great! Fresh ground coffee costs more than instant, but it's worth the price for me. It provides a higher-quality taste, smell, and morning experience I have grown to love and enjoy. In this case, the smell and taste are the determining factors of the high quality of the coffee.

If the organization delivers a *service*, quality will be determined by such factors as safety, courtesy, speed, competence, accuracy, and convenience. Examples include healthcare, plumbing, dry cleaning, hotels, airlines, consulting, teaching, law enforcement, and government. In a service organization, the customer's perception of quality is largely determined by personal interactions with the service provider.

Some tangible products are involved in the delivery of the service, but the service is the main thing. In healthcare, the service is care. In plumbing, the service is fixing a leak. In dry cleaning, the service is cleaning the clothes. In hotels, the main service is a good night's sleep. In airlines, the service is travel by air. In consulting and teaching, the service is the transfer of knowledge and the improvement of capability. In law enforcement, the service is protection and order. In government, the service is the well-being of the community. Service organizations are highly relational, and their perceived quality depends heavily on interpersonal interactions.

A few years ago, my eighty-year-old dad was having a routine heart catheter procedure. His local cardiologist discovered that one of his main arteries was 90 percent blocked and immediately (speed) sent him to the closest heart center (convenience). When we arrived, we had a pre-op consult with the surgeon who would be performing Dad's bypass surgery. There were only two questions I wanted to ask the surgeon at that moment. How many of these have you done (competence), and did anyone die as a result (accuracy and safety)? In this service experience, we defined the quality of Dad's care by the interactions with the two doctors involved. Had his cardiologist not responded quickly to the discovery of the blockage and had the surgeon lacked experience with a good track record, our perception of the quality of the experience would have been very poor.

Whether you provide a product or a service, you must clearly define the look of quality from the customer's perspective. Next, you need to know how to *measure* your quality.

At the organizational level, there are several measures of quality. We've already mentioned a few of them. Foremost is customer perception. You must clearly understand how your customer perceives your quality. The best way to know is to ask them. You can conduct a formal survey of your customers on a regular basis, you can survey them at the point of delivery, or you can contact a sampling of them following a purchase or interaction. You may choose to do all of the above. Anything less than an excellent rating needs attention.

Most organizations measure quality in terms that describe what they don't want—number of accidents, defects or errors, rejected or reworked products, product shortages, and waste. I prefer to measure what we do want—number of days or transactions conducted safely, products produced accurately, products delivered successfully. When you focus on what you want, you're more likely to get it. Measurement is funny that way. Be careful if you choose to measure what you don't want. Specific measurements will vary depending on the type of product or service you deliver.

At Blue Ridge HealthCare, for example, organizational quality is defined in the charter document as "providing *patient-focused care that makes best use of our clinical resources* for high-quality, cost-effective care." It is measured in the following ways:

- the patient's perception of overall quality of care as determined from a survey
- number of hospital-acquired condition rates (never events)
- inpatient mortality percentages
- performance on thirty-one indicators of appropriate care
- length of stay in days
- number of patients who left the emergency department without receiving treatment
- infection rates
- medication reconciliation percentages
- Medicare readmission rates

Most of these measures are related to industry standards and enable the organization to benchmark its quality against similar healthcare organizations around the country. They deal mostly within the areas of error, speed, and inaccuracy of delivery of care. Since healthcare is a service business, the patient's perception of quality is largely driven by the service provided by the doctors, nurses, and assistants. We'll talk more about that under the service pillar.

Disney and Ritz measure quality predominantly through guest perception, repeat business, cleanliness, complaints and compliments, and customer loyalty. A furniture manufacturer might measure quality using customer perception, defects, reworked items, customer returns, product appearance standards, and repeat business.

I asked the chief operating officer of a project management company how he knows whether or not he has delivered high quality to his customer. He shared four main measures their customers use to rate the quality of their service.

1. Did they complete the project on time (speed)?
2. Did the customer perceive it with high quality (customer perception)?
3. Did they complete the project on budget (cost and value)?
4. Did the customer perceive a high quality of communication (service and courtesy)?

The key at the organizational level is to clearly understand how your customer measures quality and to develop strategies and tactics to meet and exceed those needs.

Team Quality

In teams, quality looks very much like it does at the organizational level. The team needs to assess its impact on quality as the organization defines and measures it.

How does what we do affect the quality outcomes of our organization?

If the team is directly involved in the production of the product or the direct delivery of the service, quality will be defined very similarly as it is at the organizational level. If the team is in a support role for operations or production, they're actually functioning as an internal service department, and the quality of that service is determined like a service organization's quality.

In healthcare, nursing teams are involved in the direct delivery of the care. Therefore, their quality is defined in terms of patient's perception, infection rates, mortality rates, and so on. The only difference is that the nursing team will focus on the quality they deliver to the patients that come to their team, and the organization will focus on quality that is delivered to all patients. The difference is a matter of scope, not definition.

In the furniture factory, the first step in the process is to cut the wood. There's a department set up to do nothing but cut wood. For this team, quality is measured mostly by accuracy—cutting the wood to the defined specifications. This team sends the cut wood to the sanding department to smooth the rough edges. For the sanding department, quality is measured primarily with touch and appearance. From sanding, the wood goes to the assembly department, where pieces are fit together and the furniture begins to take shape. If cutting and sanding deliver a poor-quality product to the assembly team (i.e. cut to the wrong lengths and not sanded smoothly or correctly), the pieces will not fit together properly and will have to be reworked or sent back to the cutting or sanding department. Therefore, the cutting and sanding departments can also measure quality with rework and defects, both of which are also organizational measures in that business.

Teams directly involved in the operation or delivery of the service have quality definitions and measurements similar to those at the organizational level. However, internal service teams (human resources, quality control, education services, food services, and housekeeping) will use service definitions and measurements for quality because they function like a service organization on a smaller scale.

> *39. Every team member must understand his or her impact on the quality of the excellence experience.*

My learning team used the learning customer's *perception* of the quality of the learning experience as the main measure of quality. Our philosophy was that when we delivered high-quality learning services to nurses and direct care providers, they in turn provided a higher quality of care to the patient, causing the patient's perception of quality to improve. Our impact on organizational quality was determined by the quality of the learning service we provided to nursing operations. It was an indirect impact.

Every internal sub-group or team that is not directly involved in the production of the product or the delivery of the service must be able to map his or her impact on organizational quality. Additionally, *every* team member must understand his or her impact on organizational quality, whether direct or indirect.

Church Quality

What does excellent quality look like in the church environment? Christian A. Schwarz, director of the Institute for Natural Church Development, led the most comprehensive research project on the causes of church growth that has ever been conducted. From 1994-1996, more than a thousand churches of all types, sizes, and styles participated in the study. From this extensive research, Schwarz was able to discern eight quality characteristics of growing churches. Described in detail in *Natural Church Development*, these characteristics provide us with an excellent picture of quality in the church environment.

The NCD Eight Quality Characteristics

1. **Empowering Leadership**
    - Leaders of growing churches help Christians develop greater degrees of empowerment. They equip, support, motivate, and mentor individuals to become all that God wants them to be.

2. **Gift-Oriented Ministry**
   - The role of church leadership is to help its members identify their gifts and integrate them into ministries that match their gifts. According to the research, no factor influences the sense of joy in living the Christian life more than if we are living it according to our spiritual gifts.
3. **Passionate Spirituality**
   - Effective ministry flows out of a passionate spirituality. Spiritual intimacy leads to a strong conviction that God will act in powerful ways. Faith is actually lived out with commitment, fire, and enthusiasm.
4. **Functional Structures**
   - The church is the living Body of Christ. Like all healthy organisms, it requires numerous systems that work together to fulfill its intended purpose.
5. **Inspiring Worship Service**
   - Is the worship service an inspiring experience for those who attend it? People who attend inspiring worship services unanimously declare that the service is actually fun, and they attend out of a sincere desire to worship God rather than to fulfill a Christian duty.
6. **Holistic Small Groups**
   - Growing churches have developed a system of small groups where individual Christians can find intimate community, practical help, and intensive spiritual interaction.
7. **Need-Oriented Evangelism**
   - Growing churches share the gospel in a way that meets the questions and needs of non-Christians.
8. **Loving Relationships**
   - Unfeigned, practical love endows a church with a much greater magnetic power than all the marketing

efforts in the world. Real love spreads that mysterious scent that few can resist.

The NCD Institute can help a church survey its membership to assess quality in the eight areas. Using data from the assessment, the church can develop priorities for action to improve the quality of the church experience for its members. To locate those materials, access the NCD website at http://www.ncd-international.org.

Family Quality

A high-quality family environment is loving and harmonious. Disagreements are settled calmly with an attitude of mutual benefit. Family members seek win-win outcomes with one another, and instances of hurting one another are minimal. The home and grounds remain clean, orderly, and in good repair. The family works together to meet one another's needs and the needs of the family unit as a whole.

To assess the quality of the family environment, family members need to be able to express their individual perceptions of the quality of the family experience. Reaching that level of clarity requires that the family specifically defines quality and commits to make it happen. With a clear definition and assessment of its current state, strategies and tactics can be implemented to improve the quality of the family experience.

Debbie and I identified five quality characteristics of our family environment. We measure our progress by discussing these areas with one another on a regular basis.

1. Every family member views the home experience as generally loving and harmonious (perception of quality).
2. Disagreements are settled calmly with an attitude of mutual benefit. Family members seek and generally achieve win-win outcomes (courtesy).

3. Instances where one family member hurts another are minimal (safety).
4. Family members respect one another's space and property (respect).
5. The home and grounds remain clean and in proper order (appearance).

Individual Quality

The definition of a high quality of life at the individual level is a highly personalized thing. Each person may define it differently. I learned a quality of life planning system from Zig Ziglar many years ago that I still use today. He defines seven areas of life to consider and assess:

Quality of Life Areas

1. Physical—maintain good health
2. Spiritual—positively develop your relationship with the supreme being
3. Social/emotional—cultivate positive relationships with others
4. Family—maintain positive connections
5. Career—cultivate purposeful work you can be passionate about
6. Mental—continually challenge the mind with learning and growth
7. Financial—wise stewardship of all that is entrusted to you.

How's the Ride?

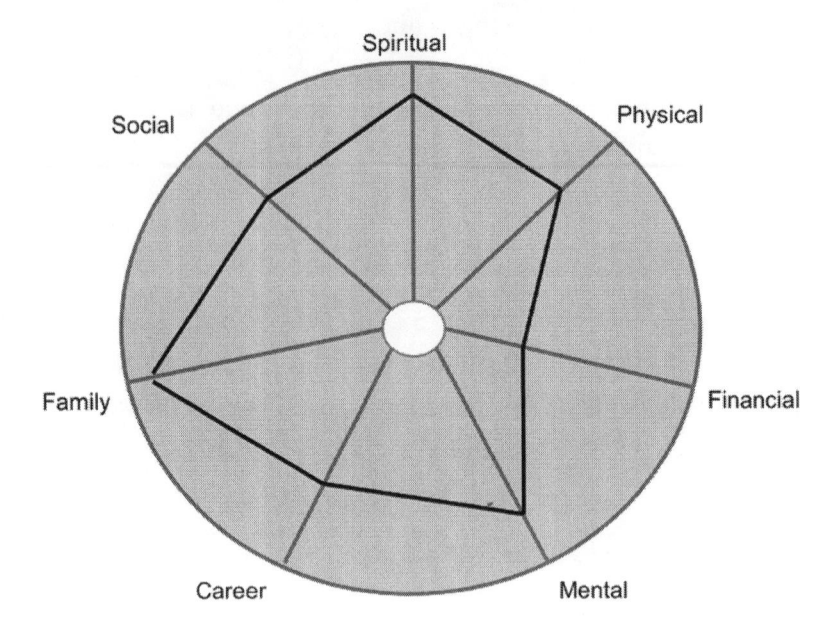

[Wheel diagram with seven spokes labeled: Spiritual, Physical, Financial, Mental, Career, Family, Social]

To assess the seven areas, Zig provides a wheel with a one-to-ten scale on each of seven spokes. You are to assess your quality in each of the areas on the scale, plot your number, connect the dots, and then see what kind of wheel it produces. Your goal is to have a balanced life in all seven areas as high on the scale as possible. When you plot your scores on the wheel, how balanced is the picture and how large is the wheel? If you would ride on that wheel, how smooth would the ride be? You can locate all of Zig's materials for success on his website at www.ziglar.com.

Remember that the essence of excellence lies in the quality of the individual's performance; it's where the quality of all of life's endeavors begins. The organization, the team, the church, and the family are all comprised of individuals like you. Therefore, you, the quality of your life, and the quality of your performance are the essence of excellence.

However you define and measure quality, it must remain the first priority in your framework for planning and execution. Excellent quality is the only appropriate goal. Poor quality will rapidly derail any effort of excellence. Work with your team to define your quality and determine how best to measure it so you will know when you're on the right track. Quality really *is* job one.

Summary of Chapter 8

1. The five-pillar framework provides a method of planning and execution with balanced clarity of focus.
2. High quality is the first priority in a culture of excellence.
3. The definition of quality at the organizational and team levels will depend upon whether you produce and sell a tangible product or deliver a personal service. Product quality is determined by safety, durability, strength, comfort, style, usefulness, and appearance. Service quality is determined by safety, courtesy, speed, competence, accuracy, and convenience.
4. Quality at the church level can be defined and measured with the NCD's eight quality characteristics of growing churches.
5. Quality at the family and individual levels is highly personal.
6. *You* are the essence of excellence in any endeavor. The success of your organization, team, church, and family depends upon the quality of your life and performance.

Take Action

1. Define excellent quality as it relates to your environment. Are you providing a product or a service? Who is your customer and how do they define quality?
2. Determine how you will measure your delivery of high quality.

3. Since the essence of excellence lies in the quality of your performance in whatever you do, make sure you clearly define your personal and individual quality measurements. Assess your progress on a regular basis (at least annually).
4. Add these descriptions to your Blueprint for Excellence.

CHAPTER 9

The Service Pillar

> The only way we can deliver an excellent guest
> experience is to see things through the eyes
> of the customer.
> —Jake Poore, President, Integrated Loyalty Systems

Everyone is a service expert. We experience acts of service in retail stores, restaurants, grocery stores, and doctor's offices every day—simply by going about our normal daily activities. Acts of service happen all around us all the time. Someone serves us with something every day.

Quality refers to the product or service being delivered, whereas service refers to *how* that product or service is delivered. Service is the act of one person or group providing assistance to another. It involves a relationship, a connection between two people. *Service* is the second pillar of focus in a house of excellence.

The Navy Blue Blazer

In 1994, I ventured into my own consulting business and was booked to speak at a regional convention in Atlanta. I wanted a new sport coat so I would look sharp for the meeting. I decided to go to the best men's clothing store in town. Benjamin's was a bit pricy for my taste, but I wanted the best. Ralph Lane, an accomplished professional in the clothing business, fitted me in a navy blue double-breasted blazer. It looked sharp! Benjamin's didn't have my size on the rack, and Ralph had to special order it. He told me it would take about ten days to arrive, which would be just in time for my trip. Ralph said he would give me a call when my jacket arrived.

Ten days passed, and I hadn't heard from Ralph. I called the store. The owner, Ben Belton, answered the phone. He told me Ralph had taken ill and would be out for quite some time. I shared the jacket story with Ben, and he said he would check into it for me. A few minutes later, Ben called back to inform me that there had been a mix up with the order—and it wouldn't arrive for ten more days. Obviously, that posed a problem. Today was Thursday and my presentation was in Atlanta on Monday.

Ben said, "No problem, Dave. Just come on in, and we'll fit you into a jacket off the rack. I'll have our seamstress alter it for you, and you can take it with you to Atlanta. When yours arrives, we can trade them out, and all will be well. Will that be suitable for you?"

"That would be awesome!" I replied. "I'll be right in."

After fitting me for the alteration, Ben told me to come by anytime on Saturday to pick it up.

What a relief, I thought. Ben was known for this type of excellent service, and I was experiencing it firsthand.

> *40. Excellent service with excellent quality leads to growth and sustained success.*

On Saturday, I was busy with yard work and family activities. At eight o'clock that evening, it hit me. I had forgotten to pick up my jacket. I immediately called Ben at home and franticly shared my dilemma.

Ben said, "Don't worry Dave. Realizing you hadn't visited the store when I left this evening, I put your jacket in my car in anticipation of your need. I'll run it over to you now, if that's convenient for you."

I was blown away by Ben's response! He remembered I was leaving for Atlanta the next day and realized I would not have a chance to pick up the jacket before departure. He was even willing to bring it to my home himself at eight o'clock on a Saturday evening. I was flabbergasted!

I've told that service story to thousands of people since then. Ben set the standard for me on the kind of service required in a culture of excellence.

Your goal in the service pillar is excellent service, defined as an act of service that will motivate others to talk about it positively. Excellent service creates a desire in the customer to repeat the experience. Repetition builds *loyalty*—repeat business. A *satisfied* guest is not necessarily a loyal one. Satisfaction is the enemy of loyalty. You must create a profound positive memorable experience for every guest every time. Excellent service builds guest loyalty. Ben Belton delivers excellent service, and his business still thrives today. He transformed a dead business location into a thriving, successful enterprise. He has expanded into multiple locations, and his wife has joined him with a women's line. Excellent service with excellent quality leads to growth and sustained success. Service *is* the difference.

41. Excellent service builds guest loyalty.

What happens when you fail to deliver excellent service? Each service failure demonstrates one of three forms—terrible, indifferent, or good. A service failure occurs if you mistreat a guest, behaving rudely or harshly toward them. A service failure occurs if you treat the guest with an attitude of indifference, as if you don't care about them. A service failure can also occur when you provide good service, but not good enough that the guest will be motivated to tell anyone about it.

In a culture of excellence, *good enough* is a service failure. Good service is the most dangerous type of service failure. It can lead you to believe everything is okay. To motivate your guests to talk about their service experience positively, you must provide an experience that stands out in their minds. It must differentiate you from all their other service encounters. You must strive to *wow* your guests just as Ben Belton did for me with the blue blazer. Let's consider the three types of service failures and explore what will happen in each case.

> *42. Good enough is the enemy of excellent service.*

Service Failure

Terrible Service

If you treat your guests rudely and harshly, what could happen? Some may simply walk away and never come back. Some may engage you in debate and argument, and then walk away and never come back. In either case, the experience will become the topic of conversation at tonight's dinner table. A rude or harsh service experience motivates people to talk about it negatively to others. It creates negative *word-of-mouth* advertising, enough of which will eventually put you out of business. Terrible service will devastate excellence.

Some years ago, I had my mortgage loan through a major American bank. My annual property taxes were included in my monthly mortgage payment, held in escrow, and were paid by the bank each year. One year, the bank failed to pay them, and I called to inquire. The customer service representative was pleasant and said he would fix the problem.

Several weeks went by, and nothing happened. I called again to express my concern, and the bank representative said they would take care of it. Again, several weeks passed and nothing happened. By this time, my name had already appeared in the local newspaper as being delinquent on my taxes. To avoid any further legal action against me, I paid the taxes myself and informed the bank that I would deduct the amount from my next monthly mortgage payment. They told me they would report me as missing a payment if I did that. I requested that they work it out. The bank representative became very agitated with me, and I was with him. The conversation turned very ugly.

After speaking to a few more bank reps over the next several weeks, they finally agreed to my approach. During the process, several of the bank employees were very rude to me, seeking only to follow company policy rather than fix my issue. It was the most frustrating experience I've ever had, and I have sworn to never do business with that bank again. I've also used this story hundreds of times as an example of one of the worst customer service experiences I've ever encountered. I was so frustrated that I mailed a letter to the CEO of the bank to explain what had happened. In response, one of his secretaries called me with reasons and excuses—but never an apology.

Following this experience, I renegotiated my mortgage loan with another bank, the North Carolina State Employees Credit Union. By contrast, this bank serves as the best example of excellent customer service in banking I have ever experienced. I will keep my banking business with NCSECU for as long as I can. Their continued excellence in service has made a loyal customer out of me. One bank pushed me away with their terrible, uncaring, rude service and motivated me to tell anyone who will listen about it. Another bank treated me like family and created positive memorable experiences, motivating me to talk positively about them to anyone who will listen.

> *43. Excellence requires a relationship.*

Indifferent Service

If you treat your guests with an attitude of indifference, what could happen? Mark Sanborn, in *The Fred Factor*, says it best. "Indifferent people deliver impersonal service. Service becomes personalized when a relationship exists between the provider and the customer."

Excellence in service requires a relationship, a special connection between provider and receiver. Indifferent service ignores the relationship and simply focuses on the task being performed.

I recently took my dad to the doctor's office for a checkup. When we approached the counter, two ladies were working. After a few seconds, one of the ladies asked Dad's name, checked her schedule, and told us to have a seat. "We'll be with you in a few minutes," she said. She didn't smile or make any eye contact. She seemed preoccupied.

We sat down. The lady at the desk performed her duties as she was expected to do. We were taken care of and everything was proceeding normally. Dad completed his doctor visit, and we went home. We didn't think too much about it—and *that's* the problem. The experience we had was *normal* and *mundane*. It was an experience of *indifference* that did not stand out in our minds at all. Most of the service experiences I encounter are of this type. They are ordinary, routine, and unnoticeable. My needs are met, but it seems like the service providers have other things on their minds. I feel like an intrusion. Notice the words of mediocrity in this paragraph—normal, mundane, ordinary, routine, unnoticeable, intrusion. When you experience service indifference, you may be motivated to talk negatively about it—or you may simply find another place to go. Indifferent attitudes *can* lead to lost business.

Good Service

If you provide *good service* to your guests, what could happen? In the example above, if the receptionist had simply looked at us with a smile, greeted us warmly, maintained a pleasant attitude during the interaction, and appeared interested in our needs, I would've rated it as a good service experience. However, I would probably not be motivated to talk about it to others. For me to talk about it positively to others, I must view it as a profoundly distinguishable experience. It must be better than good.

Excellent Service

Moving from good service to excellent service may simply be the result of small acts of kindness, courtesy, or consideration that differentiate the experience in the mind of the guest. One hotel had a custom of cleaning the windshields of the cars in the parking lot during the night. When guests got into their car the next day, imagine the pleasant surprise.

Many times, when I stay in an Embassy Suites for several nights in a row, the housekeeping crew will notice my preferences and customize their service to cater to them. They see which side of the bed I sleep on, where I put my towels, how I arrange the television and chair, and where I keep the remote. They leave things where I put them and clean up around them rather than putting everything back where it was before I arrived. Their free cook-to-order breakfast and nightly manager's reception stand out as well. I can rely on their cleanliness and ease of check-in and check-out. Consequently, Embassy Suites has distinguished itself in my mind to such an extent that I tell people about it and look for them whenever I travel.

Disney is a master at differentiation in many small ways. Their housekeepers configure the room towels in likenesses of animals to welcome you back to the room. Small things can turn a good service experience into an excellent positive memorable experience. Find small ways to differentiate yourself from your competitors.

Your goal in the service pillar is to deliver excellent service to *every* guest *every* time. We define excellent service as an act of assistance that creates a positive memorable experience that the guest will be motivated to repeat and talk about to others. If you fail to provide excellent service, your guests may respond in a variety of ways—from negatively talking about you to others to quietly finding somewhere else to go. Poor service leads to poor business.

Service applies to everyone. Everybody serves somebody with something. Many people, especially those deep inside large organizations, fail to realize this reality. To deliver excellence in service, it's critical to understand who you're serving and the type of service you're providing them.

> *44. Everybody serves somebody with something.*

Four Types of Guests

There are four types of service guests—direct, indirect, external, and internal. A *direct* guest is someone who is the direct recipient of your product or service and with whom you have direct personal contact. An *indirect* guest is someone who is served directly by someone else. You do not make actual face-to-face contact with your indirect guests but serve them by serving someone else who does. An *external* guest is someone you serve who is outside of the organization of which you are a part. This is what we usually think of when we talk about guest service. An *internal* guest is someone you serve that is inside the organization of which you are a part. Examples include other members of your team, other departments or committees, and other leaders.

In Ben Belton's clothing store, I was his *direct, external* guest. He was dealing with me face-to-face, and I was not a part of his organization. He was providing me with the service of helping me find the right item of clothing to meet my need. When Ben is coaching one of his employees about better service skills, he is providing a service to his *internal, direct* guest. The employee is his coaching customer and is an internal member of his organization. Ben is in a direct, face-to-face encounter while coaching. In this case, I have become the *indirect* guest that Ben is trying to influence by coaching his employee. It's important that every member of the organization understands who they're serving and what type of service they provide.

Service Behaviors

Excellence in service can be universally applied to any endeavor. Since service involves an encounter between two people, you can apply specific behaviors to every service encounter to create an excellent service experience. The twelve key service behaviors are revealed below.

The CARE Model of Service Excellence

Connect with every guest.
- Stop, focus, and give them the moment. Pay attention to the guests.
- Smile when appropriate and make friendly eye contact.
- Introduce yourself. Greet them warmly and use their names whenever possible.

Anticipate the guests' needs.
- Offer directions and escort them to their destinations.
- Describe how long it will take for you to serve them.
- Listen and engage them in conversations. Look for simple ways to *wow* them.

Respond compassionately to questions and requests.
- Explain activities that need to occur during the service encounter.
- Answer all questions eagerly and respond promptly to requests.
- Take ownership of *service recovery* when discovered.

Exhibit professional behavior at all times.
- Always portray a neat, clean appearance.
- Always use open, positive, and appropriate body language.
- Always thank them for allowing you to serve them.

Service Recovery

Notice the phrase "take ownership of *service recovery* when discovered" in the model above. A service recovery plan is important because *all* human beings make mistakes. Although your goal is to create a positive memorable experience for every guest every time, no one is perfect. You're going to mess up sooner or later. When you do, it's best to have a plan in place for how to respond so you can quickly correct the error. If you do nothing, it's very likely that you'll upset your guest enough to motivate them to talk negatively about you to others.

Conversely, if you impress them with service recovery, you can literally turn a service failure into a loyal guest. Service failures are opportunities to create guest loyalty. The guest can be so astonished by your response to the service failure that they'll be motivated to talk about it positively to others. A strong service recovery effort can create a profound positive memorable experience.

> 45. *A service failure is an opportunity to create quest loyalty.*

Blue Ridge HealthCare uses an acronym for its service recovery model. It's easy to remember and apply. Their mantra is to approach service recovery with *heart*.

H.E.A.R.T.

Our objective is to deliver excellence in service and care, but when we make a mistake with a guest or fail to meet their expectations, we must act immediately to make it right. All care team members are expected and empowered to act appropriately in response to a service failure.

Recently, a patient's breakfast arrived a little late—and his coffee was cold. He told his nurse, and she ordered a fresh cup. Good service would end there. But excellent service means the nurse got a Blue Ridge HealthCare coffee mug from the service recovery toolbox and brought it to the patient along with his fresh cup of coffee. The patient was so surprised and pleased that he poured his fresh coffee into his new mug. He told the nurse that in the future every time he drank his coffee from his mug, he would remember the excellent service he received at BRHC.

This true story is an example of the service recovery plan in action and is just what the doctor ordered to improve patient loyalty. Our guests enthusiastically tell others when they receive excellent patient care and service at our facilities. But when we turn a service failure around, as illustrated in the example above, we solidify a committed guest for life who will tell ten times as many people about the experience. That's the power of effective service recovery.

When you observe a service failure, respond with **H.E.A.R.T.**

- **H** = **Hear** the concern
- **E** = **Empathize** with the guest
- **A** = **Apologize** to the guest
- **R** = **Respond/Resolve** the issue
- **T** = **Toolbox/Track**: record the activity

The Wow Factor

Good guest service is not good enough for excellence and loyalty. You must strive for a *wow factor* in your delivery of excellent service. Creating a wow factor requires thinking outside the box to develop unique and unexpected methods of impressing your guests. The wow factor creates a powerful memorable experience that will motivate your guests to voluntarily talk positively to others about you.

In 2001, my parents treated my family to a Walt Disney World vacation in Orlando, Florida. We stayed at the Caribbean Resort. On the first day of our trip, we experienced the classic Magic Kingdom. The kids had a blast and purchased several of the stuffed Disney characters as souvenirs. We returned late that night to the room and crashed for a good night's sleep.

The next morning, we arose early and ventured to EPCOT. After another full morning of fun, we returned to the room to change clothes for a visit to one of the waterparks. When we arrived, one of the stuffed animals was perched in the window, waving to us as if to welcome us back. The housekeeper had arranged all the stuffed animals on the bed facing the television and had turned it on as if the stuffed characters were watching. None of us had ever experienced that type of unique service and the kids still talk about it today. The Disney housekeeper wowed us with her unique and personalized service such that we are motivated to talk positively to others about it every time we have an opportunity.

Most men, if they're wise, remember to do something for their wife on the anniversary of their wedding. Getting flowers, candy, or perfume would be something that is probably considered normal and expected by most wives. What if you surprised your wife one morning with breakfast in bed, a red rose on the nightstand, and an envelope with two plane tickets to a destination she had always wanted to visit. Would it create a wow experience she would talk about positively for many years?

One thing I like to do for my wife is to acknowledge the first day we met. Most men acknowledge their wedding anniversaries, but few remember the first day they met. It always impresses Debbie when she gets a dozen roses delivered on November 4. When people ask her why she got roses, they can't believe her response. It creates a unique experience that she often talks positively about to others. Plus, it scores me some much needed wife points in the process.

Let's explore the concepts of service excellence, service recovery, and the wow factor in each of our five environments.

Service in the Five Environments

Organizational Service

What does excellent service look like at the organizational level? Since service is such a personal act, it takes on more of a strategic role at the organizational level. The organization strategy must include five important steps:

1. Establish service standards.
2. Teach them to every member of the organization.
3. Require that all team members take accountability for exhibiting the standards.
4. Reinforce excellent service behaviors at every opportunity.
5. Require that leaders model the way.

Blue Ridge HealthCare corporately defines its service pillar objective as "making BRHC a great place for patients and residents to receive care by providing superior service in the most pleasant, caring environment possible for patients and their families." To help accomplish this, they use a service model created by the Studer Group called AIDET, an acronym for five key service behaviors.

1. Acknowledge the patient.
2. Introduce yourself.
3. Duration—describe how long the procedure will take.
4. Explain exactly what's going to happen to them.
5. Thank them.

Studer Group's research has proven that if nurses use this model properly with their patients, it will reduce patient anxiety and improve clinical outcomes. Excellent service leads to higher-quality care.

Disney talks about creating *awesome arrivals* and *fond farewells* to help create the wow experience for guests. Ritz-Carlton teaches Three

Steps of Service as part of their Gold Standards of behavior for guest service (see chapter 7).

Many healthcare organizations develop detailed service standards covering areas such as the sacred encounter, personal appearance, environmental ownership, communications etiquette, escorting etiquette, telephone etiquette, elevator etiquette, e-mail etiquette, response to call lights, and guest waiting.

To reinforce great acts of service, many organizations use formal programs to encourage everyone to notice them and respond. Blue Ridge HealthCare created a Wow Card Program just for that purpose. Patients and care team members are encouraged to complete a Wow Card anytime they witness an act of service excellence. The cards can be redeemed for gifts and prizes.

Each year, the organization selects a few dramatic acts of profound excellence in service and awards the Merit of Excellence in a special meeting with the board of directors. The marketing department collects stories of service excellence and prints them in the company newsletter. Find ways to recognize and reward behaviors of service excellence.

Zig always said, "Behavior that is recognized and rewarded will be repeated."

Measuring Service

The most common method of measuring service at the organizational level is guest surveying. There are many excellent survey companies that can help. To be considered best in class, your goal is to deliver service at the ninety-fifth percentile or better, meaning you are better than 95 percent of the organizations surveyed.

You should also pay attention to guest compliments and complaints. They provide insight into the quality of the service being provided and can be an excellent source of service stories you can share with others. Remember that stories define and perpetuate your culture. You should master the art of storytelling.

The Ellen Avery Effect

On Sunday, March 12, 2006, our doorbell rang at five o'clock in the morning. Debbie's former husband brought news that their twenty-one-year-old son, Curtis, had been tragically killed in a car accident. Shocked and dazed, we made our way to Grace Hospital in Morganton. When we arrived, the emergency department staff quickly settled us into the private waiting area and summoned the house supervisor to our side.

Within minutes, nurse supervisor Ellen Avery joined us. Over the next several hours, Ellen stayed by our side. The cell phone calls kept coming, and she quietly and discreetly handled each one. It made us feel as though we were the only ones present in her care. Her loving, caring voice and touch were healing to Debbie as they navigated together through the myriad of steps required to process Curtis's death.

Debbie wanted to view the body, and Ellen took us to the morgue. I was amazed by how, in this most tragic and difficult of moments, she remained calm, compassionate, and caring. As busy as she was running the entire hospital that morning, Ellen allowed us to dictate the schedule, taking as much time with us as we needed to work through the pain and emotions.

As family members continued to arrive, Ellen returned to the morgue with us many times. Each time, she remained calm and sensitive to the needs of the moment. When we were finally ready to return to our home, Ellen asked if she could lead us in a prayer. She wept as she prayed, and I knew we had been in the care of someone special—someone who was genuinely connected to what she was doing and sincerely cared about helping us through our tragic ordeal. I didn't know Ellen very well before that day, but now I consider her one of my favorite service heroes. Debbie and I have a warm and tender memory of Ellen and Grace Hospital because of her care. Ellen made a significant difference in our lives that morning as she led us through our maze of emotion, trauma, and grief.

We will never forget the angel God sent to minister to our needs that Sunday morning. Ellen Avery unselfishly and humbly served us with great purpose and worth. She demonstrated to us the power of excellence in service when delivered with honest, humble intent.

About two weeks later, Debbie and I were sharing a few moments of reflection. As Debbie reminisced about the events of the past two weeks, she made a comment that captured my attention. She said she had a positive memory of the experience at Grace Hospital on the morning of the accident. Ellen Avery had created a positive memorable experience for Debbie on the most tragic day of her life—the day she lost her baby boy to a horrific car accident. When she said those words, I realized the tremendous power an act of excellent service can have on someone's life. We will never forget Ellen Avery for the powerful positive impact she had on our lives that day.

The next year, we received a card from Ellen sharing her thoughts and prayers with us on the memory of that sad anniversary. Debbie wept as she read it. Ellen Avery had carved a permanent place in our hearts with her unselfish act of service. Now that's *wow* service!

Disney claims to have what they call the *Disney Magic*. They're referring to a magical experience they strive to create for their guests. I admire and respect the wonderful job they do. However, I would suggest that the Disney magic, as powerful as it is, pales in comparison to the magic Ellen Avery created through her personal service that tragic morning in March of 2006. Your goal should be to do the same. What a wonderful world this would be if we all could find a way to create the *Ellen Avery Effect* for every guest we serve. The Ellen Avery Effect creates a positive memorable experience your guests will never forget.

Team Service

Team service will look very much like it does at the organizational level. The team needs to assess its impact on service as the organization defines and measures it.

How does what we do in our team affect the service outcomes of our organization?

If the team is directly involved in the production of the product or the direct delivery of the service, service will be defined very similarly as it is at the organizational level. If the team is in a support role to operations or production, they're actually functioning as an internal service department, and the operations groups they support will determine their service. The only difference at the team level is that the team will focus on the service they deliver to the guests that come to their team, and the organization will focus on service that is delivered to all guests. The difference is a matter of focus, not definition.

In our furniture factory example, the cutting department serves the sanding department, who serves the assembly department, and so on. They are internal service departments whose direct customer is another department inside the factory. Ultimately, they all focus on serving their primary external guest, the person who purchases an item of furniture.

My learning team used an interdepartmental survey to gather guest perception feedback and paid close attention to the compliments and complaints received from our direct learning guests. When we deliver a high level of service to nurses and direct care providers, they provide a higher level of service and quality of care to the patient, thereby causing the patient's perception of quality and service to improve.

Our impact on organizational service is determined by the service we provide to our internal guests—nursing operations. It is an indirect impact. Every internal sub-group or team that is not directly involved in the production of the product or the delivery of the service must be able to map its impact on organizational service in the same manner. Additionally, every team member must understand his or her direct or indirect impact on organizational service.

Service in the Church Environment

What does excellent service look like in the church environment? In a church, the concept of service is typically known by a different name—*ministry*.

Defined as the act of serving others, ministry should be the natural outcome of a growing church community. In *The Purpose Driven Church*, Rick Warren defines ministry as demonstrating God's love to others by meeting their needs and healing their hurts in the name of Jesus. Each time the church reaches out in love, it is ministering to others. According to Warren, the church is to minister to all kinds of needs: spiritual, emotional, relational, and physical.

Service in the church environment means reaching out to others in the community and meeting their needs. *What are the needs of the people in your community? Are you working to help meet those needs?* If the needs are being met, the church is successful. If the church ignores them, it is failing to fulfill one of its main purposes.

Recently, a leader in the church brought a community need to the church administrative council. Ken had learned there was no shelter in the community for homeless women and children during the winter months. The church had recently completed construction of an all-purpose activity building. Ken wanted to use it to house homeless women and children during the winter. He brought it before the council, the council voted to proceed with the fact-finding, and Ken was off and running with a new ministry opportunity for the church. There were many social and legal issues to work out, but Ken was committed to the goal—and it was certainly a community need. This is a good example of how the church should respond to expressed or discovered needs in the community.

It's important to note that every ministry must have a minister—someone who is willing to lead the ministry effort. The purpose of every Christian includes discovering how God has uniquely designed them to serve. Therefore, every member of the church should be involved in a ministry of some kind—and no one person should be involved in all of them. Every individual is wonderfully and uniquely designed for ministry. An individual church member who understands his or her unique design can begin to discover ways of serving that align with that design. When that occurs, the individual church member begins to experience a life of service excellence. When the majority of the members of a church reach that level of spiritual maturity, the church ministries will flourish, and the church has an opportunity to deliver service excellence in the community.

There are two main measurements of excellence in church ministry. In my home church, we discovered that only 40 percent of the people listed on the church membership roles attended church services on a regular basis. Only 16 percent of the membership was involved in something more than the Sunday morning service. *Active involvement* is the first measure of service excellence in the church. The second measure is to identify the number of ministries the church is providing to the community and assess their impact quality. I'll discuss this more in Section 4.

Family Service

Family service takes on two dimensions: the impact of the family on the neighborhood and the impact of the family members on each other. A family that is a positive contributor to its community makes sure its property and grounds remain clean and aesthetically pleasing to others. They manage their lifestyles so that other families in the community enjoy having them as neighbors. They don't disturb others, they pay their taxes, and they help other families in the neighborhood when needed. Others in the neighborhood view them as good neighbors. The family with a mindset of service excellence goes out of its way to make sure others in the community have positive experiences in the neighborhood. When the collective synergy in the neighborhood is at its peak, there is a sense of security and strong fellowship that makes everyone in the neighborhood feel safer and better.

Internal family service is very personal. It wows my wife when I get up early on Saturday morning to fix her favorite breakfast in bed—homemade French toast, fruit, and cold, fresh milk. It really wows her when I take initiative to fix something around the house before she notices it or before she has to ask me. (The handyman role is not my area of strength.) Debbie wows me when I come home from work and she's prepared something special for dinner. She wows me when she cleans the house. She wows me when I see the beautiful flowers she planted in the front yard. She wows me when she purchases the occasional box of Breyers Oreo cookie ice cream that I love so much.

It wows me when Debbie and I come home from a meeting at church to find that my son, Samuel, has vacuumed the carpet or washed the dishes while we were gone. It wows me when he pays his car insurance bill without me having to ask or offers to help me put up the family Christmas tree at the holidays. It wows me how, after a big family meal, the kids will offer to do the dishes so Debbie and I can relax and enjoy the family company. It wowed me when my daughter, Callie, so willingly and voluntarily stayed by my Mom's side during Dad's final week of agony, serving and ministering to them during that tough time. It wows me when my son, Isaac, sweeps up the leaves in his grandmother's driveway without having to be asked or willingly takes her to the post office to get her mail each day.

Excellence in service at the family level can create a positive home environment that brings joy and peace to everyone in the family. When family members put the needs of others above their own, great things happen. Excellent family service creates a home that family members want to be a part of. If you want to know how you're performing in the area of family service, just ask the members of your family to tell you. Usually, they'll be more than happy to share.

Individual Service

What does excellent service look like at the individual level? Are you a positive impact on the world around you or a negative one? Do others like having you on the team—or would they rather you took a hike? Your level of excellence in individual service is easily discerned by the way others treat you. Do they dread it when they know you're going to be around—or do they look forward to spending time with you?

Remember that the essence of excellence is found in the quality of the individual's performance. It's at this level that you should pay most attention to your goals and measurements. Since every team and organization is comprised of individuals, you want to be an individual who others want on their teams. Are you? Identify every team and every individual with whom you come in contact and begin to identify behaviors that will wow them in those moments of truth. This action, more than any other, will have the greatest impact on your overall quality of life. Refer back to the CARE Model of Service Excellence. It's a great place to start.

Summary of Chapter 9

1. Service is the second pillar of focus in a culture of excellence.
2. The goal of service is to create a positive memorable experience your guest will be motivated to repeat and voluntarily share with others. This leads to guest loyalty.
3. Everybody serves somebody with something. The CARE Model of Service provides twelve key behaviors that lead to service excellence in any environment.
4. Since service involves human beings interacting with one another, mistakes will happen. It's critical to have a service recovery plan in place to provide guidance in the event of a service failure. A service failure is an opportunity to create guest loyalty.

5. Good service is not good enough. The service encounter must wow the guest so they will be motivated to speak positively to others about it. Strive to create the Ellen Avery Effect.
6. Team service is comprised of two elements—service to others outside of the team and service to one another within the team.
7. Church service is called ministry and seeks to meet the needs of the community.
8. Families serve both the community of which they are a part and the individual family members.
9. Excellence in individual service creates a desire from others to want you on their teams.

Take Action

1. Define excellent service as it relates to your environment. Plan the behaviors that will lead to service excellence in every guest encounter.
2. Determine how you will measure your progress on your delivery of excellent service. Consider soliciting the feedback of your guest on a regular basis. Pay attention to compliments and complaints as well.
3. Add these descriptions to your Blueprint for Excellence.

CHAPTER 10

The People Pillar

> Any company trying to compete must figure out a
> way to engage the mind of every employee.
> —Jack Welch, former CEO of General Electric

> Many companies know that their ability to find and
> keep talented employees is vital to their sustained
> success, but they have no way of knowing whether or
> not they are effective at doing this.
> —Marcus Buckingham, *First, Break All the Rules*

The Selection

Carrie was impressed by the ad in the paper. Learning team seeking a unique individual who wants to help make it a great place to work!

Carrie thought, *I don't know if I've ever worked at a place I would consider great.*

She was curious and filled out the online application. The website was unique. Navigating to it was easy. She remembered the trouble she had finding that link on many other company websites. This website had a very warm, friendly appeal and made her feel like they were different somehow.

A few days later, Carrie received a call for an interview. When she arrived, she noticed the building and grounds were immaculate and well landscaped. As she made her way to the human resource (HR) department, she passed several people who wore special badges with the company's name on them. She was impressed by how friendly everyone was and how each one of them made eye contact, smiled, and said hello. Several of them asked her if they could help her find something or someone. One of them escorted her to the HR department, and she met a pleasant lady at the door.

"You must be Carrie," the lady said. "We've been expecting you."

Her visit to the HR department was extremely positive. Everyone she met seemed so interested and excited to be a part of the team. She'd never before experienced such energy and enthusiasm in a first interview.

Carrie had two interviews with HR staff, two with the department manager, and a group interview with a panel of employees from the learning team. She had to complete several online tests and surveys and make a presentation to the learning team. She was told that all of her references would be thoroughly checked. The process took several weeks to complete and made Carrie feel as though this company was very serious about who they invited to join them. She'd be lucky to receive a job offer, she thought, and she was hopeful.

A few days later, the department manager called with the offer. Carrie was elated and accepted it right away. Shortly following, a member of the HR team called Carrie to work out the details of her arrival. "Everyone who joins our organization starts with our nationally recognized orientation program called Connections," the HR team member said.

Nationally recognized orientation program? Carrie thought. *What is this all about?*

HR informed Carrie that her initial orientation experience would take place at the Learning Center and would consume the first week of her new job.

Five days of orientation? What would they possibly do for five days?

The week before Carrie was to start her new job, she received an interesting card in the mail. It was a colorful computer-generated note from her new teammates saying how excited they were that she was joining the team. Everyone on the team had signed the card and written a short, personal note to her.

This is different. I've never had anyone treat me like this before. I haven't even started yet!

In addition to the note, she received a phone call on Friday from her new manager. He relayed his excitement and told her he would be there personally on Monday morning to greet her. "Remember to park in the large parking lot to the left of the Learning Center. Your car will be safe there. And just to remind you, dress for Connections is business casual. No jeans or open-toed shoes are allowed. We'll also be providing a hot buffet breakfast for you; make sure you come hungry. I know starting a new job can be a very anxious experience, and I want to make sure we do everything we can to help you relax. Do you have any questions before Monday?"

Carrie was blown away. *No new boss has ever treated me like this. Can it really be this good?*

The First Week

On Monday morning, Carrie made her way to her new place of work. Arriving about 7:35, she was pleasantly surprised to see that her manager was already there. He was waiting for her outside of the building, holding a white placard with the words "Welcome, Carrie." It reminded her of what she had seen at the airport at the bottom of the escalator when a limo driver was looking for a passenger.

Her new manager escorted her into the building across a red carpet entrance to the registration table. Several familiar faces from the HR team and her new learning team were there to greet her. She also noticed several other employees that she didn't recognize. They all had huge smiles on their faces and said, "Come on in. We've been expecting you!"

Some were even dressed like the crew of a cruise ship and said, "Welcome aboard!"

There was lively music playing and people moving around. Carrie smelled fresh bacon and noticed other new employees settling in with their hosts. It was a very exciting and energetic atmosphere.

After signing in at the registration table, Carrie's manager escorted her into the meeting room and helped her settle in. She noticed a nameplate on the table identifying her seat. Also on the table was a packet of material and her new name badge. Hanging on the side of her chair was a travel bag sporting the company's logo. This was hers to keep, and it housed all the materials she would need for the next five days of orientation. Her manager helped her put on her new badge and said, "Don't sit down yet, Carrie. We're just getting started. There are several things I need to help you do before we get comfortable. Just relax and come with me."

Carrie's manager escorted her out of the room to an interesting display where she had a picture taken. It was like a picture taken on a cruise ship that is ready to set sail.

Her manager escorted her to the time clock so she could officially clock in to be paid for the day. They navigated their way to the buffet table and helped themselves to a hot breakfast of scrambled eggs, bacon, sausage, hash browns, biscuits, gravy, and fresh fruit.

Her manager said, "May I get you some coffee or juice, Carrie? Or would you prefer water or a soft drink?"

"Coffee would be fine," responded Carrie. *I never remember any boss of mine offering to get me coffee. It was always the other way around everywhere else I've worked!* Carrie was impressed with the humble service attitude of her new boss.

The time flew by as Carrie and her boss chatted over breakfast. Carrie had a chance to meet some of the other new employees as well.

A gentleman dressed like a ship's captain got everyone's attention and announced, "We'll be casting off in about two minutes. If you have anything you need to do before we start, now's the time!" The hosts began to excuse themselves from the table, and a few of the new employees refreshed their coffees.

All of a sudden, the room went completely dark. An image of a spaceship appeared on the big screen at the front, followed by several images of flying through the heavens and landing on a beautiful beach. *2001, A Space Odyssey* was playing in the background.

As the ship landed on the beach, an image of a beautiful cruise ship appeared with the words "Welcome Aboard!" plastered across the screen. A deep, resonant voice proceeded to welcome the new employees with words of excitement and anticipation. "You're about to embark upon the journey of a lifetime, Our Journey to Excellence! We have selected you to join us on this journey because of the unique talents and capabilities you possess. So sit back, fasten your seatbelts, and prepare yourself for the most exciting journey you've ever encountered—our Journey to Excellence."

A spotlight appeared at the door and focused on a nurse shouting to the captain that someone had been injured. "We need to airlift them to the emergency department right away!" she cried. She dashed through the room and out the exit door. Just at that moment, she appeared on the screen in the ship's doctor's office.

The doctor agreed that the patient should be sent to the emergency department. For the next fifteen minutes, Carrie witnessed the continuum of care for the patient who had experienced a stroke on the cruise ship. The patient journeyed through the emergency department, inpatient services, the nursing home, and the wellness center for rehabilitation. It was Carrie's chance to observe the important work the good people of the healthcare organization did every day. They called it their *sacred work*.

This was a powerful and impressive beginning for Carrie. Over the following days, Carrie experienced one incredible presentation after another as the learning team escorted her and the others through all the necessary *excursions* to introduce them to their new culture and team. The entire week was themed like a cruise trip. Members of the learning team played captain, cruise director, and ship's crew as they entertained, informed, and welcomed the new team members. Repeatedly, they spoke about the Journey to Excellence, and how they would need Carrie and all the new team members to understand the organization's mission and vision, agree to uphold its principles and standards, and do everything they can to be a positive contributor to the journey. Excellence in quality of care and service to their patients depended on it.

The week was filled with tours, games, exercises, presentations, and activities; they were all designed to provide a fun, informative, and exciting introduction to the new organization. It was the most incredible first week on the job Carrie had ever experienced. She knew she had made the right decision in joining the team.

On Friday, during the celebration lunch, Carrie's boss presented her with her *Passport to Excellence*, a beautiful certificate with a picture of all the "shipmates" who started their new job with her that week. She had completed the first step in her personal Journey to Excellence with her new organization and team. Next, it was on to phase two of this five-part new care team member orientation process.

The First Ninety Days

The following Monday morning, Carrie joined the others at the facility where she would be working. Phase two was called *Facility Connections*. The guide, one of the directors in the facility, gave the new team members a tour and an introduction to the safety protocols and unique expectations of being a part of that facility.

At the end of the experience, Carrie's boss met her and escorted her back to her new department, where she would spend much of her time in her new role. For Carrie, this began phase four of her orientation, *Care Team Connections*. Some of the other new team members had to complete phase three. *Direct Care Provider Connections* was designed for those new team members who would be working directly with the patients as nurses, nursing assistants, and other support roles.

46. Excellence creates a place where people want to be.

For the next ninety days, Carrie was introduced to all the expectations of her new team and role. Her new boss assigned a mentor to work closely with her and show her the ropes. Each week, Carrie had a meeting with the boss and the mentor to talk about her progress and ensure she was receiving everything she needed to be successful in her new role. Her boss taught her all about the mission, vision, principles, and standards of the team. The expectations were high, but everyone on the team was committed to helping Carrie learn her new role and become a positive, productive member of the team. They made her feel welcomed and appreciated. Her new team members modeled everything she had learned about the organization's expectations and standards. They worked very hard to create a special place in which everyone wanted to be a part. Carrie wanted to be a part of this team too. She worked very hard to learn her new role and follow the principles and standards.

At the end of ninety days, Carrie was ready for phase five of her orientation experience, *the Ninety-Day Checkup*. She was invited back to the place where it all started for a fun-filled review and *reconnection* with the others from her *Connections* class. They enjoyed a hot breakfast together, reminisced about their first ninety-day experiences, and joined in a lively review of the fundamentals of excellence in their new *culture* of work. It was a chance to celebrate the completion of their *Connections* experience and earn recognition as a permanent member of their new organization.

A Great Place to Work!

Would you like to be a part of an organization that treats new team members like this? Perhaps you are already. If so, then you know how powerful and fulfilling it can be.

The main objective under the people pillar is to create a *great place to work, live, or be*. This begins at selection as described above. The focus of the people pillar is on the *team member*. The two main measurements for the people pillar are team member *turnover* and team member *commitment*. People stay longer at places they view as great places to be. They also become more committed to the mission and vision if they feel valued and are treated respectfully. In a culture like this, people are more apt to give their best every day and work to help the team accomplish its objectives.

Since team members are responsible for delivering high-quality products and services and serving the customer, excellence in the people pillar becomes the main strategy for achieving excellence in the quality and service pillars. Each member of the team must be fully engaged in the team's purpose.

A 2006 study by Gerard Seijts and Dan Crim said, "An employee's attitude toward the job and the company had greater impact on loyalty and customer service than all other employee factors combined."

Leaders must take care of the people who take care of the guests. The people pillar is the third and center pillar of focus in your house of excellence.

> *47. Leaders must take care of the people who take care of the guests.*

When I ask team members to describe what a great place to work means to them, they tell me it's a place where leaders practice what they preach and regularly show appreciation to others for the work they do. People are treated fairly and with respect, making them feel like valued members of the team. It's a safe place to work with competitive pay and benefits. There's a positive attitude about the work and people help each other without having to be asked. Communication is clear and comprehensive. Everyone knows what's going on with the business. There's also an air of transparency, causing team members to feel as though leaders aren't hiding anything. There's recognition for great work—sometimes monetary, sometimes not.

Many of the team members describe it as a family-type environment where everyone treats each other with respect and protects the interests of the family. Perhaps most importantly, relationships with bosses are positive and productive with mutual trust and respect. These are the types of things that characterize a great place to work, live, or be. We should all strive to make this type of environment a reality in any team of which we are a part. The best strategy is to be the kind of teammate others want to have on their teams. Making it a great place to work, live, or be is everyone's responsibility.

> *48. Be the kind of teammate others want to have on their teams.*

Conversely, if you're unsuccessful in making it a great place to work, turnover will be high and commitment will be low. High performers in the culture will not stay very long. Quality and service will suffer due to the increase in turnover and lack of highly competent, skilled team members. Morale will be low, and getting every team member to give his or her best every day will seem impossible.

In a culture of excellence, the majority of team members view it as a great place to work, live, or be and are *fully committed* to doing their best every day to help the team get where it wants to go.

The Commitment Continuum

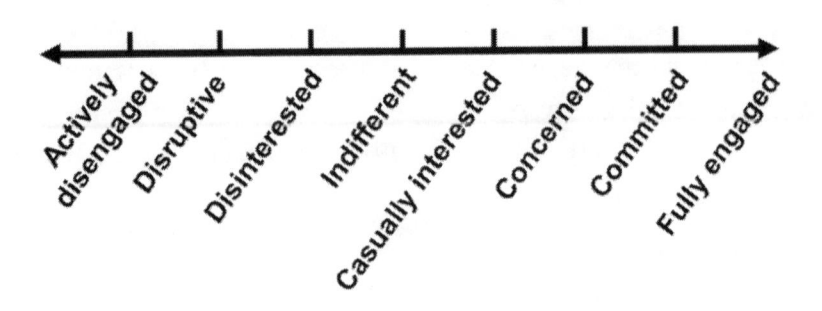

Actively disengaged — Disruptive — Disinterested — Indifferent — Casually interested — Concerned — Committed — Fully engaged

In the figure above, as you move from left to right on the continuum, the commitment level increases from actively *disengaged* to fully *engaged*. Team members who are actively disengaged make it their business to disrupt the work of the team. They talk negatively about the leader, other team members, and the organization. They complain frequently and try to pull others down with them. In front of the leader, they may appear very supportive. Behind the leader's back, they weave a web of destruction.

Your goal should be to identify the actively disengaged and either move them to the right side of the commitment continuum or get rid of them altogether. Those who have chosen to actively disengage rarely make the conversion back to full engagement. It's the right thing to help them do so, but don't waste too much time in the process. If you don't see immediate progress in the positive direction, you'll most likely have to release them from the team. From the rest of your team's perspective, the sooner you take care of it, the better (more on that in chapter 17).

> *49. Excellence requires the full commitment of everyone on the team.*

Before you can lead others to full engagement, you must be fully engaged yourself. Where are you on the commitment continuum right now? Are you fully engaged in what you're doing? If not, you must determine what it will take for you to become fully engaged.

One of my favorite bosses, Tim Crane, said, "If I'm not committed, I'm ineffective!"

You must become fully committed to the journey, and you must lead others on your team to do the same.

People in the Five Environments

The People Pillar from the Organizational Perspective

Every year, *Fortune* identifies one hundred companies as the *best places to work*. In 2010, the top ten companies were SAS, Edward Jones, Wegmans, Google, Nugget Market, DreamWorks Animation, NetApp, Boston Consulting Group, Qualcomm, and Camden Property Trust. Also on the list were Microsoft, Nordstrom, Mayo Clinic, Men's Warehouse, American Express, General Mills, FedEx, Starbucks Coffee, Aflac, CarMax, Stew Leonard's, Mattel, Marriott, and Colgate Palmolive.

Fortune partners with the Great Place to Work Institute to conduct perhaps the most extensive employee survey in corporate America; 343 companies participated in the 2010 survey. Two-thirds of a company's score is based on the results of the institute's Trust Index survey. The survey asks questions related to employee attitudes about management's credibility, job satisfaction, and camaraderie. The other third of the scoring is based on the company's responses to the institute's Culture Audit, which includes detailed questions about pay and benefit programs and a series of open-ended questions about hiring, communication, and diversity. Any company that is at least seven years old and has more than a thousand American employees is eligible. For more information, refer to www.greatplacetowork.com.

When you investigate the things that make these companies great, you see common themes in their cultures. They all have leadership cultures that model the way with humility and integrity, and they place team member engagement high on the company's priority list of strategies. Here are a few examples from the website.

- **Stew Leonard's**, a supermarket operator in Connecticut, introduced phased retirement: In their last year of service, employees work three days and get paid for five. Senior managers froze their salaries so that other employees could get raises (4 percent for hourly folks, 3 percent for salaried) and the company could maintain its no-layoff policy.
- **SAS**, a software company headquartered in Cary, North Carolina, boasts a laundry list of benefits—high-quality child care at $410 a month, 90 percent coverage of health insurance premiums, unlimited sick days, a medical center staffed by four physicians and ten nurse practitioners, a free, sixty-six-thousand-square-foot fitness center and natatorium, a lending library, and a summer camp for children. The architect of this culture is Jim Goodnight, its cofounder and the only CEO that SAS has had in its thirty-four-year history. SAS is highly profitable and ranks as the world's largest privately owned software company. Turnover is the industry's lowest at 2 percent.
- **Men's Warehouse**, headquartered in Houston, Texas, was noted for avoiding layoffs. CEO George Zimmer took a 20 percent pay cut in 2009; senior vice presidents, 5 percent; and members of the board of directors, 10 percent.
- **Baptist Health South Florida,** in Coral Gables, is South Florida's largest private employer and just keeps growing. The workforce is up 20 percent in the past three years. BHSF offered annual bonuses of $1,500 to $4,000. In 2009, the organization invested more than $2 million in new benefits

and programs focusing on work-life balance, retention, and leadership development.

(Retrieved November 23, 2010, from http://money.cnn.com/magazines/fortune/bestcompanies/2010/)

The People Pillar from the Team Perspective

The team is simply a smaller version of the organization. The criteria that make it a great place to work, live, or be at the organizational level also apply at the team level. The key measures of excellence for the people pillar at the team level are also employee engagement and turnover.

Greatness requires the leader to develop a relationship with each team member. Team member engagement occurs when the leader selects the right person for the role, develops clear expectations for them, provides them the tools, equipment, and training they need to do the job, and effectively supports them along the way.

Marcus Buckingham, a former executive with the Gallup organization, discovered that great managers learn how to focus an individual's talents toward clearly identified behavior outcomes and then let them achieve those outcomes in their own ways. Great managers simply provide the support and coaching necessary to help them get there. This sounds like a simple approach to team member engagement. However, it's reported that only 29 percent of employees across the country describe themselves as fully engaged in their work? (http://en.wikipedia.org/wiki/Employee_engagement)

The answer to team member commitment can be found in the leader's behavior. Leading a team of excellence requires connection with the individual team members. Most leaders choose not to invest the time to create that special connection. Consequently, most teams achieve varying levels of mediocrity, not excellence. Excellence at the team level is largely dependent upon the leader. As the leader goes, so goes the team. According to Buckingham, managers trump companies. While all the things the one hundred best companies do to create a great place to work are important, the manager's relationship with the employee is even more important. Leaders should be measured on the level of team member engagement they create and on the percentage of turnover on their teams as compared to similar teams.

> 50. As the leader goes, so goes the team.

I offer a word of caution for those who lead other leaders, such as directors, senior leaders, vice presidents, and CEOs. Don't think for a moment that I've just let you off the employee engagement hook. It's the manager's job to build a strong relationship with the employees in their team, but whose responsibility is it to make sure the managers do their jobs?

Too often, leaders of leaders think the engagement equation doesn't apply to them. Leaders of leaders must engage their subordinate leaders—or employee engagement will be left up to chance. It's the responsibility of upper managers to build engagement at the manager level. Leaders of leaders must model the way.

The People Pillar from the Church Perspective

The concepts of making it a great place to be, member engagement, and member turnover apply in this environment as well. Three of the church's main purposes relate to the people pillar initiatives—worship, fellowship, and discipleship. People look for a church environment where they enjoy the worship style, the way other members relate to them, and the opportunity to grow in their faith. The church must meet these needs. Each church member must become fully engaged in his or her personal growth process and strive to be a positive member of the church team, commonly referred to as the *congregation*.

Engaged members attend church on a regular basis and find ways to add value in ministry and service to the church and the community. They volunteer eagerly for opportunities that align with their unique gifts and talents and are excited to serve in those connected ways. Engaged church members actively and regularly participate in worship services, study the Bible on a regular basis, invest daily private time with God, give freely of their time, talents, and treasures, strive to obey the Word of God and share with others what God has done in their lives.

Leadership in the church plays a significant role in creating this engaging environment. The Natural Church Development Initiative identified *empowering leadership* as one of the keys to excellence in church growth. A church has empowering leaders when they equip, support, motivate, and mentor individual members to become all that God has created them to be.

If church leaders fail to create this type of engaging environment for their members, members may leave the church and join another one. At best, members will become complacent and stop doing things to grow the church's influence in the community. Either outcome is bad for the church and will lead to eventual church death.

Church member turnover is a good measure of commitment in this environment. People will stay longer where they are engaged and connected. Since church attendance is voluntary, it can provide insight into member engagement. Low attendance equals low engagement. High attendance equals high engagement. Creating an engaging church environment that encourages members to fulfill their God-given purposes in life is critical to excellence in the church initiative.

The People Pillar from the Family Perspective

Excellence is defined here more by the engagement of the family members in the family unit than with turnover. You can choose your friends, but you can't choose your family. Parents should consider what type of home environment they desire, document it, and discuss it openly with other family members.

Most families would describe a great place to live as one in which family members express unconditional love and respect for one another. The environment is characterized as one of joy and peace where family members cooperate with one another in unselfish ways. These are more adult-like characteristics that have to be taught to young children—and they take time and patience to develop. Making it a great place to live is not an easy thing to do, but it can certainly be accomplished if two parents committed to making it happen lead the family. As with any other team or organization, excellence in the family environment requires a long-term commitment coupled with unwavering persistence.

Shortly after my twenty-year-old son moved back home with us, he asked me how I thought the living relationship was going. He was seeking to measure my perspective of the home environment as a great place to live since he had moved in. Naturally, he didn't think of it that way, but in our context, that's exactly what he was doing. I told him his moving in had brought me great joy and that it was a pleasure having him live with us again. I thanked him for the way he cleaned up after himself, cooked for us at times, kept his room straight and clean, helped out around the house, and respected our principles and standards. And then I gave him a big hug. It was difficult for me to hold back my tears of joy. Having a chance to live with my son again after being apart for thirteen years was awesome! He responded in kind, and thanked me for letting him join the family. There's nothing in life better than that.

It's tragic to consider what happens in the family environment when we fail to make it a great place to live and be. The divorce rate for first marriages in America ranges from 41 to 50 percent. On the second marriage, the rate increases to 60 to 67 percent. On the third marriage, it increases to 74 percent (http://www.aboutdivorce.org/). We don't get better with practice.

Between 1 million and 1.5 million children run away from home each year. Somewhere between 20 and 40 percent will become involved in high-risk behaviors, including drug use, prostitution, pornography, or starvation (http://www.crisiscounseling.com). Instances of child and spousal abuse have skyrocketed in recent decades. According to the US Department of Health and Human Services, there were approximately six million children reported as victims of child abuse in 2008 (http://www.acf.hhs.gov).

This is strong evidence of the possible breakdown of the family unit. Many believe the core strength of American society has been found in the strength of the family unit. It's the family leader's responsibility to create an environment in the home that prevents these tragic results. Granted, this has become more difficult to accomplish with all the negative influences affecting our kids, but it's even more reason for family leaders to strive for excellence in the creation of strong, positive family environments.

To measure your progress with *engagement* in the family environment, solicit feedback from family team members on a regular basis. I've found it best to simply talk it out at every opportunity. When I see my son doing something that demonstrates our principles and values, I point it out and thank him. When my wife does something that makes me feel good or demonstrates her respect for me, I point it out and thank her. It's important to reinforce those desired behaviors and express love for one another in the process. Working together, the family can make it a great place to live.

The People Pillar from the Individual Perspective

The objective at the individual level to is to become a positive team player who others want to have on their teams. When I ask team members in the work environment to describe the characteristics that make a team member someone they would want to have on their teams, here's what they say.

An MVP (most valuable player) is someone who can be depended upon to pull his or her weight on the team, performing assigned duties at a high level of excellence on a regular basis. They follow through on their commitments and volunteer to help others when needed. They are pleasant to work with, have positive attitudes about life and work, and encourage others to do the same. They have integrity and strive to do the right things at all times. When they mess up, they acknowledge it and ask for forgiveness from those they've wronged or hurt. They are humble in spirit but confident in action. They are trustworthy and are considered role models of personal excellence.

Your objective is to have others describe you in these ways. Ask them often to provide you feedback on what they think. Encourage them to be honest with you and demonstrate to them your commitment to continuous personal improvement. Making it a great place to be is everyone's responsibility. You do your part when others see you as one of the MVPs on the team.

51. Excellence requires every member of the team to strive to become one of the team's MVPs.

Summary of Chapter 10

1. Excellence in the people pillar is the third priority in a culture of excellence.
2. The main objective in the people pillar is to create a great place to work, live, or be for every member of the team.
3. The two main measurements in the people pillar are team member turnover and team member commitment (or engagement).
4. Only 29 percent of employees report they are fully engaged in their work.

5. While all the things the 100 Best Places to Work do to create great places to work are important, the leader's relationship with the team members is even more important.
6. The concepts of turnover and commitment apply to the team and church environments as well.
7. It's everyone's responsibility to make it a great place to work, live, or be. You do your part when you become one of the team's MVPs.

Take Action

1. Define excellence in the people pillar as it relates to your environment.
2. Determine how you will measure your progress toward people pillar excellence.
3. Add these descriptions to your Blueprint for Excellence.
4. Assess your personal level of commitment to your team and organization. If you are not fully committed, develop a plan to become so.

CHAPTER 11

The Growth Pillar

>It's all about progress, not perfection!
>—Kenneth W. Wood, former CEO, Blue Ridge HealthCare

>It is not the strongest of the species that survive, nor the most intelligent, but the one most responsive to change.
>—Charles Darwin

>Gone are the days when innovations were incremental in scope and sequential in nature. In their place is perpetual unrest, unending fundamental changes.
>—Daryl Conner, *Managing at the Speed of Change*

>There is nothing more difficult to carry out, nor more doubtful of success, nor more dangerous to handle, than to initiate a new order of things.
>—Machiavelli

To grow or not to grow, that is the question. To experience excellence, forward progress must occur. Has anything great ever been accomplished while maintaining the status quo? The objective in the growth pillar is to grow forward, to progress in a positive direction. If all you do is maintain, you decrease. The only constant is change. Are you changing for the better or for the worse? Growth means *forward progress*, changing for the better.

Change is inevitable. Its pace is increasing exponentially. In 1990, automobiles took six years from concept to production. By the year

2000, they took two. Ninety percent of Miller Beer's revenues come from beers that didn't exist a few years ago. Today's computer chip has a life cycle of about eighteen months. Since the invention of the telegraph, the pace of change has experienced exponential growth.

Growth connotes change. Change is required for progress to occur. Zig said, "If you keep on doing what you've been doing, you'll keep on getting what you've been getting!"

To realize a different result, you *must* change.

> ## 52. Excellence demands the pain and pressure of development.

Significant growth requires *development*, which can only occur when pressure is applied. Pressure is usually painful. So is forward progress. Think about it. Something can grow naturally, without any pressure applied. Evidence a plant, an animal, a human, or practically any living thing. Growth occurs from the natural life process. When a baby is born, it begins to grow, as long as it receives air and food and is not intentionally neglected. But if a man wants his muscles to develop, he must apply pressure against them over a period of time. The muscle will develop more rapidly when there is pain from the applied pressure.

The more pain we experience, the greater the development. An organization is the same. An organization will grow naturally, and if no pressure is applied for it to develop in a positive direction, it will grow to mediocrity and eventually decline and die. For an organization to develop in a positive direction, leaders must apply pressure that will most likely be painful. To develop a culture of excellence, you're better served to expect the pain and pressure of development than to fight it or become frustrated by it. You must learn to welcome the pain and pressure that comes from positive development. Challenges, frustrations, and painful experiences are necessary and beneficial for growth; it is through them that we learn the most.

> 53. Excellence requires an attitude of continuous improvement.

There are two types of change—change that happens to you and change that you initiate. Initiating positive changes is called *personal innovation*. Without an attitude of continuous improvement, you're destined to experience a life of mediocrity. You must master the skills of change and lead those around you to do the same. Have you noticed that everything we've discussed in this book thus far deals with initiating positive changes? Remember that great leaders don't leave excellence up to chance. They make it an *intentional* objective and initiate action that leads to excellence.

Many times, however, change comes to us unexpectedly from an outside source. When my healthcare organization decided to renovate two hospitals at a cost of $120 million, no one asked for my advice. I had nothing to do with that decision, but I—and everyone else in the organization—had to cope with all the changes that came about as a result. We didn't *choose* the change that occurred to us, but we could choose our responses to that change. I could gripe and complain about all the inconveniences the renovation projects caused, but where would that lead me? My attitude about the change was *all* I could control.

Congress recently passed new overwhelming healthcare reform. No one in Congress asked me for my opinion about the reform before it was passed. Most of them didn't even read the two-thousand-page bill before passing it. I could gripe and complain about what they had done, but what good would that do? I had no control over the sweeping reform that had been thrust upon me, but I could control my response to that change.

> ## 54. Excellence requires positive change.

Rather than complain about unexpected changes, a more conducive approach may be to search for the benefits of the change and determine what you can do personally to become productive in it. Perhaps you could even help others work through the challenges of the change and thereby have a dramatic positive impact on your entire environment.

Resilience is the ability to positively and productively respond to change, to bounce back quickly from change and adversity. According to change expert Daryl Conner in *Managing at the Speed of Change*, resilience isn't a characteristic that is either present or lacking. It is a combination of traits that each of us possesses in various measures. It is a *continuum*.

> ## 55. Excellence requires resilience and innovation.

On one end of the resilience continuum is the view of change as danger. On the other end is the view of change as an opportunity. Danger orientation is characterized by fear, denial, feeling threatened or victimized, lacking purpose, and reactionary. Opportunity orientation is characterized by viewing change as positive, responding with a flexible, focused, organized, and proactive approach. You must master these five characteristics of resilience to be effective in today's environments. You must become highly resilient.

To initiate forward progress, you must continuously improve and innovate. To respond to unexpected changes positively and productively, you must become resilient. Developing *innovation* and *resilience* in yourself and others will produce an environment that is advantageous to positive growth.

Growth in technologies, facilities, and people is required to build and sustain a culture of excellence. The key to excellence in this pillar is to understand that growth is a natural outcome of focus in the first three pillars. That's why it's pillar number four in our priority order. You will move forward if you use innovation and resilience to initiate positive progress in quality, service, and people pillar initiatives. If you don't, you will decline. It's important to understand how to measure growth and to have goals that make sense in your environment.

56. Focus on the doing, not on the getting.

It's important to keep the end result in mind. However, the main thing is to focus on the *doing*, not on the *getting*. If you focus on results and forget about your principles and values, you may achieve growth—but you could forfeit your soul in the process, and your good results won't last. Focus on the doing (building high quality, delivering excellent service, and making it a great place to work, live, or be) and the getting (growth) will take care of itself.

Growth in the Five Environments

Organizational Growth

At the organization level, leaders must clearly identify what *forward progress* looks like and how to properly measure it. Such consideration will include market share, product lines, product volumes, guests served, employees on the payroll, facilities in operation, technologies employed, the capabilities of the people on staff, and revenue growth.

In a healthcare environment, growth is typically identified in terms of patient volume, market share, and growth in the different service lines. The organization sets a goal for the number of patients it hopes to serve in the coming performance period. Market share refers to the percentage of the potential market the organization is serving. If there are one hundred thousand potential customers in the market and the organization is serving seventy thousand of them, it has a 70 percent market share. Leaders then set a goal to grow the market share percentage. Service line growth refers to the number of total cases or patients served in a particular line of service, such as surgery, cancer, cardiology, or gastroenterology.

In the furniture factory, growth is defined as the number of pieces of furniture sold, the number of customers served, the number of factories in operation, the number of employees on the payroll, revenue growth, and market share. In a theme park, growth is defined primarily by the number of guests served, the number of attractions offered, the size of the property, and ticket sales. For a car manufacturer, growth is measured by the number of vehicles sold, the number of manufacturing and retail locations in operation, the number of employees on the payroll, and market share. In a volunteer charity organization like United Way, growth is identified primarily in the number of volunteers, the amount of donations received, the number of donors, and the number of people served.

Organizational leaders must clearly identify the goals and measures of growth and remember that the way to achieve them is through focusing on the quality, service, and people pillar initiatives—the doing. These types of measures for growth will enable the organization to understand and measure its forward progress effectively.

Team Growth

In a smaller team, growth definitions and measurements will vary, depending on the type of team being considered. If the team is an operational unit, it may have growth goals that are similar to the organizational growth goals that relate to the department's activity. For example, in the healthcare environment, one organizational growth goal might be to increase the number of surgeries performed in the coming period. That organizational goal should directly cascade into the surgery team's goals for tracking and measurement.

The surgery team is an operational unit that is directly involved in delivering service to the patient.

If the team is not directly involved in the delivery of the product or service to the guest, its growth goals may look a bit different. In the furniture factory, the sanding department will measure its growth by how many pieces of wood it sands during the period. This goal indirectly relates to the number of furniture products sold by the company but will not be specifically noted on the organizational scorecard. Sanding is one process that leads to the finished furniture product, but it is not the entire process. The organization focuses on the whole, and the department focuses on the part.

In my learning team, we measured our growth by the number of learning guests served, hours of learning delivered, learning events delivered, and performance improvement. These team growth goals did not directly relate to the organizational growth goals but measured activity that improves the quality of clinical care provided, thus helping the organization grow. It's important to realize, however, that activity goals do not necessarily translate into improved quality and service. Just because we delivered more learning events and served more learning guests did not necessarily mean we improved the overall quality of care. In this learning example, the learning must be transferred into performance improvement on the job in order for the impact on quality of care to be realized. Therefore, we asked organization leaders to measure the performance improvement of their staffs during the period to give us a better idea of our overall impact.

Depending on the work your team performs, you may need to seek the advice of industry experts for relevant growth measures. Find a model of growth measurement if needed or connect directly to the organization's growth goals if possible. Every team member must understand how growth in the team is defined and be able to map his or her personal impact on organizational growth. Perhaps even more importantly, the team leader must cultivate the skills of resilience and innovation in themselves and others to enable the team to effectively initiate and manage forward progress.

Church Growth

In the Christian church, growth takes on a slightly different perspective. The handbook for church living, the Bible, clearly communicates that it is the church's responsibility to serve and share Christ with others, but God is responsible for the results of those efforts. Considering this, it becomes critical to remember to focus on the *doing*, not on the *getting*. Having said that, however, it makes sense that if the church is doing what it's supposed to do, there should be objective, measurable results of those efforts. Those results should include some or all of the following:

- an increase in the number of church members
- an increase in the number of members involved in church fellowship activities
- an increase in the number of members attending regular worship services and small group Bible studies
- an increase in the number of ministry activities and events in which members are involved in helping others in the community
- an increase in the number of people served in the community by church members
- an increase in the number of members active in church life beyond the once-per-week main worship service
- an increase in the number of people with whom church members shared the message of Christ
- an increase in the number of professions of faith of nonmembers

It's relevant for church leadership to keep these growth goals in mind, but they must remember to leave the results up to God. Focusing too much on results has a tendency to remove God from the equation. Leadership must guard against this. One church may plant while another may harvest. That's how God works. To him, the church includes all Christians throughout the world, not just one local church body. Here's how one church I worked with stated this principle.

> We acknowledge that our role is to focus on the process God has given us to grow the church, but the results of actual church growth are in his control. Our role is to fulfill the Great Commandment (ministry) and the Great Commission (evangelism) and leave the results of converted lives and numbers to him. However, we also acknowledge that if we, the church members, are being effective in our ministry and evangelism efforts that we should expect to see some increase in our own churches results—membership, attendance, number of ministries offered, number of people we share Christ with, etc. Our main question is "How do we help our church members become as effective for Christ as possible so that we grow our church in the direction God would have us to go?"

Church growth depends upon church member growth. In *The Purpose Driven Church*, Rick Warren presents a wonderful path for Christian growth. If every church member completed this path, the church would grow. Oak Hill United Methodist Church in Morganton, North Carolina, used Warren's Christian growth path to connect the stages of Christian growth to the mission of the church as illustrated in this diagram.

The Development Process
Building a life & church of learning, growing, serving, & sharing

Our purpose: To be an instrument, empowered by the Holy Spirit, representing the Lord Jesus Christ, fulfilling the Great Commandment & the Great Commission.

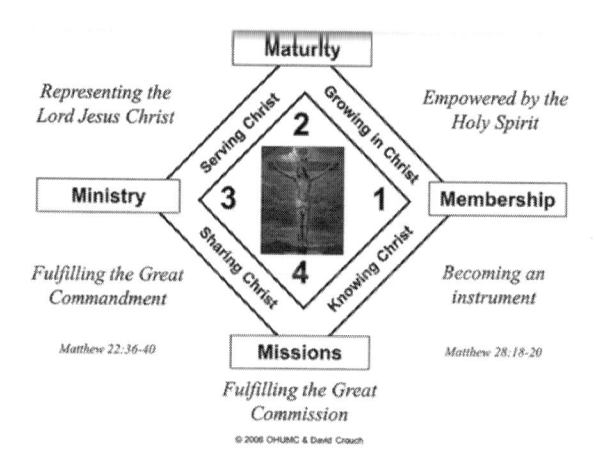

Maturity

Representing the Lord Jesus Christ — Serving Christ — **2** — Growing in Christ — *Empowered by the Holy Spirit*

Ministry — **3** — **1** — **Membership**

Fulfilling the Great Commandment — Sharing Christ — **4** — Knowing Christ — *Becoming an instrument*

Matthew 22:36-40 — **Missions** — Matthew 28:18-20

Fulfilling the Great Commission

© 2006 OHUMC & David Crouch

Family Growth

When my family and I considered the question of family growth, we answered it with a simple statement. *We want to move in a positive direction.* How do you measure forward progress in a family?

Family growth can take on several perspectives. It can be as simple as each individual family member growing personally and becoming a positive contributor to the family team. It can include specific definitions and expectations for personal growth as family members age and mature. It can also include goals and measurements for family income, investments, housing, and activities. Here's an example from my own family that focuses on teenage growth.

The Excellent Teen

Who does God want me to be?

At Home
Respect Mom & Dad
Get along w/siblings
Help around the house

At School
Respect your teachers
Make your best grades
Explore your opportunities

Clean up after yourself
Put things back where you got them
Close the door behind you
Turn everything off

**Glorify God
Respect Others
Do Your Best!**

Clean up after yourself
Put things back where you got them
Close the door behind you
Turn everything off

At Church
Respect your leaders
Get involved
Open your heart to God

Community
Respect the leaders/law
Get involved
Learn about it

What can I do to make it a better place?

We used this model to guide our children through their teen years. We identified four environments and developed three growth goals in each environment. I won't lie to you and tell you that this made everything work out perfectly for my three teenagers, but I will tell you that it gave us a good foundation for discussion. At least they knew what Mom and Dad expected of them.

Their teen years weren't perfect by any means, but all three graduated from high school with honors, entered college without any trouble with the law, and made it through without hurting anyone else. Those parameters became *have-to-do's* that served as simple guidelines. We used the model as a basis for regular discussion about how to have an *excellent* teen experience.

Today, all three are finding their ways in life very well and working to add value to the world around them. I'm very proud of them all. Our model of growth helped them experience forward progress as teens. Undoubtedly, we need to encourage our young people to find ways to make positive differences in the world. Our futures—and theirs—depend upon it!

Individual Growth

Resilience, innovation, and an attitude of continuous improvement are the keys to a life of individual growth. You must become a *lifelong learner*. I was impressed when I learned that Bill O'Reilly, the famous antagonistic anchor of *The Factor* on Fox News, reads three books a week. I thought I was doing well when I set the goal several years back to read three books a year. Now I read about a book a month. My goal is to read one book per week. Since I'm a slow reader, it can take a while to get through a book. Earning my graduate degree in 2009 at age fifty-two rekindled my love of learning. The five-year journey dramatically changed me and motivated me to write this book. Here's a note from my personal journal about that particular growth journey.

Tuesday, January 13, 2009

When I started this master's journey five years ago, I had no idea of the impact it would have on my life. When asked if I had a master's degree, I used to tell people that I had earned a master's degree in experience—that I didn't need the formal schooling to prove it. I feel differently now. While that was partially true, that my experience had prepared me for a lot, it was not the whole truth. The master's journey has served well to round out my knowledge and understanding of my chosen field of practice, organizational development. It has confirmed my experiences in some ways and has expanded and completed them in others. It has brought credibility to my experiences and new learning applications to my work. I really had no idea how it would impact my relationships with my three teenage kids. It has connected me to them in a way I could have never anticipated. We talk more now about all kinds of things. Lately, as my boys have begun to contemplate the journey of life, they have brought me into those discussions and have expressed value in what I have to offer. The master's journey has created for me an academic connection with them that is yielding bountiful results in the quality of our conversations and relationships. What an unexpected blessing for which I will be forever thankful.

The individual growth journey is very personal. Those who have known me for a long time express surprise at the evolution of mine. High school came easy for me, and I was accepted early decision to the University of North Carolina at Chapel Hill in the fall of 1975. It was the only place I ever wanted to go.

> *57. You must become a lifelong learner.*

The college learning journey was quite different. Because the As came so easy in high school, I had not developed good study habits. I struggled to maintain the proper focus on schoolwork. The many distractions of college and fraternity life didn't help. I graduated in four years with a very *mediocre* grade point average—but not without adding several summer school sessions. I was happy to finally be out of school, and I set a goal to be a millionaire by age thirty.

Having majored in business administration, I knew I had to start my own business. I began studying success gurus like Zig Ziglar, Napoleon Hill, Dale Carnegie, and Og Mandino. A year of traveling around the country as a leadership development consultant with my national fraternity helped me learn and grow further in my understanding of leadership principles and behaviors. When I moved back to Chapel Hill to start my first business, I wrote a business plan and convinced my father to cosign a $10,000 personal loan to get started. Six months later, I was broke, distraught, and in debt. I had failed miserably and had to get a job to make ends meet.

I moved back home to live in my parents' basement while I worked seven days a week running a convenience store. After a couple of years, I received an offer from a friend of a friend to come to Orlando to sing on radio commercials. I thought it was the break I needed to catapult me to millionaire status. I packed up my Honda Civic and moved to Florida.

With the business debt, car payments, and living expenses, I needed more money than an occasional singing gig could produce. I lost twenty-five pounds, was living on eggs and bread, and was falling behind on my rent. My dad graciously loaned me $500 to attend bartending school, and I earned my certificate as a certified mixologist. This landed me a job at a new restaurant on International Drive near Disney. It wasn't long before I realized I wasn't a very good bartender. A new Bennigan's restaurant opened near my apartment in north Orlando, and I got a job waiting tables. At this, I was pretty good.

Again, economics caught up with me. I needed to use the business degree to secure a higher-paying job. On a whim, my friend Tony and I moved to Atlanta to start new careers. After one day on a sales job, I quit. I hated the work. That was my first clue that sales was not for me. Fortunately, Atlanta had several Bennigan's restaurants, and I returned to waiting tables for the time being. Bennigan's accepted me into their management training program and sent me to Huntsville, Alabama, and Greenville, South Carolina. I was pretty good at managing the restaurant. I had responsibility for eighty employees and learned how to work with them to get them to give their best. It was my first lesson in finding out what people want and then helping them get it. I would later learn this was a key principle of excellence.

> ## 58. *Find out what others want and help them get it.*

By age twenty-seven, the restaurant manager life was wearing me down. The seventy- and eighty-hour workweeks began to take their toll on my health. I returned to a wholesale sales job but still wasn't very good at it. In short time, I was laid off and out of work. Again, I learned that selling stuff was not my thing. On the other hand, I also knew that if I was ever going to become a millionaire, I had to sell something to someone. That brutal fact presented me with a perplexing dilemma. If becoming a millionaire would require me to sell something and I'm not good at sales, how would I ever be able to become a millionaire? The realistic possibility of becoming a millionaire by age thirty was growing dim!

After a few more feeble and failed attempts to get rich, I landed a decent job in my hometown of Morganton. Tired and frustrated, I abandoned the millionaire goal. My new wife and I decided to dedicate our lives to God—to begin living a life that would glorify him instead of pursuing our own selfish desires for wealth and things. In retrospect, it was one of the most pivotal decisions of my life. The next ten years brought prosperity and growth. Work was worthwhile. Becoming a father was awesome! Building my new family, faith, and career became a daily walk of personal, spiritual and professional growth. Life was exciting, challenging, and fulfilling. After seven years working for a successful entrepreneur, I had the opportunity to venture into my own consulting business. For two years, business was good. Then disaster struck.

Due to my poor sales skill, my business began to decline. At the same time, my wife left the home. It was a dark time. Within a year, I lost my business, my home, my family, my church, and my friends. I was at rock bottom with occasional thoughts of suicide and despair. I wondered why God had allowed these things to happen. I was angry with him and gave him the cold shoulder for several years. I declared bankruptcy and finally secured a job as a human resource director for a furniture manufacturer. One day, as a giant cockroach crawled across my small, sawdust-covered office floor, I reached an epiphany. It was the most important turning point of my life. I gave up—not on life, but on my attempts to control it! I gave my life totally to God and committed to follow him wherever he would lead.

A few months later, I was promoted to director of training for the corporate office. In a few years, I was recruited to serve in an organizational development role with a global manufacturing company. That experience led to securing the director of organizational development position with the healthcare organization I've referenced so much in my writings.

No doubt, I've been blessed beyond measure. I haven't made it to the millionaire level *yet*, but I am a very wealthy man. My definition of personal excellence has changed. I no longer seek money or material possessions. I seek love, joy, and peace—and a chance to make a positive difference in the world around me. I walk in love every day and experience the fullness of God in my life. Nothing wanted, nothing needed, nothing missing.

Today, I write with joy what I've learned from those life experiences, both good and bad. Life is good—or should I say *excellent*! Seizing every opportunity to learn and grow makes the difference.

59. Never give up!

The personal growth journey is perhaps the most important of all the environments we've discussed. Since the essence of excellence lies in the quality of the individual's performance, all excellence emerges at the individual level. It begins with you. Stephen Covey's habit #7 of highly effective people states we should constantly *sharpen the saw*. Make lifelong learning one of your values today. Remember that it's all about progress, not perfection. With an attitude of continuous personal improvement, your life can progress forward. It's been said that the only difference between a successful man and an unsuccessful man is getting up one more time.

Never give up! The only way to guarantee failure is to quit. *Never give up!* Keep on keeping on. *Never give up!* Forge through, go around, tunnel under, and do whatever it takes to keep going. *Never give up!* A life of excellence will emerge if you remain persistent. You must *never* give up!

Summary of Chapter 11

- Excellence in growth is the fourth priority in a culture of excellence.
- Growth connotes change and change is inevitable. You must develop the skills of innovation and resilience in order to initiate and sustain forward progress.
- Growth is a natural result of focusing on the doing. You will grow when you initiate positive changes in the first three pillars (quality, service, and people).
- At the organizational and team levels, growth is typically defined and measured in terms of market share, product or service lines, product or service volumes, guests served, number of team members, facilities in operation, technologies employed, the capabilities of the people involved, and revenue.
- Team growth definition and measurement depends upon the type of work the team performs.
- Church growth is God's business, but there are things church leaders can do that will lead to growth.
- Family growth is personal and unique.
- The most important environment for growth is the individual level. All other forward progress emerges from there.

Take Action

- Define excellence in the growth pillar as it relates to your environment.
- Determine how you will measure your progress in the growth pillar.
- Add these descriptions to your Blueprint for Excellence.
- Meditate on your personal life growth path. Note the pivotal turning points in your personal journey. Consider how your decisions have developed you into the person you are today. How do you feel about what you see? What brings you joy about your journey? What would you like to do differently from now on?

CHAPTER 12

The Finance Pillar

We don't do what we do for the money, but we sure need the money to do what we do.
—Kathy Bailey, CEO of Blue Ridge HealthCare

Make all you can, save all you can, give all you can.
—John Wesley, founder of Methodism

These two leaders express a perspective on finance I admire. Too often in our world's capitalistic economies, the concept of finance is driven to the extremes of greed and selfishness. There seems to be something in the human nature that drives us to want more money and things as if its accumulation will bring us joy and fulfillment. However, if we just look around us, we see that quite the opposite is true.

Bankruptcies have become normal to resolve financial trouble. According to the American Bankruptcy Institute, filings have steadily increased since 1980, peaking in 2005 at almost two million nationwide. Most of them were filed by individual consumers. The lust for money in the business environment has crippled once strong and viable companies. Spending beyond her means is bringing America to its knees, subjecting her to the servitude of her debtors, both foreign and domestic. Huge government bailouts around the globe have become the norm to stave off impending financial collapse.

After the 9/11 toppling of the World Trade Centers, President Bush told us the best thing to do was to go out and shop. We followed his advice and put most of the spending on our credit cards. According to Cardweb.com, a service that tracks credit card trends, the average debt per American household with at least one credit card is on a steady climb. By 2002, the last year for which they have accurate data, it had risen to $8,940 per household.

60. *The love of money is the root of all evil.*

The Bible says the love of money is the root of all kinds of evil (1 Timothy 6:10). Is the love of money a prevailing attitude today? It appears so from the observable evidence. Timothy goes on to say that people who want to get rich fall into temptation and a trap and into many foolish and harmful desires that plunge them into ruin and destruction. We're out of control in our spending and debt financing habits because of the desire to get rich with money and things. That attitude prevails in too many families, businesses, and governments today.

Please don't misunderstand me. I'm a fan of capitalism. I believe it has provided the best way of life for the human condition so far. It only becomes bad when human pride, greed, and selfishness take it to its negative extremes, exploiting its principles purely for personal gain rather than for the good of the whole. Today, the words *capitalism* and *socialism* are being thrown around quite freely. The differentiating factors between capitalism and socialism are found in who owns the property and who reaps the benefits. In capitalism, the private individual or company owns the property and receives the rewards of their labor. In socialism, the state owns the property and redistributes the rewards to everyone equally. Between these two choices, I unequivocally promote and support the capitalistic viewpoint. The American capitalistic economic system has provided more opportunity, creativity, innovation, and progress than any other that has come before it. But like anything else, when taken to negative extremes fueled by selfishness and greed, capitalism too can turn sour.

The goal in the finance pillar needs to be something other than simply making money or the pursuit of more. Daniel Pink's *Drive: The Surprising Truth about What Motivates Us* introduces a new concept emerging in today's business environment. It's called the LC3 Corporation. An LC3 operates like a for-profit business, but its primary objective is to offer noteworthy social benefits. It appears we're collectively evolving to want more from life than mere profit. We're seeking the highest level of Maslow's hierarchy of needs—self-actualization, the opportunity to make a difference for the good of mankind.

There's nothing wrong with making money or wanting more. However, when making money becomes the only end goal, the greedy side of human nature has a tendency to take over and pursue *more* above all else with disregard to established foundational principles. Therein lies the rub. When pursued in the context of service, integrity, humility, and the greater good for all, capitalism is good. But when pursued in a context of selfishness, greed, and an insatiable desire for more, capitalism can turn bad. Maintaining the foundational elements of excellence is critical in this regard. That's why I discussed the foundation first—and it's why I place the finance pillar last.

Like growth, excellence in the finance pillar is the natural result of focus on quality, service, and people. When pursued from this perspective, capitalism still affords the best opportunity for excellence. Since the essence of excellence lies in the quality of the individual's performance, it's critical to maintain an environment that encourages the human spirit to strive for excellence. When you keep the financial elements in proper perspective, excellence can emerge and thrive and can produce benefits for everyone involved. Make money the chief aim, and excellence will be unsustainable and will hurt many people in the process.

Keynesian Economics

The pursuit of *more* appears to be the main goal these days. For businesses, it's more profit or earnings per share for stockholders. For a team, it's more budget allocation. For a church, it's more tithes and offerings. For a family, it's more household income and stuff. For an individual, it's more personal income and stuff. We think that if we can only generate more money, everything will be better. Current evidence suggests that in practically all environments, greed rules. Should *more* really be the goal in finance? Do the concepts of greed and more lead to a culture of excellence?

The general statistics on personal and organizational debt and irresponsible financial behavior may lead us to believe that all is out of control. However, a deeper look into those statistics reveals quite the contrary. The majority of individuals and households in America are not overextended and practice good habits of frugality.

According to Liz Pulliam Weston, a financial columnist for MSN Money, most Americans owe nothing to credit card companies. She reports that only one in twenty American households owes $8,000 or more on credit cards. Most individual Americans understand financial prudence (i.e. living within their means), and they simply expect our larger organizations and institutions to mirror those values.

It's mostly the expanding governments, Wall Street executives, large financial institutions, huge mega-corporations, and progressive politicians who have developed the attitude that debt is good and more is better. According to Wikipedia, this attitude has its roots in the philosophies of a British economic philosopher by the name of John Maynard Keynes, who became President Roosevelt's economic hero during the 1930s. Keynes believed that savings was demonstrative of hoarding and greed and that paying down the national debt and balancing the budget was counterproductive to economic growth. He claimed that the main objective of economic activity was consumption, and the solution to economic troubles was spending. His economic philosophy became known as *Keynesian*

Economics and promoted the idea that government control and spending should be used to control economic activity.

Following FDR's leadership, sustaining an ever-growing economy at any cost became the goal of American government and big business rather than financial prudence and frugality. Most Americans, however, portend quite the opposite.

> *61. Excellence requires you to keep the financial perspective in proper balance.*

The main goal in the finance pillar must be effective *stewardship*, not more. Stewardship is defined as effective management and administration of finances and other property for others. It invokes a moral responsibility for the careful use of money, time, talents, and other resources with respect to the principles or needs of a community or group. When exercised effectively, stewardship will bring about optimum results in *efficiency* and *productivity*. Revenues will be optimized and costs will be controlled.

Following a leadership example of good stewardship, people will be inspired to behave more efficiently as they make wise use of the organization's resources. *Frugal behavior* yields the best possible financial results. Stewardship combines the moral responsibility of service and frugality with the organization's practical need to balance the books and prosper. A goal of excellent stewardship in the finance pillar combined with commitment to a strong foundation will keep human nature in check and yield the greatest rewards for everyone involved.

Interesting Footnote About Money

Before the creation of money to be used in exchange for goods and services, people would barter (trade one item or service for another in order to get what they needed). Early bankers realized that people preferred to use a more common method of exchange to buy and sell goods, establishing our current monetary system. The paper note we call a dollar bill is a promise from a bank to pay and is only valuable if you and I believe it is. The paper money supply was once backed up by gold, but that system was abolished in 1971 under President Richard Nixon (source: Wikipedia).

Today, paper money is only valuable as long as people believe it is. If that belief is ever lost, paper money will become useless—and the world's financial system could collapse. That's one reason Congress voted to give banks a $1 trillion bailout in 2008 from the US public treasury, our tax dollars. They were afraid that if the huge banks failed, people would lose faith in the money supply, and it would cause a run on the banks that could lead to collapse.

About 97 percent of our current money supply exists in electronic form only, digits in a computer or on a bank statement. Only about 3 percent of the money supply exists in actual bills and coins. Under our current fractional reserve banking system, banks are only required to keep 10 percent of their outstanding loans and obligations in actual cash in the bank. The rest is fictional and doesn't actually exist. If everyone decided to take their money out of the banks at the same time, banks would not have the money to pay their obligations—and the system would collapse. It's a monetary system based on faith.

Finance in the Five Environments

Organizational Finance

Publicly traded for-profit organi-zations like Walmart, Disney, Toyota, and Southwest Airlines need to generate a return on investment for their stockholders greater than the stockholders could earn by investing their money in the bank. Privately held for-profit organizations like the local barbershop, florist, restaurant, and smaller companies need to generate a fair profit for the owners and/or investors. Nonprofit organizations such as governments, healthcare organizations, the United Way, the Red Cross, the Boy Scouts, the Optimist Club, and other charities need to cover their costs and fund growth. The specifics of those objectives will be determined by preferential variables within each group. A nonprofit hospital system determined that a profit of 4-5 percent was needed to fund future growth and financial viability. A local retail entrepreneur determined he needed at least 10 percent profit to fund growth and meet his investors' objectives. Boards of directors and Wall Street speculators heavily influence the specific earnings needs of publicly traded companies.

The responsibility for effective stewardship at the organizational level resides with the top leader and the senior team. If subordinate team members observe top leadership demonstrating good stewardship, they'll respect them and be more likely to follow in like manner. Conversely, if top leadership spends lavishly on their own perks and selfish desires without regard for the impact their behavior has on others, they'll lose respect and earn a reputation as hypocrites. Business is a game of follow the leader. As the leader goes, so goes the team.

Every organization encounters difficult financial times sooner or later. It is how leadership behaves that makes the difference. When times are tough, leadership behavior is under a microscope. Many leaders fail to recognize this important reality. When company X fell on tough times, the president issued a decree that everyone must cut

10 percent from their budgets and take a 10 percent pay decrease. The next week, the president pulled up to the corporate office in a new Mercedes Benz. While the president had every right to do those things, his behavior had a devastating effect on the rank-in-file employees. He lost respect and fueled the perception that he didn't care about his workers. It appeared the rules didn't apply to him. Leaders must carefully consider how their actions affect those they lead, particularly in tough financial times.

When the economy tanked and company *X* began to suffer financially, the senior team implemented cost-cutting measures to save money. One of the measures was to cut all internal food use. Internal catering had a tendency to get out of control because it was so easy to use it for parties and meetings. There was nothing wrong with this directive. It was wise, and everyone knew it. The only problem was that when an employee walked by the executive offices where the senior team worked and met, they would witness senior leaders enjoying elaborate food buffets and catered meetings. This created a perception of hypocrisy, which fueled an attitude of disrespect and loss of credibility for leadership. Employees began to think, *If the rule doesn't apply to them, then why should it apply to me?*

These employees would gradually begin to order catering services again. Incongruent leader behavior sabotaged the organizational goal of frugal spending. Waste continued to climb. Especially in financial areas, leaders must model the way they want others to go.

There are many ways to measure excellence in the finance pillar at the organizational level. The easiest and most common is bottom line results. Revenue minus costs equals profit. Many times, however, that simple equation doesn't tell the whole story. Strong revenues cover a multitude of sins. When times are good, most people take their eyes off the microscope, allowing waste and extravagance to emerge. Other financial measures can help. They include earnings per share, cash flow margin, operating margin, expenses as a percent of revenue, dollars of expense per employee, performance to budget, overhead costs as a percent of revenue, operating cost as a percent of revenue, cost per unit, and profit per unit. This list is certainly not exhaustive, and the exact methods you choose will vary depending upon your particular needs. The important thing to remember is to measure your financial performance in a way that enables you to avoid hiding excessive spending and accurately measure efficiency, productivity, and effective stewardship.

Team Finance

In the team environment, finance will look very much like it does at the organizational level. The objective is the same—effective *stewardship*. Teams should be good stewards of all the resources entrusted to them, performing their duties with *efficiency* and optimum *productivity*. Team leaders are accountable for the team's financial performance and must work to instill an attitude of efficiency and good stewardship with each member of the team.

If the team unit directly generates revenue, the simple profit equation may work. Some examples would include a cancer unit at the hospital, a sales department, a specific unit of a national chain like Walmart or CVS, or a local Ford dealership. If the team does not produce revenue, like my learning team, an accounting unit, a human resources department, or a sanding department in the furniture factory, performance to budget will provide a better measure.

It's also important for a team to discern the most effective productivity measurement expressed in terms of revenue, cost, or profit per unit of output. For my learning team, it was cost per learning hour delivered. Our main unit of production was a learning hour, and our main financial measure was cost.

Our team did not produce revenue. By tracking this metric over time and comparing it to like areas in other companies, we were able to set reasonable goals for our team's productivity. The lower the cost per learning hour we delivered, the more productive and efficient we were.

In *Good to Great,* Jim Collins calls this concept the economic engine dimension of the hedgehog principle. According to Collins, a hedgehog concept is an understanding of what you can be the best at and was one of the six attributes of great companies he discerned from his research. Collins learned that great companies founded their strategies on a deep understanding of three key dimensions that focused and guided all their efforts.

1. What are you deeply passionate about?
2. What can you be the best in the world at?
3. What drives your economic engine?

Great companies discovered what drove their economic engines and expressed it in terms of profit per x. Great teams need to discern what drives their economic engines, express it as profit, revenue, or cost per x, and track it.

Teams must remain responsive to organizational needs. When the hospital asked all department heads to cut 10 percent from their departmental budgets, I assembled my team together with a copy of our budget and general ledger that detailed all expenses over the past year. We studied the general ledger line item by line item to identify everything we thought we could eliminate and made the corresponding changes in our spending behaviors. The bosses were pleased, and we reduced our budget as requested while striving to maintain balance in quality, service, and the team experience.

Church Finance

> Keep your lives free from the love of money and be content with what you have, because God has said, 'Never will I leave you; never will I forsake you.' So we say with confidence, the Lord is my helper; I will not be afraid. What can man do to me?
> —Hebrews 13:5

The church invented the concept of *stewardship*. Churches are typically nonprofit organizations that need to cover the costs of their activities. The simple profit equation will work but with a goal to break even rather than make money. It's helpful to measure revenue per member as individual giving provides the main source of church income. It also provides insight into the spiritual health of the membership.

The main difference in the church environment is the spiritual perspective of money. Money is mentioned in the Bible more than two thousand times. Jesus spoke of it often. Reaping what you sow is a core principle of Christianity. Zig used to say, "You can have everything in life you want if you just help enough other people get what they want!"

In the church environment, the concept of giving is fundamental. Attitudes about money are also a strong indication of a believer's maturity about his or her faith. The Bible says a believer should tithe 10 percent of their income to the church. If every church member obeys that spiritual command, the church would never struggle financially. It's virtually impossible to know exactly what the tithing percentages are since giving is private—and the church typically has no knowledge of the actual household incomes of its member families. However, most churches report revenue per member indicating that not all members are tithing at 10 percent. For example, one of my churches had 428 members, which included children. If a third of the members are children with no personal earnings, there would be 286 members to tithe. The annual budget was about $250,000, yielding a *revenue per member* of $874 per year. If that represents 10 percent of the income of the 286 members, the average annual income of the members of my church would be about $8,740, far below the poverty line and almost certainly inaccurate. Most churches report similar numbers.

Churches around the world do wonderful work. How much more could be done if all of its members tithed 10 percent? If we use a conservative average household income of $30,000 and assume this church represents about 175 households, a 10 percent tithe would generate $525,000 per year—more than twice what we actually received. Apply that conservative estimate to the approximately 330,000 churches in America. That's a big number. It seems reasonable to suspect that government welfare could be dramatically reduced or even eliminated if the church would resume responsibility for that ministry as it once did. Perhaps poverty could be dramatically impacted if all church members tithed 10 percent of their incomes. How much different would our local communities be if all church members gave 10 percent of their incomes to their local churches?

Tithing in the church environment, like financial results in the business environment, is a result of focus on the quality, service, and people pillars. If church leadership focused more on effective discipleship by teaching and training its members in the ways of the faith, tithing would be a natural outcome of a developing believer. Churches, like all other environments, should focus on the *doing*, not on the *getting*. If each member of the church learns the ways of God and pursues a personal development path toward those ways, church growth and financial performance will take care of themselves—or should I say they will be taken care of by God?

Family Finance

Like the church environment, most families want to at least break even and prefer to have money left over for savings and investments. However, many families struggle. America has developed a culture that encourages debt financing. We've become a people who want it now and hope to be able to pay for it later. That attitude has led many families into bankruptcy court. The more debt financing a family has, the more of their incomes go to interest payments on the debt. The attitude of *pay-as-you-go* must be developed and adhered to for most family purchases. I realize in this day and time that it is hard to imagine. Debt financing should be limited to large necessary purchases such as homes and automobiles. The better approach for the purchase of other family items such as televisions, stereos, boats, and computers is to save the money ahead of time, earning interest on the savings rather than paying interest on borrowed funds. You must become a good steward of the resources entrusted to you. Again, effective *stewardship* is the key.

When my kids were young, we tried to instill in them the concept of *working to earn your way*. We were a family of five living on one income of about $40,000 a year. We had to be frugal. We maintained a strict budget and were not able to enjoy many of the luxuries most Americans have come to take for granted. We seldom dined out, had many yard sales, attended many yard sales, rented a small, two-bedroom house, and rarely traveled. When one car burned its transmission, we went without it for several months until we could save the money to fix it. It was a lean time.

When my kids reached driving age, I made a deal with them about their car expenses. Their grandmother purchased each of them a used starter car when they turned sixteen. If they wanted to keep and use the car, they had to work and earn money to pay for the maintenance and upkeep. I paid the insurance until they reached nineteen. When it came time to go to college, they each found a way to pay for their own college expenses with scholarships, grants, and school loans. I told them that if I were in a financial position to help them when it came time to pay back any loans, I would try my best to do so. I encouraged them to manage their college finances as if I would not be able to help. I'm very proud of how they managed to get through college with a minimum amount of loans. It helped that they were smart and able to qualify for many of the financial aid mechanisms in place. They learned to manage their finances on their own with minimal help from Mom and Dad.

Crown Ministries has a *Money Map* that can help families get their financial pillar in proper focus. They recommend the *pay-as-you-go* approach. According to the map, the first destination for the family is emergency savings. Crown Ministries recommends at least $1,000 in a special emergency savings account. The second destination is to pay off all credit cards and increase savings to one month's living expenses. Destination three is to pay off all consumer debt, including everything but the home, and increase savings to three month's living expenses. The fourth destination is to save for major purchases like a home or automobile, begin saving for retirement, and begin saving for children's education. If you want to start your own business, begin saving for it here as well. Destination five is to buy a home and begin investing. Purchase an affordable home, begin prepaying the home mortgage, and begin investing wisely. Destination six is to pay off your home mortgage, have your children's education fund fully funded, and confirm that your estate plan is in order. Destination seven is to have your retirement fund fully funded. Crown Ministries offers many resources to help you reach these seven destinations. You can access them all at www.CrownMoneyMap.org.

One critical tool you will need in order to reach any of your family financial goals is a *budget*. You can find budgeting tools on the Crown Ministries website as well. I've personally maintained a family budget since 1987 and have found the following budget categories helpful:

Budget Categories

1. Revenue accounts to include income from a job or business and any other revenue that makes its way into the family accounts.
2. Expense accounts to include the major categories of spending (plus anything else you feel is necessary to track). Examples include the following items:
    a. Deductions from your paycheck, such as taxes and insurances

b. Giving, such as tithes, offerings, and philanthropic contributions
c. Contributions to savings and investments
d. Home expenses, such as mortgage, repairs and maintenance, and utilities (electricity, natural gas, phone, cable, and Internet services)
e. Car expenses, including payments to the bank, maintenance, gas, oil, tires, car insurance, and major repairs
f. Food and supplies for the home, including grocery expenses, dining out, and miscellaneous household supplies
g. Medical expenses, including anything not covered by insurance (copays, professional fees, pharmacy, lab, and facility fees, eye care, and dental expenses)
h. Miscellaneous personal and family expenses (travel and entertainment, cash spending, gifts, and spending on children's needs)
i. Tax accounts, including anything you will want to capture to report on your IRS income tax return (reimbursable clothing expenses for work, work-related education expenses, job-hunting expenses, home office expenses, and unreimbursed work-related travel and entertainment)
j. General miscellaneous to cover anything you haven't covered so far. If this category gets too big, you will need to track what you're allocating to this account and break it out separately in a new category of its own. Otherwise, this account can become a money pit for uncontrolled spending.

The best way to measure your family's financial performance is to prepare a budget at the beginning of each year and track actual expenses against it on a monthly basis. Sticking to a budget requires discipline and self-control. It's best for the husband and wife to both be involved in the process. Usually, one spouse is better at keeping the checkbook than the other one is. Choose which of you is best. Have a financial planning session each month to review your spending habits compared to your budget. Be honest with one another and make whatever adjustments are necessary to stay on track. You'll be tempted to want to blame one another for things that go wrong. Avoid that temptation. Maintain mutual respect and tact in your financial conversations.

In our family, my wife controls the checkbook because she is less prone to impulse buying than I am. I'm better at tracking spending on the computer, and I allocate our actual spending from the checkbook and credit cards into the appropriate expense accounts in an Excel file. Debbie and I review our spending monthly and have a conversation about how we're doing. Sometimes it's not fun, but we've learned to agree on our financial objectives at the beginning of the year and tactfully and respectfully take accountability for our behavior against those goals on a monthly basis. The result is that we have no credit card debt, we spend within our means, and we are accumulating savings and investments according to the Money Map plan. We're certainly not perfect, but it sure is a better way to live. It also serves to keep the peace in our marriage relationship.

Financial problems are listed as the leading cause of divorce in America. As one of the casualties of divorce, I understand the devastating consequences it imposes on the family environment, both financially and otherwise. While excellence in the family environment is certainly possible in the midst of divorce, it's much more difficult to navigate. If you desire to avoid divorce and want to experience lasting excellence in your family, you must develop strong financial stewardship habits.

Individual Finance

Stewardship is also the goal in the individual environment—to make wise use of all that is entrusted to your care. Good stewardship habits rooted in a foundation of strong principles will lead to a life of excellence. It's so easy to say—and sometimes so difficult to practice. The desire for things accompanied by the societal pressure to have them now is strong.

Most people agree with the wisdom of personal financial prudence. However, it's so easy to forget that wisdom when you're staring at a fifty-inch flat-screen television on sale at Best Buy. You've wanted a digital flat-screen for a long time. Everyone else has one, but you're still suffering with your old analog TV. Best Buy is offering a payment plan that enables you to take it home today without having to pay a dime for two years. The temptation is strong. The lure is enticing. In our affluent, debt-financed society, it happens every day in many ways. To develop habits of good stewardship in our *buy-it-now-pay-for-it-later* culture is not easy. Nothing worthwhile is. Excellence is not easy either. There's a principle of nature that says nothing of value is free. Instant gratification never leads to excellence. Sometimes, this lesson is very hard to learn.

> *62. Instant gratification never leads to excellence.*

For me, it took three failed businesses, one bankruptcy, the loss of my family through divorce, and two periods of unemployment to learn it. Now, I live a life of stewardship. I'm not saying I do everything cheap and never do or buy things we want to do or buy. What I am saying is that the only debt we have is our home, and we have developed the habit of patience to be able to afford something before we buy it—most of the time.

> *63. Excellence lives frugally, spends rationally, and saves fervently.*

Today, I take my own advice on stewardship and regularly analyze the way I make decisions about what I do and buy. I've learned that a life of excellence has nothing to do with how much money or how many things you have. It has *everything* to do with what you do with what you have and finding contentment in whatever state you're in.

Debbie and I have found a way to maintain peace and joy in our hearts regardless of our financial situation. We have built our life of excellence on a foundation of faith and trust in God. I am *rich* now, whether my bank account says so or not! Balance in the financial perspective is a critical element for a life of excellence. Effective stewardship will take you there. America's founding fathers said, "Live frugally, spend rationally, and save fervently" (Beck, *Broke* p. 66).

Tip: Author Dave Ramsey has an excellent course on managing your personal finances called *Financial Peace*. You may want to check it out.

Summary of Chapter 12

1. Excellence in the finance pillar is the fifth and final priority of focus.
2. Organizations, teams, and individuals must guard against the human tendency to allow greed and selfishness to motivate financial behavior. Instead, they should seek to exercise thrift and frugality in financial matters.
3. Excellence in the finance pillar is a natural result of proper focus on quality, service, and people. You must keep the financial perspective in balance.
4. The main goal in the finance pillar is stewardship, the effective management and administration of finances and other property for others. It invokes a moral responsibility for the careful use of money, time, talents, and other resources with respect to the principles or needs of a community or group.

5. Great organizations and teams need to discern what drives their economic engines and use it to measure efficiency and productivity.
6. Since tithing is the natural outcome of a mature believer and the major source of revenue for the church, churches should focus on developing their members to full maturity in the faith.
7. Families and individuals need to measure their financial performances against sensible, realistic budgets.
8. Everyone at all levels should live frugally, spend rationally, and save fervently.

Take Action

1. Define excellence in the finance pillar as it relates to your environment.
2. Determine how you will measure your progress in the finance pillar. Include in your measurements that which drives your economic engine. You may need to study in more detail Jim Collins's Hedgehog Concept explained in *Good to Great*.
3. Add these descriptions to your Blueprint for Excellence.
4. Check out the family and personal financial planning resources from Crown Financial Ministries, Inc. at www.CrownMoneyMap.org.

Summary of Section 3

Balanced Clarity of Focus

The structure or framework for execution I've described in this section enables you to work toward *balanced clarity of focus* as you go about trying to achieve your mission and vision on a daily basis. It provides balanced clarity of focus for the senior leaders of an organization. It provides aligned balance clarity of focus for teams and team leaders within the organization. It provides aligned balanced clarity of focus for individual contributors to the team and organization.

A Priority for Action

The pillar structure is also organized in *priority* order and clarifies a priority of thought and action that can be applied on a daily basis to guide behavior in a moment of service or interaction with others. The priority in the quality pillar is *safety*. Quality really is job one. No action should ever be taken that will jeopardize the safety of anyone involved. The service pillar determines the second priority—*courtesy*. Given that no one's safety is in jeopardy, no one should ever be treated rudely or inappropriately. Even in a situation where a safety concern is present, rudeness is not necessary. People should always be dealt with tactfully and respectfully.

The third pillar is people, and the priority is creating a *positive memorable experience* for everyone involved. Following safety and courtesy is the priority of ensuring that everyone is behaving in a way that creates a positive memorable experience for guests and teammates. All actions should be focused in that direction. Fourth is the growth pillar. The priority is *forward progress*. All actions should be focused toward moving the organization, team, and individuals forward. Remember that it's about progress, not perfection.

The fifth and final pillar of focus is finance. Its priority is *efficiency*. All actions and decisions should be made with the most efficient approach as the goal, except when safety, courtesy, the positive memorable experience, or forward movement are jeopardized. Efficiency usually refers to activity that is business necessary but provides little value to the customer, such as processing paperwork, managing the electric bill, or planning business activities. Those activities are important but should never be undertaken if they jeopardize anyone's safety, cause anyone to behave disrespectfully, negatively impact the overall experience of a guest, or move the organization or team backwards. Here's how priority thinking works.

To build and maintain a culture of excellence, everyone should be taught to use the five priorities to determine how to behave in a moment of interaction by asking themselves these five questions:

1. Will this action enable everyone to remain safe?
2. Will this action enable everyone to behave with courtesy toward others?
3. Will this action positively affect the overall experience of the guest?
4. Will this action move the team and organization forward?
5. Will this action enable everyone to perform efficiently?

The five priorities of safety, courtesy, positive memorable experience, forward progress, and efficiency should be taught to anyone who joins your team and must be demonstrated by leadership in all actions taken and decisions made. The pillar structure provides balanced clarity of focus with a priority for action.

With your framework for excellence now intact, you're ready to learn how to measure progress and construct your complete Blueprint for Excellence.

SECTION 4

Assemble the Roof

> Measurement supports the alignment of desired
> behaviors. The better an organization can align these
> behaviors, the more quickly it will achieve
> desired results.
> —Quint Studer, *Hardwiring Excellence*

The roof is about setting goals and measuring your progress. It represents the ultimate end objective for your effort of excellence at the organizational, team, and individual levels. Now that you have a strong foundation that clearly communicates why you exist (*mission*), where you want to go (*vision*), how you want to get there (*principles* and *standards*), and a framework for action (*the five pillars*), it's time to measure your progress (*the roof*).

The critical concept in Section 4 is *alignment*, defined as the proper adjustment of the components of a system for coordinated performance. Everyone at every level of the organization must be aligned in thought, intent, and action. If you're trying to push a huge boulder up a hill, you need everyone behind the boulder pushing in the same direction. If you have half your team pushing on one side of the boulder and the other half of your team pushing on the opposite side of the boulder, you won't go anywhere. Everyone must be pushing in the same direction. That's alignment.

> *64. To experience excellence, everyone must be aligned in thought, intent, and action.*

SMART Goals

At the organizational, team, and individual levels, you will develop SMART goals to measure your progress. SMART goals are objective goals that can be measured by counting, rating, or ranking something. The measurement is clear and understandable. For example, one goal under the people pillar may be to increase employee engagement to 95 percent by the end of the calendar year. This is a SMART goal.

- **S**—specific (increase employee engagement to 95 percent)
- **M**—measurable (to 95 percent)
- **A**—actionable (by doing certain things, we can impact this goal)
- **R**—realistic (a stretch to achieve, but able to be achieved nonetheless)
- **T**—time focused (by the end of the calendar year)

Your goals should be purely objective at the organization and team levels, and a combination of objective and subjective measures at the individual level. I'll explain this more within each chapter of Section 4.

The Scorecard—Rating Performance

Since objective, measurable goals can be counted, rated, or ranked, I'll use a rating process that will enable you to measure alignment among the three levels of performance. *How will you know if you're properly aligned between the organization and team levels and that everyone is pulling in the same direction? How will you know that you're properly aligned between the team and individual levels and that everyone on the team is focused in the right direction?* The rating process will enable you to answer that question by quantifying your result in a consistent manner across the three levels of performance and comparing those scores to each other.

To ensure alignment, we'll use a *five-point rating scale*. The definitions of the rating categories will remain congruent throughout all three levels of performance so we can compare scorecards and assess alignment mathematically. The first two levels of the rating scale describe performances that need to improve. The last three levels describe varying degrees of excellent performances.

- **Level 1—unacceptable**; this level of performance may jeopardize your involvement with the team
- **Level 2—needs to improve**; lowest possible result that won't get you fired but needs to improve over time or a role change may be necessary
- **Level 3—fully successful**; lowest result that would be considered successful; consistent high performance over time
- **Level 4—superior**; the stretch, achievable with a strong, challenging effort
- **Level 5—distinguished**; uniquely notable performance, very difficult to achieve, only a few have made it here before

The descriptive labels are very important. You may be familiar with more common words like *meets expectations, average, does not meet expectations, below average, exceeds expectations,* or *above average.* This is typical language used in cultures of mediocrity. Our objective is excellence, so a new language and paradigm of measurement is required. The language is critical. Be very careful before you modify it.

Note that Level 3, the middle of the scale, is not average, but fully successful. Most of us are accustomed to the middle of a rating scale representing average performance. In a culture of mediocrity, that would be accurate. Don't get this rating scale for excellence confused with the A-F letter grading scale we all learned in school. In a culture of excellence, the middle of the scale is the first level of excellence, an A. It is *fully successful*. It is then followed by two more levels of excellence—*superior* (A+) and *distinguished* (A++). Your objective is to move performance toward the right end of the scale. Level 2 is performance that *needs to improve* and correlates to a letter grade of B, C, or D. Level 1 is performance that is *unacceptable*, which correlates to the letter grade F.

This one-to-five scale enables you to focus performance in the direction of excellence and create conversations that will help you get there. It may take some time to mentally adjust to this way of thinking. Remember, though, if you're already achieving the results you want to achieve, you may not need to change your way of thinking. However, if you're not achieving the results you want, you *must* change your thinking.

Using Weights to Guide Focus

Weighting your goals will help you determine focus and priority. Without weights, each goal in your scorecard is equally important. Using weights will enable you to vary the level of importance to drive focus. For example, you may find it necessary to place a large amount of time and energy in improving the quality of your product or service during a particular performance period. Increasing the weight of the quality goals will communicate to everyone its heightened level of importance in relation to the other goals in the scorecard.

General Guidelines for Setting Goals

1. Target no more than a total of eight goals on a single scorecard.

2. It's not required to have a goal under each pillar.
3. Use an action verb to start the goal statement followed by a brief description of the area being measured and tracked.
4. State the goal at the *Level 4* stretch to create stronger focus on excellence.
5. It is not necessary to state the time frame for each goal on the scorecard if all goals are related to the same time frame (i.e. the performance year). Simply note the time frame in the title of the scorecard.
6. Make sure it's a goal with which you can create a continuous numeric scale of measurement by counting, rating, or ranking the result.
7. Avoid identifying tactics as goals. If the result of the goal is stated as a yes or no, it's not a goal for this purpose; it's a tactic or project used to help accomplish a larger measurable goal. For example, you may need to implement the new information systems technology by the end of the year. This is not a goal that should appear on the scorecard since it cannot be measured numerically. You either do it—or you don't. It's a tactic to improve customer service.
8. When setting the Level 4 target, consider current performance to standard, historical trends and any other specific knowledge currently known. Level 4 should be a reasonable stretch to achieve (as defined by the general consensus of key stakeholders). Level 5 should begin where the general consensus states is truly unique and distinguishable—possible to achieve but very difficult and rare.
9. Level 3 should be set at the minimum level of performance allowed to still be considered fully successful. Oftentimes, it's stated as equal to or slightly better than the previous period's actual performance.
10. Level 2 is the lowest performance allowable that will not necessarily lead to termination of employment for those

responsible. Level 1 is anything less than Level 2—and as it states, unacceptable. Performance must improve within a reasonable time frame to at least Level 2 or those responsible will lose their jobs or be reassigned.
11. No goal should have a weight of less than 10 percent. The weight of all goals added together must equal 100 percent.

The Annual Planning Process

Goals should be set and measured on an annual basis. They must begin at the organizational level and cascade through the team and individual levels. Use the following guide to ensure alignment:

- Step 1: Assess performance for the previous period in all three levels.
- Step 2: Set organizational goals for the coming period based on your Step 1 assessment and long-range plans.
- Step 3: Communicate organizational goals to all team leaders.
- Step 4: Set team goals for the coming period that align with and enable the organizational goals.
- Step 5: Work with each team member to set individual goals that align with and enable the team and organizational goals.

In Section 4, I'll describe how to use the SMART goal-setting process to develop and align challenging but achievable goals that cascade from the organizational level to the team and individual levels within the five environments. With this understanding, you'll be ready to put it all together into a *Blueprint for Action*, your strategic plan, to guide you on your quest for excellence.

CHAPTER 13

The Organization Scorecard

>What gets measured gets done.
>—Zig Ziglar

Alignment of thought, intent, and action begins at the organizational level. It's the responsibility of top leadership to develop SMART goals that move the organization toward its stated mission and vision. With the pace of change and innovation continuing to increase at exponential levels, leaders are typically reevaluating their plans more often than in the past. Most organizations set long-term strategic goals covering a period of three to five years and break them down into annual objectives that align with the fiscal year. Annual planning and measurement should coincide with the organization's fiscal year. In the personal and family environments, the calendar year will most likely suffice. Measurement time frames should be the same for all three levels—organization, team, and individual. Anything different will impede alignment.

To allow enough time for cascading goals to the team and individual levels, organizational goal setting should begin several months prior to the beginning of the performance period. If your performance year is January 1-December 31, you should begin organizational planning no later than the previous September. In most cases, the organizational goal-setting process will need the input of many stakeholders. Assembling and processing that input takes time. Start early enough to allow time for development but late enough to have enough current year data for forward planning.

The best organizational goal-setting process will include the active involvement of key stakeholders at all levels. This will ensure that you have a well-rounded perspective on organizational issues and will enable you to gain support for the plan from everyone in the organization. A proven method to accomplish this is to create pillar teams that take responsibility for analyzing activity, setting goals, and implementing organizational action relative to the pillar.

The Pillar Team Process

For optimum effectiveness, all organizational teams should be organized under their relevant pillars. One team for each pillar should oversee all strategy and action corresponding to that pillar. The senior team has ultimate responsibility and accountability for all pillar outcomes but can be supported by an advisory team of pillar experts. Other subordinate teams may be established either permanently or temporarily to coordinate activity as deemed necessary by senior leadership or the pillar team. For example, you may determine it necessary to assign a team to plan and execute the annual company picnic. Since this team's activity is designed to make it a better place for employees to work, it should come under the oversight of the people pillar team. Each *pillar team* should be comprised of the following:

- at least one senior leader to serve as executive champion, advisor, and enabler
- one key leader to serve as team leader
- no more than seven other key players who bring value and expertise to that team's work

The senior leader should be the one who has oversight responsibility for that pillar team's activity. For example, the executive champion for the people pillar team should be the chief human resources officer. The executive champion for the finance pillar team should be the chief financial officer, and so on. With this approach, the team's executive champion will be able to quickly and efficiently authorize the team to move forward when critical decisions are made.

The team leader should be a leader who does not report directly to the executive champion. This ensures a balance of power, encourages out-of-the-box thinking, and prevents silo focus. The team members can be any *high performer* in the organization who is able to devote time and energy to serving on the team without negatively impacting his or her primary role in the organization. The pillar teams should be positioned just below the senior team on the organization chart. Pillar team membership should be viewed as a reward for high performance and should carry with it authority, reward, and recognition appropriate to its impact.

Pillar teams should meet a minimum of once per month to assess progress and deliberate action. They should be required to track organizational results against objectives and report results to the organization monthly. It's important to ensure that pillar team members are properly trained and equipped to perform their duties. It may also be beneficial to connect a portion of each pillar team member's annual compensation to the results achieved in their pillar of focus. The pillar team process serves as a viable addition to any organizational succession planning effort. Members who serve on these teams gain valuable insights into the business of running the business. It can help develop your future leaders.

The Organization Scorecard

There should be no more than eight organizational goals in any performance period. Limiting the number of goals on the official scorecard will demand focus from everyone in the organization. There may be many more goals that are set within a given performance period, but only the most critical should be included on the scorecard. This forces you to create focus, alignment, and accountability. The goals chosen should be the key outcomes that need focus and attention during the performance period.

Selecting the goals to appear on an organizational scorecard is the responsibility of the senior team with input from the pillar teams and other key stakeholders. The organizational scorecard may also need to be approved by the board of directors. At the organizational level, there will most likely be at least one goal within in each pillar of focus to ensure balanced focus and decision making throughout the performance period.

Healthcare Example
All goals to be achieved by end of the calendar year

Pillar	Goal	Wt.	1	2	3	4	5	Result	Rating	Score Wt x rating
Quality	Increase compliance on the 31 measures of appropriate care to 90%	15%	<70%	70%	80%	90%	95%	92%	4	0.60
	Reduce never events to 12	10%	>16	16	14	12	6	8	5	0.50
Service	Increase patient's perception of care to the 90th percentile	20%	<70	70	80	90	95	78th	2	0.40
People	Increase employee commitment to the 95th percentile	15%	<80	80	90	95	98	82nd	2	0.30
	Reduce employee turnover to 8%	10%	>12%	12%	10%	8%	5%	9.5%	3	0.30
Growth	Increase market share to 80%	10%	<70%	70%	75%	80%	82%	78%	3	0.30
Finance	Increase operating margin to 400k	10%	<100	100	200	400	500	360k	3	0.30
	Increase cash flow margin to 8%	10%	<7.0	7.0	7.5	8.0	9.0	8.2%	4	0.40
	Total of all weights	100%						Total score		3.10

As discussed in Section 3, specific measures will most likely be different in different industries and environments. Quality is especially unique. Many of the measures listed above are standard quality measures in American healthcare that will not relate to other industries.

While quality will usually take on a specific and unique goal-setting approach, the other pillar goals may be more similar. Every organization will most likely consider tracking guest perception under service, employee engagement, and turnover under people, market share, or volume improvement under growth, revenue, cost, or profit goals under finance.

Manufacturing Example
All goals to be achieved by end of the fiscal year

Pillar	Goal	Wt.	1	2	3	4	5	Result	Rating	Score Wt x rating
Quality	Reduce re-work by 20%	15%	<12%	12%	15%	20%	25%	13%	2	0.30
	Reduce waste to 1% of total product	10%	>1.8%	1.8%	1.5%	1.0%	0.5%	0.8%	4	0.40
Service	Increase customer satisfaction to the 85th percentile	10%	<70	70	75	85	95	77	3	0.30
People	Increase employee commitment to the 75th percentile	15%	<60	60	70	75	90	82	4	0.60
	Reduce employee turnover to 15%	10%	>22%	22%	18%	15%	10%	18.5%	2	0.20
Growth	Increase units of production by 25%	20%	<18%	18%	20%	25%	30%	15%	1	0.20
Finance	Reduce costs by 15%	10%	<8%	8%	10%	15%	20%	23%	5	0.50
	Increase units shipped/FTE/day to 12.5	10%	<10.0	10.0	11.5	12.5	15.0	10.5	2	0.20
	Total of all weights	100%							Total score	2.70

Notice the different measures for quality and the similarities in the measures in many of the other pillars. Of course, these are only examples. Your actual goals and measures will be unique to your situation.

Church Example
All goals to be achieved by end of the calendar year

Pillar	Goal	Wt.	1	2	3	4	5	Result	Rating	Score Wt x rating
Quality	Increase the score on the NCD survey to a score of 55 or more	10%	<45	45	50	55	65	62	4	0.40
Service	Increase the percentage of membership involved in ministry outside the church to 35%	20%	<25%	25%	30%	35%	45%	47%	5	1.00
People	Increase average weekly attendance at the main worship service to 250 members	10%	<175	175	225	250	300	245	3	0.30
	Decrease member turnover to 5%	10%	>10%	10%	8%	5%	3%	6.4%	3	0.30
Growth	Increase conversions or professions of faith by 50%	40%	<10%	10%	30%	50%	100%	63%	4	1.60
Finance	Increase giving/member to $1000/member for the year	10%	<825	825	875	1000	1100	$847.50	2	0.20
	Total of all weights	100%							Total score	3.80

The Team, Family, and Individual Environments

Chapter 14 will focus on the team and family levels. Chapter 15 will focus on the individual level. In those chapters, I'll cover everything you need to know in order to cascade the organizational goals into those areas.

Tactics

Your next task is to identify key organizational *tactics* you believe will enable you to accomplish your goals in the coming performance period. *What do we need to do to achieve this goal?* This is where many yes/no types of activities may reside. If your goal is to improve customer satisfaction, one major strategy may be to implement training for all customer service personnel.

Many, if not all, of your organizational tactics will cascade down into specific team scorecards. Make sure that you're not trying to boil the ocean in one performance period. Make sure your organization and team have the capability and resilience capacity to handle whatever changes you intend to implement during the period.

Summary of Chapter 13

1. The five-pillar framework provides a method of planning and execution with balanced clarity of focus.
2. The key concept in Section 4 is alignment. Goals, tactics, and time frames should be consistent at all three levels of measurement—organization, team, and individual.
3. There should be no more than eight goals on any one scorecard.
4. The five-point rating scale enables you to create mathematical measurements at all levels to ensure alignment.
5. Using weights to drive focus within a particular scorecard can help communicate to everyone in the organization the

priority of what's most important during the performance period.
6. There are general guidelines that help to enable high-quality goal setting at all levels.
7. The five-step annual planning process can be used to ensure alignment by cascading goals from the organizational level through the team level to the individual level.
8. Alignment of thought, intent, and action begins at the organizational level.
9. The best organizational goal-setting process will include the active involvement of key stakeholders at all levels. The pillar team concept can help accomplish this.
10. Specific goals will vary with different industries and environments.

Take Action

1. If you're responsible for developing measures at the organizational level, begin thinking about what you'll need to measure under each pillar and what the Level 4 measure should be for the coming performance period.

CHAPTER 14

The Team Scorecard

> No goal is really a goal by default. If you don't set a
> goal, you've already set it and the goal
> is to stay the same.
> —Rick Warren

Aligning goals between the organizational and team levels is a core strategy for excellence. Quint Studer, a consultant in the healthcare industry, says his company will not even consider working with an organization unless they agree to align organizational goals with team goals. Studer considers it the single most important tactic for excellence that leadership can implement.

> 65. *People are much more apt to support
> what they help create.*

To ensure *alignment* and *quality* in the cascading process, it's best to organize a series of goal-setting sessions with middle managers and senior leaders. Each senior leader should meet with the managers and directors under his or her supervision at or near the beginning of the performance period. The senior leader can present his or her annual goals to the leadership team first. Next, each subordinate leader should present his or her goals and explain the methodology behind the numbers. Peers then have the opportunity to ask questions for clarity and accountability.

The meeting should continue until each leader has had the opportunity to present his or her goals for the period and the group is satisfied that goals are equitable and aligned. Once approved by the senior leader, the goals are set for the period. Once the performance period begins, changes should be avoided if at all possible and made by extreme exception only.

The team leader's annual measurement cycle should look something like this:

1. Understand the organizational goals from senior management.
2. Seek any specific direction from your immediate supervisor.
3. Study your team's historical trends and current performance. Benchmark them against similar teams in other organizations within your industry.
4. Use your research to develop a rough draft team scorecard.
5. Meet with your team for brainstorming and feedback. Involving your team at the beginning of the goal-setting process enables you to actively engage them and garner their support toward achieving the goals during the performance period. Remember that people are much more apt to support what they help create.
6. Present your rough draft team scorecard to your management group (immediate supervisor and peers).
7. Revise your scorecard based on feedback from your management group.
8. Seek final approval of your scorecard from your immediate supervisor.
9. Develop tactical plans on a monthly or quarterly basis to help you achieve your goals.
10. Track and report actual results to your management group on a monthly basis.
11. Use the actual final results achieved for preparing the next period's scorecard.

If this sounds like a lot of work, it is. Anything worthwhile takes effort. Excellence is no exception. Creating an excellent team takes hard work. The most important process to ensure team excellence is the team's measurement system. I realize that many leaders juggle many important daily tasks. Everyone has a full plate. *What do you allow to be on your plate?* One of the most important skills for a team leader to master is prioritizing his or her work.

Your measurement system (*team scorecard*) should serve as the method you use to prioritize your work. This is not one of the tasks you want to leave off of your plate. It's the master task that determines exactly what goes on your plate. If you skip this critical activity, you risk everything else that can be accomplished by your team.

John Wooden, the legendary coach of the UCLA Bruins basketball dynasty, said, "Never mistake activity for achievement."

Your job as team leader is to get results. Your measurement process is the way to do it. Prioritize setting goals at the top of your annual to-do list. It will help ensure that you effectively manage what's on your plate and invest your time in the right things that drive excellence.

> *66. Excellence requires a serious commitment to accountability and discipline.*

Accountability in the goal-setting process is also extremely critical. As usual, senior leaders must lead the way. Do not let the first month of the performance period end without having team scorecards finalized. Venturing further into the actual performance year without goals clearly established is counterproductive.

If you're not going to commit to the process, forget about moving your organization forward toward excellence. It just won't happen. Leaders will lose faith in the value of the process if top leadership fails to take it seriously. If that happens, you'll be worse off than you were before you started. You will have earned yourself the reputation as a hypocrite. Excellence requires a serious commitment to accountability and discipline. This is such an essential concept in a culture of excellence that I've devoted an entire chapter to it toward the end of the book.

The Team Scorecard

Again, there should be no more than eight team goals in any performance period. The goals chosen should be the key outcomes that need focus and attention during the period. Selecting the goals to appear on a *team scorecard* is the responsibility of the team leader with input from team members as appropriate. Involving your team in team goal setting is a wise approach. Typically, the team scorecard will need the approval of the team leader's immediate supervisor. At the team level, having goals under each pillar is *not* required. Team activity is generally more narrowly focused than organizational activity.

Let's look at some examples of team scorecards that connect to and align with an organizational scorecard. To simplify the discussion, we'll consider one pillar at a time and show an organizational goal followed by several team goals that could support it. At the end of the chapter, I'll put it all together in a scorecard and show you some actual examples.

The Quality Pillar

Overarching objective: to improve the quality of the products and/or services offered; to build and sustain high-quality products and/or services.

In healthcare:
- Organizational goal: Increase compliance on the thirty-one measures of appropriate care to 90 percent in calendar 2010 as measured internally by the quality department.

- o Nursing team goal: Improve medication reconciliation match between the discharge summary and the patient list to 95 percent as measured by internal process.
    - *Medication reconciliation is one of the thirty-one measures of appropriate care. This team needs to improve its performance in this specific measure. By doing so, it will help the organization achieve its goal under quality.*
- o Learning team goal: Achieve a perception of quality learning score of 4.95 on a five-point scale from nursing leadership for all nurse learning events delivered during calendar 2010 as measured by a survey of nurse learning participants and leaders.
    - *By delivering high-quality learning to all nurses, nurses learn what they need to know in order to perform well on the thirty-one measures of appropriate care, thus enabling higher performance on that organizational goal.*
- o Bio-Medical team goal: Achieve corrective maintenance completion rate at 93 percent as calculated internally from the equipment management database for all patient-related equipment.
    - *By keeping bio-medical equipment in proper working order, nurses have the tools they need to meet the thirty-one measures of appropriate care targets.*

In manufacturing:
- Organizational goal: Reduce waste to 1 percent of total product by December 31.

- o Engineering department goal: Increase accuracy of product design that goes to the shop floor to 99.5 percent as measured by internal process.
  - *By ensuring the shop floor gets an accurate product design, the opportunity for waste in the production cycle is decreased.*
- o Assembly line department goal: Reduce rework to 1 percent of total product output as measured by internal process.
  - *Rework is a result of the product not being built right the first time and is a major contributor to waste. By reducing rework, a shop floor department reduces waste.*
- o Shipping department: Reduce shipping supplies wasted to 1 percent of total supplies used as measured by internal process.
  - *The alignment here is obvious.*

In the church:
- Organizational goal: Increase the Natural Church Development (NCD) survey score to fifty-five or higher by the end of the calendar year.
  - o Administrative team goal: Increase the NCD survey score on the category of "Functional Structures" from thirty-five to forty-five.
    - *Functional structures are one of the eight characteristics of healthy churches measured by the NCD survey. It is the responsibility of the administrative team to ensure that the processes and systems of the church are effective.*
  - o Leadership development team goal: Increase the NCD survey score on "Empowering Leadership" from twenty-nine to forty.

- *Empowering leadership is also one of the eight characteristics of healthy churches measured by the NCD survey. The leadership development team can address the issues associated with empowering leadership and implement tactics to improve that outcome.*
  - Evangelism team goal: Increase the NCD survey score on "Need-oriented Evangelism" from thirty-seven to fifty.
    - *Need-oriented evangelism is another one of the eight characteristics of healthy churches and is the responsibility of the evangelism team to improve.*

In the family:
- Organizational goal: in this case, the organization is the community of which the family is a part. An objective in most communities is to improve the overall quality of life of its citizens. With that in mind, each family team within the community has a responsibility to help make that happen. One typical measure of a community's quality is the crime rate; an organizational goal may be to decrease the crime rate by 15 percent.
  - Possible family team goals include:
    - Every family member will describe the quality of life in the family experience as excellent as measured by informal survey.
    - Every family member will testify that the home experience is loving and harmonious as measured by informal survey.
    - Ninety-five percent of all disagreements are settled calmly and with an attitude of mutual benefit. Family members seek and usually achieve win-win outcomes.

- Instances where one family member hurts another are less than 2 percent of total interactions.
            - Home and grounds inspection scores average 95 percent or higher for the year. The home and grounds remain clean and in proper order.
    o With these family quality goals, the family becomes a positive force in the community and serves to improve the quality of life for those around them. If all families would adopt and work to accomplish these goals, the entire quality of life in the community would be greatly improved.

The Service Pillar

Overarching Objective: to deliver excellent service to every guest every time.

In healthcare:

- Organizational goal: Increase patient satisfaction to the ninetieth percentile by the end of the performance period as measured by the external survey company.
    o Nursing team goal: Increase patient satisfaction to the ninetieth percentile by the end of the performance period as measured by the external survey company.
        - *Since direct care teams are the ones responsible for the direct delivery of care and service, the goal at the team level is very similar to the one at the organization level. The specific team goal may vary depending upon where the specific nursing team is starting from and what would be considered a reasonable stretch target for the performance period.*

- o Learning team goal: Achieve 90 percent excellent ratings on the annual learning services customer service internal survey.
  - *Learning services provides service to direct and indirect care groups within a healthcare organization. Therefore, their contribution to this organizational goal is measured by the employee perception of the learning service delivered.*
- o Bio-Med team goal: Achieve 90 percent excellent ratings on the annual bio-med services customer service internal survey.
  - *Like the learning team, bio-med provides services to the nursing group.*

In manufacturing:

- Organizational goal: Increase customer satisfaction to the eighty-fifth percentile by December 31 as measured by the official customer service survey.
  - o Engineering department goal: Increase customer satisfaction to the eighty-fifth percentile by December 31 as measured by the official customer survey.
    - *If the organization conducts an official customer survey, there can be one or more questions included to have the customer provide his or her perception of the engineering department's services. The engineering department may also want to survey its internal customers for the service provided to the shop floor departments.*
  - o Assembly line department goal: Achieve 90 percent excellent ratings on the internal customer service survey.
    - *Assembly line departments provide a service to the next department down the line. Feedback*

             from the receiving department is important to the continual cycle of service excellence along the production line.
    o Shipping department goal: Increase customer satisfaction to the eighty-fifth percentile as measured by the official customer service survey.
        ▪ *The shipping department actually has two customers—the recipient of the shipped product and the internal group ordering the shipment. They should survey both.*

In the church:
- Organizational goal: Increase the percentage of members involved in ministry outside the church to 35 percent by the end of the calendar year.
    o Administrative team goal: Increase the number of messages on "finding your ministry" from four per month to eight per month.
        ▪ *With more messages being communicated on the purpose and impact of each member finding his or her ministry gifts, more members will become involved in ministries.*
    o Leadership development team goal: Increase the number of members trained on leading a ministry.
        ▪ *More trained leaders will yield more ministries.*
    o Evangelism team goal: Increase the number of members being assessed by the SHAPE profile to 50 percent.
        ▪ *The SHAPE profile is a method introduced by Rick Warren in* The Purpose Driven Life *that helps the individual understand how God has uniquely designed them to serve others in ministry (see chapter 17). By increasing the number of members who understand their*

SHAPE *profiles, more people will become involved in ministry and evangelism outside the church.*

In the family:
- Organizational (community) goal: Increase the community perception of service to 60 percent excellent ratings as measured by the annual citizen perception survey. *(Wouldn't it be great if communities would do this?)*
    - Possible family team goals:
        - Every family member will describe the relationship with each other member of the family as loving and harmonious and would choose to live together even if they didn't have to.
        - Ninety percent of other citizens impacted by our family will describe us as a close-knit, loving family who adds value to the world around us.

The People Pillar

Overarching Objective: to make it a great place for people to work, live, and be.

In any business organization:
- Organizational goal: Reduce employee turnover to 8 percent by the end of the performance period as measured by the human resource department.
    - *Employee turnover is one of the easiest goals to cascade throughout the organization. Every team of ten or more will most likely have a turnover goal on their scorecard. The only reason they wouldn't is if the team has stabilized turnover so well over the past few years that it*

requires little or no focus from the leader and the team. Use the past performance periods as a baseline to set the Level 4 stretch goal.
- Possible team goal: Reduce turnover to 8 percent by the end of the performance period as measured by the human resource department.
  - *The actual team goal will vary based on recent trends. Teams may want to consider measuring certain aspects of turnover such as voluntary, involuntary, high performers, and low performers. Turnover of low performers may be healthy for the team. Be careful to set goals so that desired results are not penalized.*

In the church:
- Organizational goal: Increase average weekly attendance at the main worship service to 250 by the end of the calendar year.
  - *If this is a great place to worship, people should be drawn to the main worship hour—and attendance should improve. With that in mind, several church teams can have an impact on that outcome.*
    - Fellowship team—increase the number of members serving in the main worship hour greeting team.
    - Discipleship team—increase the number of members successfully completing the "sharing your faith" curriculum.

In the family:
- Organizational (community) goal: Increase citizen engagement to the eightieth percentile.
    o Possible family team goals:
        - *The family objectives mentioned earlier will also serve to support this community goal. An additional family objective here may include getting involved in the community in some way. Involvement is a precursor to engagement.*

The family goals are not as objectively solid as in the other environments. Typically, the family environment is a smaller group of people, and developing more solid measures of perception and team interaction is more challenging. In the family environment, the best way to ensure it's a great place to live and be is to maintain strong, honest, open communication with one another. It's the parents' responsibility to make that happen.

The Growth Pillar

Overarching Objective: to progress; to move forward toward your vision.

In healthcare:
- Organizational goal: Increase market share to 80 percent by the end of the performance period as measured by an external marketing firm.
    o Nursing team, learning team, and bio-med team—no growth goal. *Nursing's job is to serve the patient and provide excellent quality of care. The learning team's job is to provide excellent personal development for internal employees. Bio-med's job is to keep equipment in excellent working condition when nurses and patients need them. Positive word of mouth about nursing care*

will certainly drive growth, but this is already being measured under the service pillar and therefore, does not need to be repeated here. Organizational growth may be impacted by other teams more directly involved in the organization's growth initiatives, such as marketing, service line growth areas, and other revenue or volume-generating areas.

- Marketing team goal—Increase overall hospital admissions by 20 percent as measured by internal admission records.
  - *Marketing may also accept primary responsibility for the organizational market share goal.*
- Cancer center goal—Increase cancer center treatments by 20 percent as measured by internal records.
- Surgery center goal—Increase surgery cases by 5 percent as measured by internal records.
- Cardiology department goal—Increase interventional cardiology procedures to 240 as measured by internal records.

In manufacturing:

- Organizational goal: Increase units of production by 25 percent by the end of the performance period as measured by internal production records.
  - Engineering department goal—Increase new product designs by 10 percent as measured by internal records.
    - *Engineering, typically seen as the creative group, can increase units of production by bringing new product designs to market. It will depend on how the organization views the role of engineering, whether or not there is also a research and development group, etc.*

- o Assembly line department goal—no growth goal.
  - *Assembly line's focus is to produce the work that's brought to them with the highest of quality.*
- o Shipping department goal—no growth goal.
  - Like the assembly line, the shipping department needs to focus on their quality of shipments, the volume of which is determined by other areas, such as sales.
- o Sales department goal—Increase units sold by 25 percent as measured by internal records.
  - *In manufacturing, it's primarily the sales group that drives volume growth. The volume goals will be an important part of their team scorecard.*

In the church:
- Organizational goal: Increase professions of faith by 50 percent by the end of the calendar year as measured by internal records.
  - o *According to Colossians 2:19, church growth is God's will. The church grows when new members accept Christ. So the main purpose of the church is to share the good news of the gospel so that others come to know Christ. In a growing church, the evidence of effectiveness is changed lives and public professions of faith. With that in mind, several church teams can have an impact on that outcome and every church team should make this goal its ultimate aim.*
    - Discipleship team goal—Increase the number of members being trained on how to understand their unique SHAPE for sharing the gospel.

- Evangelism team goal—Increase the number of evangelistic outreach activities designed to share the gospel with seekers.
- Worship team goal—Increase the number of opportunities for seekers to receive Christ during the worship services.

In the family:

- Organizational (community) goal: Increase the population by 10 percent by the end of the calendar year as measured by official community census.
    - *The teams in the community organization that would be responsible for this outcome would most likely be part of the governmental structure of the community; i.e. business development, economic development, etc. The family team, as a sub-group of the community, may not have a goal under growth in this context. The family's contribution to community growth is expressed in the goals under the quality, service, and people pillars already discussed.*

The Finance Pillar

Overarching Objective: to be good stewards of all resources entrusted to your care.

In healthcare:

- Organizational goal: Increase operating margin to $400,000 by the end of the performance period as measured by the internal accounting group.
    - Nursing team, learning team, and bio-med team goal—Perform at (x) percent of budget for the performance period as measured by the internal accounting group.

> - *The exact percent of budget will be determined by the size of the department's budget. Consult your accounting or finance department for guidance.*
>   - Revenue-producing departments may have revenue targets or operating margin targets. The accounting group should help the department manager determine the best financial measure for the period.

In manufacturing:
- Organizational goal: Reduce costs by 15 percent by the end of the performance period as measured by internal accounting records.
  - All departments—reduce costs by 15 percent unless otherwise directed by senior management or the accounting group.
    - *This type of goal may apply to all internal groups or may need to be adjusted, depending on specific conditions in the organization.*

In the church:
- Organizational goal: Increase giving per member per year to $1,000 for the performance period as measured by internal records.
  - Discipleship team goal—Increase the number of learning opportunities about tithing.
  - Evangelism team goal—no goal needed.
    - *Since the work of the evangelism team is to bring in new members, a growth pillar goal, the evangelism team's contribution to increasing church revenue is covered there. The work of the evangelism team may even serve contrary to this finance goal for the church if the new members*

brought into the church don't give at all. Therefore, it is primarily the responsibility of other church teams to focus on this goal. The evangelism team may, however, have a goal to operate within budget just as all other cost departments and groups have in other nonprofit organizations. They may also have a goal to increase their own team's budget through their own fundraising efforts, independent of the church's overall budgeting process.

In the family:
- Organizational (community) goal: Operate within budget for the fiscal year as measured by validated community accounting documents.
    - As with the growth goals, the teams in the community organization that would be responsible for this outcome would most likely be part of the governmental structure of the community; i.e. the county or community accounting office, and each functioning team or department in the community structure would have a budget goal similar to the one described under the business section. The family's responsibility in this scenario would be to pay its portion of taxes levied.
    - It may be more sensible to consider the family's finances independent of the community structure. In this case, the family goal becomes similar to the church or community—to operate within budget. The family may, however, add a goal to increase family revenues and then determine a set of tactical things to do to work toward that goal. Whatever the family revenue goal becomes, operating within budget should always be a target.

Team Scorecards

Let's put it all together in a format similar to the organizational scorecards we created in chapter 13. Here are examples based on the material in this chapter.

Nursing Team in HealthCare

Pillar	Goal	Wt.	1	2	3	4	5	Result	Rating	Score (Wt x rating)
Quality	Improve medication reconciliation to 90%	15%	<80%	85%	88%	90%	95%	92%	4	0.60
Quality	Decrease the fall rate to 0.27/1000 patients.	15%	<.35	0.35	0.3	0.27	0.25	0.21	5	0.75
Service	Increase patient's perception of care to the 90th percentile	30%	<70	70	80	90	95	75%	2	0.60
People	Increase employee commitment to the 95th percentile	15%	<80	80	90	95	98	87%	2	0.30
People	Reduce RN turnover to 8%	15%	<12%	12%	10%	8%	5%	9.3%	3	0.45
Growth	No growth goal									0.00
Finance	Achieve 98% of budget	10%	>102	102%	100%	98%	95%	93%	5	0.50
	Total of all weights	100%							Total score	3.20

Assembly Line Department in Manufacturing

Pillar	Goal	Wt.	1	2	3	4	5	Result	Rating	Score (Wt x rating)
Quality	Reduce re-work by 20%	15%	<12%	12%	15%	20%	25%	22%	4	0.60
Quality	Reduce waste to 1% of total product	10%	<1.8%	1.8%	1.5%	1.0%	0.5%	1.75%	2	0.20
Service	Achieve 90% excellent ratings on interdepartmental survey	15%	<80	80	85	90	95	75%	1	0.15
People	Increase employee commitment to the 75th percentile	15%	<60	60	70	75	90	68%	2	0.30
People	Reduce employee turnover to 15%	10%	>22%	22%	18%	15%	10%	19.0%	2	0.20
Growth	Increase units produced by 25%	20%	<18%	18%	20%	25%	30%	33.0%	5	1.00
Finance	Reduce costs by 15%	15%	<8%	8%	10%	15%	20%	9%	2	0.30
	Total of all weights	100%							Total score	2.75

Evangelism Team in the Church

Pillar	Goal	Wt.	1	2	3	4	5	Result	Rating	Score Wt x rating
Quality	Increase the NCD survey score on "Need-Oriented Evangelism: to 50	30%	<37	37	45	50	60	53	4	1.20
Service	Increase the number of members being assessed by the SHAPE profile to 50%	20%	<33%	33%	43%	50%	60%	10%	3	0.60
People	No people goal									0.00
Growth	Increase the # of evangelistic outreach activities to 24/year	40%	<12	12	18	24	30	43	5	2.00
Finance	Operate at 100% of budget or better	10%	>105%	105%	102%	100%	98%	101.0%	3	0.30
	Total of all weights	100%							Total score	4.10

The Family Team

Pillar	Goal	Wt.	1	2	3	4	5	Result	Rating	Score Wt x rating
Quality	6 of 7 family members describe the home experience as loving & caring	30%	<4	4	5	6	7	7	5	1.50
Service	Increase the neighborhood perception of our family to 90% excellent	25%	<75%	75%	85%	90%	95%	94%	4	1.00
People	6 of 7 family members describe our home as a great place to live	30%	<4	4	5	6	7	6%	4	1.20
Growth	No growth goal									0.00
Finance	Increase family revenue by 20%	15%	<10%	10%	15%	20%	25%	40%	5	0.75
	Total of all weights	100%							Total score	4.45

As you may have discerned, determining the right team goals is as much art as it is science, relying heavily on sound judgment. The organization must have a strong leadership development process in place to teach leaders this fundamental skill.

Summary of Chapter 14

1. Aligning goals between the organizational and team levels is the single most important tactic for excellence that leadership can implement.
2. It is the responsibility of the team leader to ensure team goals are set and aligned with organizational goals.

3. Involving team members in the process enables their interest, support, and performance toward accomplishment of the goals.
4. Your measurement system (*team scorecard*) is the method you use to prioritize your work. This is not one of the tasks you want to leave off your plate. It's the master task that determines exactly what goes on your plate!
5. Determining team goals is as much art as it is science—with much leadership judgment involved. The organization must have a strong leadership development process in place to teach leaders this fundamental skill.

Take Action

1. If you're responsible for leading a team, begin thinking about what you'll need to measure and what the Level 4 measure should be for the coming performance period.
2. Share the organizational goals with every member of your team and begin soliciting their support and input for the team goals.
3. Use the team leaders' annual checklist in this chapter to begin your planning process.

CHAPTER 15

The Individual Scorecard

> The essence of excellence lies in the quality of the individual's performance. The key then is to create an environment in which each individual is inspired to passionately and voluntarily give their best every day.
> —C. David Crouch

> Be the change you want to see in the world.
> —Gandhi

The individual level of performance is where the excellence rubber meets the road. A board of directors and senior team can make all the plans and set all the goals they want—and the directors and managers can align the team purpose and objectives to the organizational goals all they want—but if each individual member of the team, including the leader, doesn't perform his or her role on the team to the best of his or her ability, team and organizational excellence will be only a dream. The *individual* is the fundamental element of a culture of excellence.

There's a tendency to think that when we refer to the individual contributor, we're only talking about employees in nonleadership roles. This is a fallacy. Everything we discuss here applies to any role at any level within an organization, including leaders.

Most businesses today use some sort of evaluation process in an attempt to measure individual performance. I've had the opportunity to write and implement many such processes. *Performance evaluation* is a common practice dating back to the mid-1900s. What began as a simple method of income justification has evolved into the many talent management, career management, management-by-objective, and motivational exercises in existence today. Formal performance review systems have become a multibillion-dollar industry with software and consultants on the topic too numerous to count. American business has become addicted to the notion that they can't survive without this process in place. Interestingly however, most leaders and employees claim the processes used are worthless, nonproductive, and time consuming. Everyone hates them! Yet we persist.

According to Peter Scholtes in *The Leader's Handbook*, 90 percent of managers using performance appraisals describe them as unsuccessful. There is no significant data to support their effectiveness. In my own survey conducted in 2009, 75 percent said the leaders of their organizations don't like employee evaluations or are neutral to them. Ninety-two percent said their leaders have only one performance conversation with their employees each year. Fifty-eight percent said their current system does not improve team or organizational performance, and 83 percent said their leaders don't use the process on a daily basis to encourage desired performance.

According to Salary.com's 2006 Performance Review Survey, 82 percent of managers believe they provide clear goals to their employees prior to their formal performance review, but only 46 percent of employees say the same. Eighty-three percent of employers say they include the input of their employees in the review process, but only 43 percent of employees feel their input is valued and included. Nearly half of the two thousand employees surveyed said their performance has at some time been reviewed against goals that were not previously communicated.

In 2003, I led an intense research project in search of the secret to individual performance measurement. It was very frustrating. We found no commonly agreed-upon approach in organizational practices. Most of the ones we studied were merely variations of the same old thing. Someone along the way had come up with a list of behavior characteristics or attributes they thought were important. They asked each team leader to assess individual performance against that list using some type of rating scale. We even found one organization with thirty-five variations of performance in their rating scale. That option seemed ridiculous to me—how could the organization ever defend that kind of performance differentiation in court?

Most managers and employees we surveyed hated the process they were forced to use. They claimed it served no value to the team and organization other than providing a paper trail to place in the human resource file for legal purposes. Even then, most human resource leaders claimed that the paperwork in the file was not an accurate portrayal of the individual's performance. Most leaders biased high in their judgments and lacked the skill to properly and accurately assess individual performance. This placed the organization, the human resource leader, and the manager in potentially precarious legal positions. The research clearly indicated that most people hated what they were doing but had no idea how to make it better.

Some organizations had no formal evaluation process at all. Toyota was one such example and had earned a great deal of respect for their results in the auto industry. Managers were held accountable for employee engagement and allowed to do whatever they deemed necessary to inspire, reward, and recognize performance. I found this intriguing. Was it possible to eliminate the frustrating evaluation systems of old and simply task it to the leader?

We found several problems with this approach. We learned that Toyota had invested enormous energy and resources in leadership development over the past several decades, resulting in a mature leadership culture unlike most I had worked with. The ability to totally delegate the responsibility for individual performance measurement to the leader is heavily related to the skill of the leader. Most leadership cultures haven't matured to that level.

Executives, human resource professionals, and legal departments were very concerned about the potential legal liabilities that could emerge. Nearly all organizations in our research held similar concerns. We concluded that until the culture matured, organizations needed some type of process to guide leadership behavior in the risky and legally treacherous waters of individual performance measurement. Most leaders have not developed the skill of effectively assessing performance and need a process to guide them.

This presents an interesting dilemma. Most leaders need a process to guide them in assessing individual performance, yet the processes most organizations use are ineffective. Clearly there's a problem with the way we manage and measure individual performances. Worse, most leaders feel trapped and don't know what to do about it. We've become confident in our abilities to measure organizational and team performances, but when it comes to individual measurement, we're at a loss.

Let's begin this perplexing conversation with an understanding of why we do what we do. Then we'll unpack the issue and present a new approach that will help leaders accomplish the main objective—to create an environment in which each individual is inspired to voluntarily and passionately give his or her best each day.

A Journey into the Abyss

Why do organizations invest so much time and energy in the employee evaluation process? What is it that they hope to accomplish? Those *expectations* include the following:

1. Help people improve their performances
2. Differentiate between good and bad performers
3. Create some way to link performance to pay
4. Motivate and retain high-performing employees
5. Help employees with career development
6. Identify training needs
7. Identify candidates for promotions and layoffs
8. Improve the boss/subordinate communication process

9. Create a paper trail for the human resource file for legal protection
10. Link individual performances to team and organizational performances

When you consider the list above, the reason for our struggle becomes clear. Perhaps we expect too much from our performance evaluation process. If everyone hates these processes so much, why do we persist with them? According to Scholtes, our logic goes something like this:

> We believe our process works and we can accurately and objectively identify those employees whose performance is consistently above or below average or standard. We believe that the individual's performance contributes to the bottom line, for better or worse. There are good performers and bad performers, and we're able to tell the difference between the two. Good performers make a positive contribution to the company, and bad performers are detrimental. Performance evaluation serves to clarify the individual's work responsibilities, align them with the organizations goals, hold each individual accountable for their part, and motivate them to continuously improve.

> Scholtes also contends that we approach these beliefs with underlying *assumptions*.

1. Employee evaluation will improve the employee's performance.
2. The individual being evaluated has control over the results.
3. The individual's contribution can be discerned from other individuals and teams.

4. The standards of evaluation are related to factors important to the business and are reasonable and achievable.
5. The systems and processes within which the individual works are stable and capable of delivering the expected results.
6. The evaluation covers performance over the entire period not just the period easily recalled by recent memory.
7. All evaluators are consistent in the execution of the process so comparisons can be made across teams within the organization.

These assumptions are common in business today but most often are not true. Inherent in these assumptions are certain premises and *beliefs* with which many of us would not agree.

- People cannot be trusted and don't want to accept responsibility to carry their fair shares of the load.
- Most people don't want to learn or improve; rather, they want to be left alone.
- People are withholding their best efforts and must be induced or coerced to do better through techniques imposed by their managers or other outside factors.
- Managers can and must motivate and control the workforce.

These beliefs and premises are ridiculous. Most people are trustworthy and want to do a good job. If provided a supportive environment that includes the tools and equipment they need, the cooperative support from teammates, and the skilled coaching and encouragement from a talented leader, most people will try to give their best. Perhaps it's time we think differently about the entire approach.

Daniel Pink makes a strong case in *Drive* that the commonly employed *carrot-and-stick* approach to individual motivation is no longer effective. Pink differentiates motivation based on the type of work we do. If your work is *algorithmic*, that is, largely repetitive and following a specific step-by-step process, the carrot-and-stick approach may work. But if your work is *heuristic* (creative, requiring even the remotest possibility of cognitive skill) the carrot-and-stick approach can present problems. Pink points out that in most industrialized environments, algorithmic work has largely been outsourced to less industrialized nations. Seventy percent of the work being produced in advanced environments today has become heuristic in nature. Where heuristic work prevails, leaders must find a way to tap into the individual's *intrinsic motivation*. Pink identifies three characteristics of intrinsic motivation—autonomy, mastery, and purpose. Perhaps what we need in today's environment is a way to unleash the individual's intrinsic drives.

The problem is that we've created a fatally flawed system of performance management based on algorithmic motivation and built upon inaccurate beliefs and assumptions. Today's methods harm the pursuit of excellence more than help it. There must be better way. There must be something that will help guide the leader on a value-added path of individual performance improvement. There must be a way to unleash the intrinsic motivation within.

A New Approach

My team and I introduced the process I'm about to share with you at national conferences from 2004 to 2009. As a result, many other organizations began to use it. Many executives visited us to observe it in action and learn more. One CEO claimed it was the most important factor in their excellence transformation. Aligning well with the balanced scorecard approach at the team and organizational levels, a consulting firm invited us to develop software to accelerate its execution in practice. Today, many organizations continue to use it, or some variation of it, to guide their leaders. It's adaptable to any environment, any organization, and any team. The secret to its adaptability is found in the five-pillar framework.

What are the critical behavior outcomes of an individual's effort that drive team and organizational outcomes under each of the five pillars?

This balanced approach led us to identify *eight behavior outcomes* with five categories of measurement that drive pillar performance at the team and organizational levels. It helps the leader unleash each individual's intrinsic motivation and inspires him or her to give his or her best every day.

A Magic Pill?

Many leaders yearn for a magic pill to fix their fatally flawed processes. Some oversee the performance of as many as one hundred and fifty team members—far too many for even the greatest of leaders. The evaluation processes their organizations ask them to complete take enormous amounts of time. No wonder they hate them so much. We must reduce the leader's span of control (fewer people to oversee directly) and provide him or her a reasonable and manageable way to inspire individual performance excellence. The secret lies in *accurate self-assessment*.

Imagine a world where leaders didn't have to do employee evaluations at all—a world in which employees evaluated themselves accurately. Some psychologists suggest accurate self-assessment is not possible, that most people cannot be objective when it comes to their own performances. I disagree. When we employ Dan Pink's concept of creating autonomy, mastery, and a sense of purpose, intrinsic motivation is unleashed and accurate self-management becomes a realistic possibility.

After I introduced this concept at a national conference a few years ago, a human resource executive approached me and said, "You're crazy if you think you can get people to accurately self-assess. Everyone is going to bias high in their assessment of their own performance. It's just human nature."

Do you agree with that statement? Is it impossible to expect an individual to accurately self-assess? Is this an unrealistic expectation?

I said, "Pardon me, sir, but I respectfully disagree. I've done it! Members of my own team are accurately assessing themselves on a regular basis and bringing their assessments to me for approval. Many other leaders have done it as well."

The reason most of us have not experienced this level of relationship is that we don't invest the amount of time it takes to achieve such a high level of understanding. If you commit to gaining mutual understanding of what's expected and how it is to be measured and master the concepts of intrinsic motivation, you can have each member of your team accurately self-assessing within one year's time. It requires that you master the concept of *behavior outcomes*.

Marcus Buckingham and Curt Coffman reveal the concept of the behavior outcome in *First, Break All the Rules*. In an exhaustive twenty-year study, the Gallup organization searched for understanding of what it takes to become a great leader. They learned that great leaders who consistently experience great outcomes have learned how to develop a deep level of understanding with each team member about what's expected and how it's measured. They're able to agree upon *expected outcomes of behavior* in the role. The leader then gets out of the way to allow the team member's intrinsic motivation to take over.

Great leaders have learned that most people want to do good work and are capable of doing it. They simply need someone to help point them in the right direction, provide them the tools they need to do the job, and give some positive coaching along the way. That's the kind of thinking my process is built upon. It just might be the magic pill of individual measurement that leaders have been searching for after all.

Benefits of the Process

Here's what you can expect when you harness the concept of behavior outcomes. You will:

1. Improve communication by creating daily conversation that builds individual accountability.
2. Place strong emphasis on development, autonomy, mastery, purpose, and self-discovery.
3. Focus on excellence (as opposed to mediocre performance that barely meets minimum standards).
4. Differentiate high and low performance.
5. Measure individual performance against defined standards of behavior, including many objective measures that can be counted, rated, or ranked.
6. Minimize rater and recency bias.
7. Maximize the individual's responsibility for and participation in his or her own performance improvement.
8. Align to and improve organizational and team objectives under the five pillars.

Some leaders may think it's a waste of time to worry about all this performance management stuff. I fervently disagree. The leaders' job is to *get things done through others*. The best way to do that is to create an environment in which team members clearly understand what's expected of them and how it's measured, accept personal accountability for those expectations, are positively recognized when they do them well, and are treated with respect and courtesy along the way. Inspiring others to excellence is the core leadership role. There are two key strategies for making this happen:

1. The leader must be a strong, positive role model of everything he or she expects of all team members.
2. The leader must execute effectively on a fair and relevant daily performance improvement conversation.

The leader's goal is to develop such a strong understanding of performance expectations and measurements that when the team member assesses his or her own performance, it's the same as if the leader had done it. There should never be any surprises. I realize this is a very deep level of understanding that is rarely achieved in leader/subordinate relationships. The reasons we don't achieve this level of relationship is that we don't try, we don't know how, or we don't value the activity.

If you're not getting the results you want, perhaps you need to change what you're doing to get those results. If everyone in your team is inspired to voluntarily and passionately give his or her best every day and your team is achieving the excellent results you desire, skip the rest of this chapter and don't change a thing. Otherwise, I suggest you read on.

Allow me to present my four-step process for inspiring individual excellence. I've combined the best advice from Gallup, Peter Scholtes, W. Edwards Deming, Dan Pink, appreciative inquiry experts, and academic experts such as Samuel Culbert and David Ulrich with my personal experience and insights to develop and implement a process considered a best practice today in many environments.

The P^4 Performance Process

While simple in concept, P^4 requires daily commitment to perfect. At its core are eight behavior outcomes measured in five levels of performance. The four stages are:

1. Perpetual shared understanding
2. Pay attention daily
3. Periodic summary discussions
4. Performance alignment

P⁴ Performance Process™

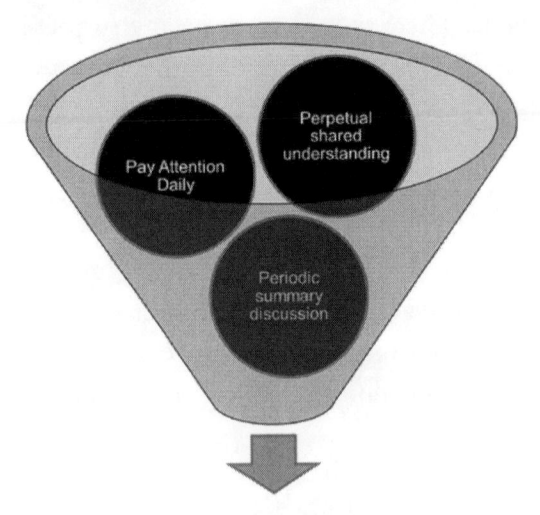

(diagram: funnel containing three circles labeled "Pay Attention Daily", "Perpetual shared understanding", and "Periodic summary discussion", with an arrow pointing down to)

Performance Alignment

Stage 1: Perpetual Shared Understanding

The objective in this step is to achieve deep understanding of what's expected and how it will be measured. *Perpetual shared understanding* is keen insight, comprehension, knowledge, discernment, and sympathetic awareness achieved between two individuals. It's a process of learning to work together that never ends.

Of course, it's the leader's responsibility to initiate the shared understanding process. It's best to begin the process prior to the team member's first day on the job. Follow the suggestions noted in chapter 9 and in Appendix E and F. Your team member will be impressed, and you will have started your relationship on the right path toward performance excellence.

> *67. Excellence requires clear and frequent communication.*

Continue your communication with an initial discussion during their first week. The general rule of thumb is *the more you communicate, the deeper your understanding.* If you're married, you know exactly what I mean. Excellence requires clear and frequent communication. At a minimum, you should meet with your team member once per week during his or her first ninety days and once per quarter thereafter. During the first ninety days, review the following things with your new team member:

1. Your team's foundational elements: its mission, vision, principles, standards, pillar goals, and how they're measured.
2. The eight behavior outcomes in detail, striving for understanding of what they specifically mean to the team member, how they translate into behavior guidelines, how they connect to team and organizational outcomes under the pillars, and how they're measured.
3. Your personality profile and leadership style. The more your team member understands you and your style, the easier it will be for him or her to relate to you.
4. Your team member's personality profile and behavioral tendencies. Use a tool like Myers-Briggs, DISC personality profile, or Gallup StrengthsFinder to help you.
5. Introduce your new team member to the rest of the group. Any time a new team member is introduced into an existing group, the group dynamics change. Take time to integrate the new team member by sharing personality profiles and conducting simple team-building activities at team meetings. Team trust must be rebuilt with each new team member introduced.

After the first ninety days, have a relaxed sit-down discussion with the team member at least once per quarter (see Appendix D). The purpose of this session is to summarize performance observations and issues during the period, celebrate successes, assess engagement, and plan forward into the next quarter. At the end of your first quarter, have the team member assess his or her own performance using the eight behavior outcomes explained below. The first attempt may not be totally accurate, but this will give you the opportunity to seek deeper shared understanding of what's expected and how it's measured. Your goal is to have the team member accurately self-assessing by the end of the first year. At each quarterly meeting, his or her self-assessment ability should improve.

Gallup recommends a quarterly discussion for the remainder of the relationship, regardless of how long it lasts. I agree. As relationships mature, team members will accept more and more responsibility and accountability for their progress. Over that time, the effort required from you will decrease. You'll know you have matured to a deep level of shared understanding when the team member is consistently and accurately self-assessing. When you reach this level of relationship, the employee is setting and achieving relevant, aligned performance goals with little help from you.

The Eight Behavior Outcomes

Achieving perpetual shared understanding will require you to have an in-depth command of the *eight behavior outcomes* and the *five levels of measurement*. Based on sound research from Gallup, world-renowned team building experts, and myself, they form the framework from which you will be able to achieve perpetual shared understanding with each individual on your team. The eight behavior outcomes are illustrated below. I'll address them one pillar at a time.

The 8 Behavior Outcomes

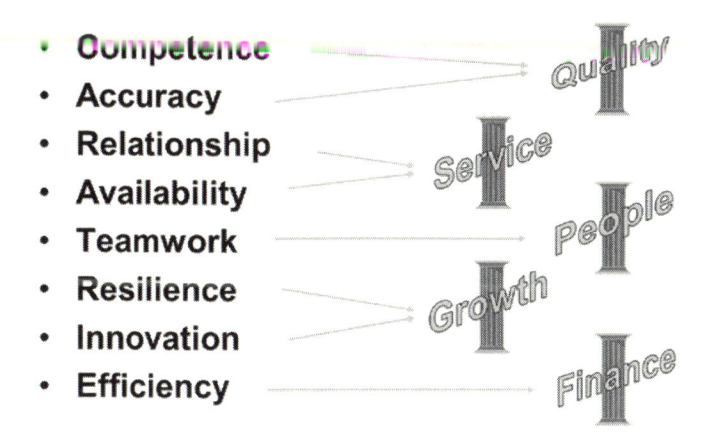

- Competence
- Accuracy
- Relationship
- Availability
- Teamwork
- Resilience
- Innovation
- Efficiency

Quality
Service
People
Growth
Finance

Quality: Competence and Accuracy

What are the critical outcomes of an individual's behavior that drive high quality in products and services delivered? Individuals must know how to do what they're expected to do (competence), and they must choose to do it right (accuracy) every time. Quality is a matter of skill and will. If an individual is lacking in skill, the remedy is training and practice. If the individual is lacking in will, the remedy is coaching or discipline.

Competence is capability, proficiency, skill, and know-how. It is being qualified and capable, exhibiting sufficient skill and knowledge to effectively complete assigned tasks. Do your guests and teammates view you as a *content expert* in your area of expertise? When an individual demonstrates superior or distinguished competence in his or her role, the leader will generally begin to rely on him or her to teach and mentor others.

It's reasonable to assume that if a person does the same thing every day, he or she should eventually become good at it—and become competent. If they don't, the leader must recognize the possibility that the person is in the wrong role and begin to take steps to transfer them to something more suitable to their talents and strengths. Achieving a high level of competence in your role within a reasonable amount of time is the expectation for every team member. The reasonable amount of time is determined by the leader and the learner relative to the role being performed. Some roles require a longer period of time to become competent. Some people are quicker learners than others and become competent more rapidly.

Accuracy is precision or exactness. It is the safe, careful, precise delivery of products and services that lacks significant errors and conforms exactly to standards and targets. Do you deliver your products and services safely, accurately, and timely? Once a person is competent, accuracy becomes a matter of choice, given that the process they are working within is a good process. If a person is performing his or her job accurately and still getting a bad outcome, the process is most likely the culprit.

> *Special note about process: I agree with the quality guru Edwards Deming that most errors are the result of a bad process, not a bad person. Like I said before, most people want to do a good job. Since this book's focus is human performance improvement, not process improvement (PI), I'm going to leave that discussion to the PI experts for now.*

The objective with accuracy is to perform the role with precision most of the time. No one is perfect, and totally error-free performance is unrealistic in most cases. I say most cases because there are times when totally error-free performance must occur or severe consequences may result. Heart surgery, assembly of an airplane, and administration of a drug are a few examples.

The key word when discussing errors is *significance*. If a nurse administers the wrong drug to a patient and the patient dies, that's obviously a significant error. If I misspell a word in this book, I've made an error but I doubt anyone will be tremendously affected by it. It may affect your perception of the quality of this work, but no one will die as a result. High performers avoid errors that have a significant impact on the creation of the product or the delivery of the service.

High quality requires each individual to accept personal accountability for his or her work and behavior. Competence and accuracy drive high-quality products and services. If everyone knows how to do his or her job and chooses to do it correctly every time, high quality will result.

Service: Relationship and Availability

What are the critical outcomes of an individual's behavior that enable you to deliver excellent service and develop loyalty with your customers?

The customer must see you as a partner in his or her situation, with his or her needs and concerns as your primary focus. They must have faith in your ability to help them get what they want. *Relationship* is connectivity created through service to others. Life itself is all about building relationships. Nothing happens in a vacuum. It always involves others. Do you build a strong, positive relationship with every guest you serve, both internal and external, and work diligently to meet his or her needs?

Whenever a customer is in your field of view (or as Disney puts it, when you're *on stage*), they should be your focus—nothing else. All of the behaviors of effective service then come into play—eye contact, courtesy, respect, tact, listening, good manners, and the sincere desire to fix any problems that occur in the exchange. It's those types of behaviors that build trust with your customers and enable them to see you as a true partner in their experiences. Building strong relationships with those you serve drives excellent service.

The other behavior outcome driving excellent service is *availability,* being within one's reach, accessible, able to be contacted. Are you fully present, fully aware, and fully available when your guest or teammate needs you? (Read *The Present* by Spencer Johnson, M.D.) The high performer is always available for a guest or customer and rarely, if ever, has attendance issues. They are focused on the guests and working to build strong relationships, fully present and fully aware that the guests are their primary concerns in that moment. You can always count on them to be available to fulfill their roles and serve their customers.

A Behavior Outcome or a Characteristic?

This is a good place to differentiate between a behavior outcome and the traditional characteristics most organizations use to measure individual performance. Let me illustrate what I mean with an example. Every evaluation system I've seen in my career had *attendance* as one of the things leaders were required to assess in their teammates. But attendance is not really the outcome we're most interested in, is it? Attendance is important, for sure, but I can be at work and not be available for my customer. Attendance is a factor in availability, but it is not the main thing.

A lady in one organization had to contact information systems to fix her computer because she had downloaded so many games to play at work that the computer froze up. She was at work (i.e. good attendance), but she wasn't available to serve her customers. She was spending so much of her time playing games at work that she didn't have time to serve her customers—to do the job she was being paid to do.

Have you ever known anyone to be *at work* but not working? We call them lazy, leeches, derelicts, thugs, and other derogatory terms. My mother called them thieves because they were stealing time from the company. She always said, "If you're on the clock, you should be working!"

An honest day's work for an honest day's pay is another way to say it. Again, perfection is not the goal—excellence is. You can achieve excellence without being perfect. Thank God for that! In the case of attendance, strive for 95 percent availability. It's okay to take a break a couple of times a day, and it's unreasonable to expect a human being to be *on stage* 100 percent of the time. We can achieve excellence in availability with 95 percent availability, but you must be sure that during the 5 percent of the time you're not available to serve your customer, someone else is.

Other excellent resources on the concept of building great customer relationships and making yourself available for them include *The Simple Truths of Service* by Ken Blanchard, *Positively Outrageous Service* by T. Scott Gross, *The Fred Factor* by Mark Sanborn, and *The Ten Critical Laws of Relationship* by Robb Thompson. Review these resources and begin mastering the art of guest service.

People: Teamwork

Everyone on the team has a responsibility to help make it a great place to work, live, or be.

Mother Teresa said, "Do not wait for leaders; do it alone, person to person."

To deliver excellence in the people pillar, every team member must become a positive team player. Working together with this mindset builds strong teamwork. *Teamwork* is collaborating effectively with others to deliver the highest-quality products and services in the most efficient manner on a continuous basis. Do your teammates view you as valuable, positive contributor to your team?

Teamwork is a huge topic. There are hundreds of resources available. One of my favorites is John Maxwell's *The 17 Indisputable Laws of Teamwork*. Patrick Lencioni identifies five keys to teamwork in *The Five Dysfunctions of a Team*. Stephen M. R. Covey in *The Speed of Trust* presents building high-trust relationships as the most fundamental element of teamwork. *Crucial Conversations* by Kerry Patterson et al will help you learn how to confront others with difficult messages tactfully and respectfully.

Perhaps it would help to paint a word picture of the high performer in teamwork. The *high performer* is a role model of team values and standards to such a point that the team leader relies on her to encourage others to emulate them. She keeps the place clean and urges others to do the same. When she sees trash or a spill on the floor, she cleans it up herself or sees that it gets cleaned up. She frequently asks questions for clarification, listens to others well, and seeks mutual understanding in all relationships. She resists the urge to gossip, walking away in the presence of it, or tactfully encouraging others to stop. She mines for conflict and resolves it productively, aggressively assisting others in doing likewise. Her word is bond. She is reliable to follow through on commitments, promises, and responsibilities. She tactfully helps the leader monitor the accountability of others. She is a go-to person, a positive contributor to her team and organization. She demonstrates strong personal initiative, acting appropriately without having to be told. She frequently volunteers to help the team and organization in ways that are outside of her defined role. She is honest and trustworthy, always striving to do the right thing—a role model of integrity.

When she realizes she has done something wrong or has wronged someone else, she owns the mistake, immediately apologizes, and seeks restitution. She requires little to no supervision to get her work done right. She is so good at what she does that the leader learns from her. She participates in most team and organizational activities, frequently volunteering to help. She is customer, team, and organization focused—a part of the solution, not part of the problem. She is results oriented and considered a solution seeker. She follows policy and procedure except when safety or quality are put at risk, at which time she does what's right for the best interest of the customer, team, and organization. She is a proactive problem solver, helping the team and organization seek viable solutions to challenging issues. She is an owner of her performance and accepts mutual responsibility for team and organizational outcomes. She is respectful of others and tactfully confronts disrespect in others when observed. She has a strong self-image but remains humble in attitude and approach, always putting the needs of others ahead of her own.

Have you ever worked with anyone like that? Does that sound like superwoman? Do *you* behave like that? Can you? Remember that excellence doesn't require perfection. No one is perfect, but everyone can strive to reach the high level of performance and behavior just described. What kind of team would it be if everyone on it behaved like that? That's a team of excellence! And that's the kind of team I want to be a part of. Don't you? Make a commitment today to be the high-performing teammate described in the previous paragraph. It can start with *you*!

Growth: Resilience and Innovation

To enable a team or organization to progress forward, each team member must learn how to respond productively to change and continuously improve his or her work. Growth connotes change. Many of the changes we're faced with each day are thrust upon us without our input. Yet we must learn how to function successfully in spite of them. That's where resilience comes into play. You must learn to assimilate changes more effectively because they're coming at you at accelerating speeds. The pace of change is increasing exponentially, and it's likely to continue in that direction.

Resilience is the ability to positively and productively respond to change and adversity. When faced with change, are you a part of the solution or part of the problem? You must become a rubber band with the elasticity to stretch when unexpected changes hit and bounce back to productivity quickly.

There's another side of growth. You can improve your work every day if you so choose. I'm not talking about giant product innovations or solutions to organizational problems. I'm simply talking about paying attention to what you do every day and maintaining a mindset of continuous improvement about it. *You* are the most qualified person to assess the work you do every day and make minor improvements to it. That's called *innovation*. Innovation means continuous improvement—offering and implementing new ideas and methods to improve products and service delivery. It also means initiating positive change to make things better. How well do you learn, grow, and improve? When everyone maintains a continuous improvement mindset, small daily innovations can be made across the team and organization, resulting in a constant progression forward.

The high performer in resilience and innovation remains positive, flexible, focused, organized, and proactive through change whether planned or unexpected (see Daryl Conner's *Managing at the Speed of Change*). He aggressively initiates positive change and helps others manage through changes effectively. He is a constant learner, always seeking personal growth and improvement and helps others do the same. He finds new ways to help the team improve processes, yielding frequent improvements in the products and services delivered.

Finance: Efficiency

Excellence in the finance pillar requires good stewardship of your time, energy, materials, money, and resources. To optimize financial objectives, each individual must master the ability to accomplish tasks with the minimum expenditure of time, materials, and money while preserving safety, courtesy, and the positive memorable experience for the guest. How well do you manage the resources entrusted to you? That's *efficiency*. The high performer is resourceful and productive and helps the team implement more efficient ways to work.

As I was teaching this concept to a radiology team in the hospital, a technician looked up at me and said boldly, "Why are you talking to us about the budget? We don't have anything to do with that!"

"Really," I replied. "Let me ask you a couple of questions. First, did you receive a paycheck from the organization last week? How about the week before that? Have you received one every week you've worked here?"

His reply to all three questions was an obvious yes.

"Well then," I continued, "what do you think that paycheck represents? When you were hired, you entered into an agreement with the hospital to deliver the services listed on your job description in return for X amount of dollars per hour, right?"

"I suppose," he hesitantly replied.

"So then, have you ever known anyone to be receiving pay and not delivering the services they agreed to deliver? In other words, they're on the clock, but not working."

"Of course," he answered, "many times."

"When the team member is being paid to work but not working, that affects our budget. The hospital pays us to do our work. When we do it well, our productivity increases, that is, we get more work done for the same amount of pay. When we do it poorly, productivity declines—less work for the same amount of money. If you don't do the work while you're being paid to do the work, someone else has to do it, and it costs the hospital more money. Payroll is the largest expense for our organization, and we can increase the value of that expense by being more productive. Can you now see now how your personal efficiency affects the budget?"

"What's the second question," he asked.

I responded, "In the course of doing your work yesterday, did you use any materials and supplies provided by the hospital?"

"Of course."

"Did you know that supply costs are the second-largest expense in our budget? When you and I use supplies and materials wisely, recycle when we can, use less expensive items when we can, turn off the lights when not in use, and take care of the equipment we have so it lasts longer, it costs the organization less money. You and I are the ones who control supply costs. Not only that, when you and I take home a pencil or a paper clip or make personal copies on the company copier, we're adding to the team's supply costs and taking things that aren't ours to take. Most people think taking a paper clip is okay. But if a paper clip is okay, how much does an item have to cost before it's not okay to take home?"

I think the rad-tech got the message.

Each individual's use of time, money, and materials entrusted to their care directly affects the financial outcomes of the team. Each person must be a good steward of his or her resources and become highly efficient for the team to achieve excellent financial results.

So there you have it—eight behavior outcomes that drive excellence in the five pillars of performance. Next, let's discuss how to measure individual performance.

Measurement

In chapter 13, I introduced a five-point scale as the way to measure results at the organization and team levels. I defined the five levels of performance, compared them to our typical letter grading scale, and briefly described the intent. At the individual level, we'll use the same five-point scale, but I need to explain how it applies to individual behavior outcomes.

Unlike the team and organizational levels where performance can be measured by purely objective criteria, performance at the individual level must use a combination of objective and subjective criteria.

My research team asked, "Is it possible to measure individual performance with purely objective criteria like we do at the team and organizational levels?"

We found the answer to be yes, but it's also incredibly complex and time consuming. As you recall, measuring service at the team and organizational levels, we survey our customers for their perceptions of service and then benchmark our results on a percentile basis against other teams doing the same. This is an *objective* measure. Can we do that at the individual level as well?

We contemplated creating an internal survey group to do nothing but document and survey customers of each team member and crunch the percentile rank data in much the same way. In an organization of two thousand people, that meant we would need to survey enough customers of each of the two thousand individuals over a year's time to obtain statistically valid data and then compare those perceptions across the organization for percentile ranking. While it could be done, we decided it would require an enormous amount of effort, time, and financial resources. But would it be worth it? Not only would it prove financially prohibitive, it's just not necessary. The juice is not worth the squeeze.

We can achieve the same results without all that effort by combining *objective measureable criteria* with more *subjective observable behavior guidelines*. These five levels of performance measurement applied at the individual level are the result of that research and testing.

The Objective

The objective for individual measurement is to develop a measurement system that will guide the leader and team member toward fair, consistent, accurate, honest, and timely feedback aligned to the team and organizational objectives that can be administered in an efficient manner. To do this, we need to provide participants with a general understanding of the five levels of performance and how they apply at the individual level. The challenge, then, is to understand the desired outcomes of behavior and then measure how well an individual performs against them.

Since individual measurement involves objective and subjective criteria, we need more descriptive language to ensure that everyone is measured against the same standards. We'll use the same definitions of the five levels of measurement and add a few caveats to clarify their application at the individual level. The key is simply to understand what to measure *(the eight behavior outcomes)* and how to measure it *(the five levels of measurement)* at the individual level. The following guidelines will help.

What to Measure

Quality—deliver high-quality products and services
- *competence*: viewed as a content expert in your area of expertise
- *accuracy*: safe, careful, precise delivery of your products and/or services

Service—create a positive memorable experience for every guest you serve
- *relationship*: build a strong, positive relationship with everyone you serve
- *availability*: remain fully present, fully aware, and fully available in the moment

People—make it a great place to work, live, or be
- *teamwork*: be a valuable, positive contributor to the team

Growth—continually improve your services, products, facilities, equipment, and people
- *resilience*: respond to change and adversity positively and productively
- *innovation*: proactively initiate positive change

Finance—be good stewards of your resources
- *efficiency*: make wise use of time, money, and materials

How to Measure It

- *Level 1—Unacceptable*
  - Immediate improvement is required or you could be reassigned or dismissed.
- *Level 2—Needs to improve*
  - Something in this area needs to improve.
- *Level 3—Fully successful*
  - There is a consistent high level of performance in your *specific role*.
  - Nothing needs to improve, keep on keepin' on.
- *Level 4—Superior*
  - You are a teacher, mentor, and/or role model in your *team*.
- *Level 5—Distinguished*
  - You are a teacher, mentor, and/or role model in the *organization*.

This five-point scale is the right mix of variation, stability, and consistency. It provides enough variation to differentiate between high and low performers, yet not too much so that differentiation becomes moot or valueless. It also conforms to the five-point Likert scale used at the team and organizational levels, enabling consistency and alignment in scoring and assessment among all three levels of performance.

We have found that most team members and leaders can reach accurate assessment performance within one year by using the guidelines in this chapter. To help grow and mature to that level of relationship, I've provided more detailed descriptions in Appendix B. Study those descriptions and master the general understandings noted below.

The Five Levels of Performance

The first two levels describe performance that *needs to improve*. The last three levels describe *degrees of excellence* in the role being assessed.

Specific Objective Measurements

Although the reality of individual performance measurement must include many subjective observable behaviors, our purpose is to identify specific objective measurements of performance that can be counted, rated, or ranked whenever practical. More objectivity is better. It enables better consistency in performance assessments. Each behavior outcome will have several aspects of performance that must be considered when determining a rating. Consider all aspects of the behavior outcome and assess accurately against the identified standards.

Level 1: Unacceptable

It's helpful to describe some examples of unacceptable performance in this area from the specifics listed at Level 3. Examples should be described in observable behavior terms. If even one area within the behavior outcome is unacceptable, the outcome must be rated *unacceptable (Level 1)* and a developmental plan is required. If performance does not improve immediately, the role is in jeopardy.

Level 2: Needs Improvement

One or more specific behaviors within the outcome need improvement. No aspects of performance demonstrated are considered unacceptable; however, performance is not *fully successful (Level 3)* in all aspects noted. Areas that need to improve should be clearly identified, and a developmental plan is required.

Level 3: Fully Successful

All aspects of performance considered within the behavior outcome should be listed here. All areas of performance in this outcome must be considered fully successful for the individual to earn a *fully successful (Level 3)* rating for the category. If even one area of performance related to this outcome is not considered *fully successful*, this area must be rated *needs improvement (Level 2)* and a developmental plan is required. If fully successful status in all areas of this outcome is not achieved in a reasonable amount of time, a job role change should be considered. Generally speaking, performance at this level deals primarily with how the team member performs in his or her *specific job role*.

Level 4: Superior

Performance is *fully successful (Level 3)* in all aspects considered in the behavior outcome and one or more aspects of behavior, but not all, demonstrate *distinguished performance (Level 5)*. The individual is a teacher, mentor, and role model to others on the team. Generally speaking, performance at this level positively impacts and influences the performance of *others on the team*.

Level 5: Distinguished

It's helpful to describe some examples of distinguished behavior in this area. All aspects of performance considered with the behavior outcome are at *distinguished* levels. The individual has met all requirements of Level 3 and 4 performance and is a teacher, mentor, and role model to others in the organization. Generally speaking, performance at this level positively impacts and influences the performance of *others outside the team in the greater organization as a whole*. By its very definition, distinguished performance, when properly measured, is very rare and difficult to achieve.

General Guidelines for Assessing Performance

To help leaders and team members gain *perpetual shared understanding*, the following information is provided in the Appendix:

- Guidelines for Individual Performance Measurement (Appendix B)
- MVP Self-Assessment (Appendix C)

Stage 2: Pay Attention Daily

Now that you're working on developing a deep level of *perpetual shared understanding*, you must *pay attention to performance daily*. For the leader, this means personally observing team member performance and saying something about it when you see it. For the team member, it means remaining constantly aware of what's expected and how it's measured so you can identify it along the way. Both partners in the performance relationship should find a way to capture observations and record them for future reference. For some, a notepad works. For others, an electronic handheld device works. For most, memory will *not* work and will likely lead to rater or recency bias.

Rater bias occurs when the one rating makes measurement decisions based on anything other than the measurement guidelines. *Recency bias* occurs when one considers only the most recent performance of an individual when measuring performance. Recordkeeping is the best defense against recency bias. Recordkeeping should be the primary responsibility of the individual. *You* are the best-qualified person to accurately assess your own performance. I tell those who report to me that if they want me to be the one to measure their performance, don't be upset when they disagree with my ratings. Individual excellence is predicated upon the notion that the individual takes *personal responsibility and accountability* for his or her own performance and does whatever is necessary to measure and improve it.

When paying attention daily, the rule of thumb is *when you see it, say it*. Communicate constantly and immediately what you see, then encourage the team member to make a note of it for reference at the *periodic summary discussion* (see Stage 3). Praise right behavior according to the individual's personal preferences and coach for improved performance in private as soon as possible after the behavior is observed.

Use the language of performance you've learned in this chapter as you communicate with one another—and be specific about what you observe. This helps reinforce what to measure and how it's being measured on a daily basis. For example, if you observe someone in an interchange with a customer and they've demonstrated fully successful performance, say something like this:

> Sally, I just observed you with the customer, and I was very impressed. You made great eye contact, used a wonderfully friendly tone of voice, and exceeded their needs by offering to follow-up tomorrow. That is truly what we mean by fully successful performance in the behavior outcome of relationship. Great job!

According to Caterpillar Safety Services, a division of Caterpillar Inc. devoted to creating and sustaining cultures of safety excellence for organizations around the world, excellence in behavior observation and feedback demonstrates five primary characteristics. The feedback must be *timely*, delivered as soon after the observed performance as possible. It must be *relevant* to the work being demonstrated and communicated with specific behaviors observed at the moment of observation. The receiver must perceive it as *sincere*. Everyone has a built-in BS detector. You can't fake sincerity. The receiver must *confirm* the observation. You need to ensure that the performer accurately understands the behavior you observed. The feedback should be *frequent*. No one has ever complained of too much positive input. Be liberal with your encouragement of what they're doing right. You should praise what's right at a ratio of seven to one over coaching for what's wrong.

Handling Difficult Conversations

Sometimes, it can be very uncomfortable and intimidating to approach someone about something they're doing that's not right. Most people dislike this type of communication and try to avoid it. An excellent leader learns how to handle these difficult discussions and conducts them immediately and effectively.

Allow me to share some simple guidelines to help you manage those difficult and challenging discussions with others.

1. Establish in advance how you will deal with difficult conversations. "I'd like us to have the kind of relationship where we can come to one another and share what's on our minds. Would you like that as well? As your leader, part of my job is to come to you when I notice you doing anything contrary to the way we've agreed things are supposed to go. That kind of conversation can sometimes feel awkward for both of us. When that happens, how would you like me to approach you?"
2. When you observe something that requires a small adjustment in performance:
    a. Preserve their self-image with a comment of encouragement.
    b. Remind them of your vision for the team and for them.
    c. Thank them for their strong, consistent performance most of the time.
    d. Make your suggestion for improvement.
    e. Ask, "How can I help you make this happen?"

  f. Reinforce their importance to the team.

  g. Example: "John, I really appreciate your hard work with the team. Our goal is to deliver the best service to our customers possible, and we expect that from you too. Thank you for the great work you do in that regard. There is one small thing I'd like to mention to you that I think you could improve. (State your suggestion.) Do you agree that would be a good idea? (If so, great. If not, discuss.) Is there anything I can do to help you make that happen? Well thanks, John. Again, you're a critical part of this team, and I appreciate you very much. Let me know how I can help."

3. For serious or repetitive problems:

  a. Don't start positive. Remind them of your prior discussions about this specific behavior. Connect back to #1 above. Ask them not to talk until you're finished.

  b. Share your observations with specific examples that demonstrate their nonsupport.

  c. Tell them how you feel about it.

  d. Tell them what you expect.

  e. Describe the consequences of continued poor performance.

  f. Follow up at an agreed-upon future time.

  g. Example: "John, do you remember our conversation about it being my job to bring things to your attention when there's a problem? That's what I need to do now. I need you just to listen for a few moments and let me talk. You came in late again today. As you know, we've had several discussions about this, and your performance hasn't changed. This morning, you arrived fifteen minutes late again. This is your fifth time in two months. (Be specific.)

That's unacceptable and must change. It angers me that you continue to behave this way in light of the many discussions we've had about it. I expect you to be on time for work just like all the other members of our team, and I need you to comply with that expectation. You coming in late cannot continue. If it does, I'll be forced to help you find employment elsewhere. Do you understand what I'm saying to you, John? Is there any reason you can give me right now as to why you cannot comply with my request? Do you understand that if you're late again, you'll lose your job? Okay then, let's get back to work and let me know if there's anything I can do to help you today. Let's touch base one week from today and make sure we're on the right track."

4. Some other keywords that may help you:
    a. "Remember our conversation earlier about how to handle difficult information with one another? I have something like that I need to share with you now. Is this a good time?"
    b. "I have something I need to talk with you about that's uncomfortable for me to share and may be uncomfortable for you to hear. Is now a good time?"
5. Remember that the more you encourage and recognize the good behavior in others, the less you have to deal with the bad. *Authentic encouragement* is the strongest catalyst for individual excellence.

> *68. Authentic encouragement is the strongest catalyst for individual excellence.*

Having a difficult conversation with someone when they're not performing well is not easy. But it's critical to success and is a life skill that can be learned. Avoiding difficult conversations will only postpone problems and perpetuate a culture of mediocrity. *Crucial Conversations* by Kerry Patterson et al is a wonderful in-depth resource on this topic. With practice, you may not learn to enjoy the process, but you can improve your competence and be able to effectively influence others to improve performance. When you do, you'll earn the respect of everyone around you and sincerely demonstrate you care.

Paying attention daily is the only way to build individual excellence in your team. If you only have one conversation per year, you'll be doing what most leaders do and be just as frustrated as they are about the performance of the people on their teams. If you want to inspire every person on your team to voluntarily and passionately give his or her best every day, you'll need to *pay attention daily* to what they do.

Stage 3: Periodic Summary Discussions

You must also conduct *periodic summary discussions* of performance progress at regular intervals. Gallup recommends a quarterly meeting. In practice, most leaders feel lucky if they get to it once per year. The more often you summarize progress, the easier it becomes to do so—and the more quickly you'll have the individual accurately assessing his or her own performance. Once per quarter is the gold standard.

I want to share a secret with you at this point that will save you a lot of time. Human beings are creatures of habit. It takes a major life event, such as marriage, divorce, death of a family member, or spiritual conversion to significantly alter habits. The more often you conduct the periodic summary discussion, the more likely it is that there will be little, if any, change in performance between discussions. The best thing to do each time you have a periodic summary discussion is to ask, "What, if anything, has changed in the performance since the last periodic discussion?"

The likelihood is that not much has changed, and you'll be able to quickly consider the elements of your assessment. You don't have to rethink it every time you do it. You can take that advice to the bank and save yourself 75 percent of the time it would normally take to reassess yourself or another person.

In Appendix D, you'll find a guideline for conducting a quarterly *periodic summary discussion*. Ask the team member to complete the worksheet before you meet. The conversation should revolve around three main areas:

1. A look back
2. Assess performance
3. A look forward

The worksheet provides some good questions to ask within each of the three areas to guide your team member in his or her self-assessment. I used Gallup's research as the basis for the guide. You can refer to the appendix of Gallup's book *First, Break All the Rules* for more detail.

Remember that the more *periodic summary discussions* you have with an individual, the greater your *perpetual shared understanding* will be—and the sooner you'll be able to mature the relationship to a level of true performance excellence. Regular communication is critical. Without it, you'll remain frustrated and stagnant in a quandary of mediocrity.

Stage 4: Performance Alignment

The only thing left to do at this point is to check for *performance alignment*. Organizational excellence is achieved when each team performs at a high level of excellence in alignment with the organizational goals. Team excellence is achieved when each individual team member performs at a high level of excellence in alignment with team goals.

If the three levels of performance are aligned, there will be a recognizable performance correlation. The aggregate of all the individual team member assessments will align with team goals achieved. Likewise, the aggregate of all team outcomes will align with the organizational goals achieved.

To illustrate this, allow me to use an extreme example. If I assess my ten team members all to be at the *distinguished* level of performance *(Level 5)*, but our objective team outcomes are performing at the *needs to improve* level of performance *(Level 2)*, something is wrong—and we are not aligned. If the aggregate of all my team members' performance is *distinguished*, the total team performance measured by the objective outcomes under the pillars must also be at the *distinguished* level. Otherwise, I am out of alignment and must investigate why. Either my team goals were not developed properly and do not accurately reflect the team's performance or I have biased high in my individual assessments, causing them not to align with actual team results. Typically, the problem exists in the latter where greater subjectivity is in play. Checking the alignment can help you prevent or reduce your instance of personal bias.

Since we've assigned numbers to the ratings, we can do the alignment check numerically. From a statistical standpoint, the objective is to be at 95 percent confidence. On the five-point scale, 95 percent alignment would require a plus or minus .25 variance in the scores between two levels of measurement. Here's an example.

1. The organizational scorecard yields a performance score of 3.25 on the five-point scale. The total score is calculated by multiplying the performance rating on each goal by its weight and adding them all together. We showed some examples of this in chapter 13.
2. The aggregate of all the team scores within the organization yields an average overall score of 3.85, which is a .60 variance from the organization score of 3.25. Since .60 is greater than

the allowable .25 variance, we are out of alignment at this level.
3. The average performance score of all the individual team members on my team is a 3.95, and my team scorecard score is 3.65, a .30 variance. I am out of alignment in my team as well.
4. Both variances were outside of the .25 variance allowed for 95 percent alignment. I must evaluate my situation to understand why and make whatever adjustments possible to reach alignment.

Since there is judgment involved in performance assessment, checking the alignment is not a definitive mathematical formula upon which you can totally rely. However, it can help you assess alignment and ask questions for understanding of your situation. It can also help you reduce bias in setting goals and individual assessments. Most importantly, it can help you ensure a high level of confidence that the performance levels you have measured are accurate and valid.

Summary of the Individual Scorecard

Gaining *perpetual shared understanding* is a continuous activity that requires regular communication and a deep level of relationship. *Paying attention daily* is critical to the constant reinforcement of the excellence you expect to see in others. Holding *periodic summary discussions* enables you to measure progress and continuously improve individual performances. Checking *performance alignment* at the end of the period will ensure that you have valid results that can be celebrated with confidence. The *P⁴ Performance Process* can help you achieve performance excellence!

In chapter 17, I'll discuss effective leadership behaviors that will help you accelerate the P^4 Performance Process. Combined with the steps in this chapter, you'll develop a skill that will enable you to consistently inspire each team member to passionately and voluntarily give his or her best every day. Without a rigorous daily focus on individual performance excellence, team and organizational excellence is left up to chance or luck. Effective leaders don't rely on luck to bring them success.

Summary of Chapter 15

1. The individual is the fundamental element in a culture of excellence.
2. It is the responsibility of the leader to create an environment in which each individual is inspired to voluntarily and passionately give his or her best every day. Performance management is the leader's core role.
3. Most leaders need a proven process to guide them in the fair and consistent execution of individual performance measurements.
4. The first stage of the P^4 *Performance Process* is to gain *perpetual shared understanding* with the individual of what's expected and how it's measured so they can always know, through self-assessment, how they're doing and what they need to do to improve.
5. The *eight behavior outcomes* of individual performance help measure and inspire performance excellence.
6. The more you communicate with the members of your team, the deeper your perpetual shared understanding will be.
7. It's the individual's responsibility to ensure that his or her own performance is measured accurately and fairly.
8. The second stage in the P^4 Performance Process is *paying attention daily*. Recognize and encourage right behaviors while coaching to improve wrong ones. When you see it, say it.
9. The third stage in the P^4 Performance Process is the *periodic summary discussion*. The shorter the time between your

discussions, the easier it is to assess. People are creatures of habit and don't change that much.
10. The fourth stage of the P^4 Performance Process is validating *performance alignment*. To gain confidence in the validity of your performance measures, check alignment between the three levels of performance at the end of the period.

Take Action

1. Study the *P^4 Performance Process* and begin thinking about how you can adapt it to your situation.
2. Take the Myers-Briggs personality profile assessment (or something like it), and encourage others to do the same. Before you can facilitate a deeper relationship with another person, you must have a clear understanding of yourself. These types of tools help you deepen that personal understanding. Google *personality profile assessments* and pick one. Many are free. Make self-understanding a life-long objective. The better you know yourself, the better you can connect to others.
3. Share the *P^4 Performance Process* with your team members. Let them ask questions and seek understanding. Discuss how it can help you build team strength in relationships and results.
4. Begin using the terminology of the *P^4 Performance Process* every day to reinforce good performance and coach for improved performance. Integrate this terminology into your daily conversations.

SECTION 5

Top It Out!

It's common in the construction industry to hold a *topping out* ceremony when the last beam is placed on the new structure. The practice dates back to a time when Europe was covered mostly by forests. Humans inhabiting the forests would celebrate the completion of their wood-framed homes by placing the topmost leafy branch from a tree used in the construction on the home as a gesture of thankfulness to the forest for the use of the trees. Eventually, European craftsmen brought the practice to America where it is still considered an important part of the construction process. Today, the custom is continued most frequently on completed structures such as bridges, skyscrapers, and major structures and signifies the successful completion of the main structure (Source: Wikipedia).

Similarly, in order to prepare your house of excellence for use, you must top it out with a strategic plan and equip your team with effective leadership to make it work.

CHAPTER 16

The Blueprint for Excellence!
From concept to application

> I know the plans I have for you, plans to prosper you
> and not to harm you, plans to give you hope
> and a future.
> —Jeremiah 29:11 (NIV)

> If you fail to plan, you plan to fail!
> —Zig Ziglar

Now it's time to put it all together into a strategic plan for you and your team. Drawing up your specific *blueprint* requires a methodology of thought that enables you to transform your situation from where it is now to where you want it to be at some point in the future. It requires an executable plan to make it happen. This is called *strategic planning*.

Strategic Planning is the process of determining the primary objectives of an organization [or team] and then acting and allocating resources to achieve those objectives. It drives transformation of an organization's [or team's] mission by identifying gaps between where it needs [or wants] to be and where it is.
—Louis Boone and David Kurtz, *Contemporary Business*

The *house of excellence* is a *strategic planning model*. If you want to build a business, improve your team, grow your church, build a strong family, or improve your personal life, you need the guidance of a strategic planning model.

The house model is different from other strategic planning frameworks. It can be applied to any environment, and its emphasis is on the human aspect of excellence. Most models fail to effectively connect the tasks that need to be performed to the inspiration of the people to perform them. The neglect of this aspect of planning is a fatal flaw—and the primary reason most efforts fail to reach excellence. Excellence depends upon the quality of the relationships that exist among the members of the team working toward it. Whereas other strategic models fail to properly incorporate this aspect, the *house of excellence* model is built upon it. The human aspect of performance is its primary focus.

The five-pillar framework demands a balance of tasks and people planning elements. There are seven steps to a successful blueprint, as illustrated by the diagram below. This strategic planning framework integrates the elements of the house of excellence with the actions needed to make it work.

Strategic Planning

- Mission & Vision
- Current State (SWOT)
- Gap Analysis
- Strategies & Tactics
- Measure
- Assess & Adjust

Principles & Standards

The Seven Steps of the Blueprint

1. **Determine Your Foundation**: create a mission and vision and determine your core principles and standards. We discussed this in Section 2.
2. **Conduct a Pillar SWOT**: using the five pillars as your guide, conduct a SWOT analysis of your current state. (SWOT is an acronym that stands for strengths, weaknesses, opportunities, and threats and is used as a way to help you conduct a detailed analysis of your current state.) Use the information in section 3 to guide you in your assessment.
3. **Conduct a Gap Analysis**: compare your current state identified in the SWOT to your desired future state described in your vision. Contrast and compare steps one and two above.
4. **Identify Tactics**: develop tactical action to transform your endeavor from current state to future state. In our discussion of the pillars and measurements, we covered many tactics that can be used to move you forward. Your list will be very specific in nature, will change from performance period to performance period, and will be affected by your unique conditions.
5. **Enable Personal Action**: translate your tactics into language that will guide personal action on a daily basis. Use the performance terminology and processes for excellence described throughout the book to identify your specific language of excellence. Ensure accountability. Make sure everyone completely understands the expectations of his or her role, how to fulfill them, how they will be measured, and how they will be rewarded.
6. **Assess and Adjust**: assess your progress regularly and make any necessary adjustments. Refer to the annual cycle of measurement for how to do this.
7. **Stand Firm**: never abandon your core principles and standards.

The house of excellence model combined with these seven steps enables you to create your customized *Blueprint for Excellence* for any environment. In this chapter, I'll apply the house of excellence concepts with the seven steps of strategic planning to create a blueprint in each of our five environments. It's my hope that by reviewing these examples, you'll be able to see how this all comes together to enable you to create and sustain your own culture of excellence in whatever you do.

Note: the standards sections are abbreviated to save space. Refer to the chapter on standards for more detail. Due to the sometimes-lengthy nature of standards of behavior, many organizations create an additional standards document dedicated only to them.

> 69. *The principles of excellence can be universally applied to any situation in any environment.*

Applications in the Five Environments

An Organization Blueprint
Blue Ridge HealthCare, Morganton, North Carolina
(Reprinted with permission)

Mission
To enhance life by excelling in care

Vision
To become the best community healthcare system in America

Principles

Commitment
Personal dedication to fulfilling the mission and achieving the vision

Respect
Polite consideration and courtesy toward others

Integrity
Steadfastly adhering to high moral principles that build trust

Excellence
An uncompromising drive to deliver outstanding performance in every aspect of responsibility

Service
Putting others above self by creating superior experiences for them at every opportunity

Standards

We are committed to improving the behaviors of our employees to assist us all in creating a great place for employees to work, a great place for physicians to practice, and a great place for patients and residents to receive care.

We believe that our employees are a caring force. Ensuring that behavior means incorporating these Standards of Service Excellence into our daily work lives.

Everyone is expected to hold each other accountable to these standards and help create an environment founded on positive **A**ttitudes, **C**ommitment, and **T**rust. How we AC'I' as team members will ultimately determine our success on our Journey to Excellence.

1. Commitment
    a. Develop a sense of personal ownership in our organization.
    b. Work to create a positive environment. Negativity affects everyone with whom you come into contact and will not be tolerated.
    c. Be responsible, take pride in your work, and create successes that we can all enjoy. Strive to do the job right the first time.
2. Respect
    a. Be respectful to everyone. Treat each person as you would like yourself or the persons closest to you to be treated.
    b. Never, never, never be rude. We believe in "zero tolerance" for discourtesy toward a customer.
    c. Recognize the value and potential of each person.
3. Integrity
    a. Be supportive of each other.
    b. Treat each other with courtesy and respect.
    c. Help coworkers feel comfortable enough to ask for your help.
    d. Have regard for each other's areas of expertise.
    e. Be honest with each other and respond truthfully, with the best interest of the organization at heart.
    f. React professionally in all situations.
4. Excellence
    a. Make sure all your personal and team work is such that you would be proud to sign your name to it.
    b. Research best practices in your area of expertise and strive to deliver "best in class" products and services to all your patients and guests.
5. Service
    a. Acknowledge each guest.
    b. Introduce yourself.

c. Duration, tell how long the procedure will last.
d. Explain the procedure in detail as you perform it.
e. Thank them for choosing us as their place to receive care.

(There are many more, too numerous to include. A separate standards document enumerates them all.)

The Pillars

All of our goals, tactics, and methods are designed to achieve excellence in the five pillars of performance. The pillars provide balanced clarity of focus for us as we try to determine how best to proceed in all our operational areas.

Our board of directors and senior leadership team use the pillars to set strategic direction each year for our organization. These strategies, tactics and goals are captured in a document called the *Corporate Scorecard.*

Managers and directors use the pillars to set strategic direction each year for their areas of practice. Leaders identify these care team goals in a document called the *Leader Performance Evaluation.*

The pillars of performance also provide structure for determining how each of us is expected to perform and behave in order to achieve individual, team, and organizational excellence. These eight behavior outcomes of individual measurement are outlined in detail in the *Care Team Member Evaluation* document.

Quality
Providing patient-focused care that makes best use
of our clinical resources
Priority is safety. All else is secondary.

Service
Making this a great place for patients to receive care by providing superior service in the most pleasant, caring environment possible for patients and their families
Priority is courtesy. Always treat others with respect and courtesy.

People
Making this a great place for people to work by attracting and retaining the best care team members; creating an environment where people continuously learn, feel respected, and are recognized and rewarded so they can perform to the best of their abilities
Priority is the positive memorable experience. Everyone works together to create it.

Growth
Capitalizing on opportunities to grow in ways that are focused, purposeful, patient-centered, and mission-driven, through two acute care hospitals and other affiliates
Priority is forward progress, leading to a more positive memorable experience.

Finance
Maintaining and protecting the financial health by focusing on opportunities, internally and externally, to perform at our best as a system
Priority is efficiency. Never let paperwork interfere with the guest experience.

Measurements
Areas for Consideration by Pillar

Quality
thirty-one measures of appropriate care
never events
mortality rate

average length of stay
left without treatment rate
infection rate
medication reconciliation
Medicare readmissions

Service
patient satisfaction percentiles
HCAHPS scores
physician satisfaction percentiles

People
employee turnover
employee engagement percentile
vacancy rates
time to fill open positions

Growth
market share
adjusted discharges
surgery cases
service area volumes

Finance
operating margin
cash flow margin
FTE's per AOB
controllable expenses
salary/wages/benefits
overtime
accounts receivable days

A Team Blueprint

My learning team in the healthcare environment

Mission
To enhance care by excelling in learning

We believe that by delivering excellence in employee education and development, we will further the mission of our organization by enabling employees to continually improve their ability to provide excellent, compassionate, high-quality care.

Vision
To enable BRHC to become a true learning organization

We believe that becoming a true learning organization will play a large role in making our organization the best small healthcare system in the country. We will create an environment and culture that promotes, encourages, provides, supports, and rewards continuous improvement through knowledge enhancement. In this culture, every employee will want to continually learn and grow. And with this culture, our organization will produce dramatically improved results.

Values
Innovation, trust, passion, fun, communication, and continuous improvement

We also support and uphold all values outlined in organizational statements.

Value Statements

1. We will always strive to do the right thing in everything we attempt and everyone with whom we come in contact.

2. We will expect and encourage excellence in all educational activities and in all services we provide to our customers.
3. We will interact with integrity, respecting all individuals with whom we come in contact.
4. We will seek to develop and maintain relationships of high trust with each other and each of our customers.
5. We will constantly innovate and strive to continuously improve the value and quality of our products and services.
6. We will strive to communicate effectively with all those with whom we come in contact and create fun and joy in all we do.

Standards
A sample

Service Pillar—Relationship
1. Guest interaction—practice CARE and AIDET
2. Answering the phone—key words: *"Thank you for calling Learning Services. This is* [your first name] *speaking. How may I help you?"*
3. Dress—director—(nonclinical) coat and tie, (clinical) business casual with lab coat or navy and white to match the nurse uniform; staff—(nonclinical) coat and tie; administrative assistant—business casual/professional look; everyone—adjust up to the audience or a notch above the audience and meet company policy at all times.
4. Class conduct: have classroom completely setup at least thirty minutes before start of class. Make sure you or a member of our team is present in the room to greet when participants start arriving. Meet and greet using CARE and AIDET standards. Make sure a member of our team opens the class, coordinates participant introductions, and introduces the speaker/teacher. Gain the speaker's permission or assurance that all is well before leaving the classroom. Make sure a

member of our team is present at the close of class. Collect the sign-in sheets and class evaluations.

People Pillar—Teamwork
1. Resolving conflicts: work together respectfully and tactfully to resolve conflicts. Bring team conflicts to the boss only after failing to resolve them one-on-one.

Pillar Measurements
Areas for Consideration

Quality
postevent reaction scores
joint commission compliance
guests' perception of quality
mandatory learning compliance

Service
interdepartmental survey score
patient satisfaction percentiles

People
team engagement score
organization turnover

Growth
none

Finance
performance to budget
cost/learning hour delivered

A Church Blueprint
For a nondenominational Christian church
Excerpts from Oak Hill United Methodist Church, Morganton, North Carolina
(Reprinted with permission)

Church Mission

To be an instrument, empowered by the Holy Spirit, representing the Lord Jesus Christ, fulfilling the Great Commandment (Matt 22:36-40) and the Great Commission (Matt 28:18-20)

Church Vision

A growing church serving and sharing Christ as God has uniquely designed us to do

Within ten years, we see a future for our church in which 95 percent of the members clearly understand how God has uniquely designed them for his service, are active in some type of ministry, and are sharing Christ with others through evangelism in the way he has designed them to love to do—or they are on a path of discipleship and personal Christian growth toward that end. That dramatic change in the personal development of the members of the church will yield many benefits for the church community, the community at large, the body of Christ, and the world we impact.

Among those benefits, we see more Sunday school classes in existence. We see full utilization of all our facilities with expanded services on Sunday and Wednesday nights, and perhaps other nights as well. Younger leaders have been mentored and developed such that they are actively leading the church in a period of dramatic growth, characterized by growing membership, attendance at services, ministries in action, testimonies being shared, and non-Christian conversions to belief in Christ being witnessed on a regular basis. The growing membership has created the need for a correlated growth in clergy to support it. The growth in ministries has enabled us to reach to greater areas of our county, the state, and perhaps even the country and the world. Our thriving, active, meaningful and energetic fellowship is inviting to others and creates a synergy of action and excitement that is contagious to anyone exposed to it. There is a full contemporary worship service in the all-purpose building with a full complement of musicians and singers ministering to people of all ages several times per week. We have created a vibrant outdoor sanctuary in nature on the property where members and visitors can gather individually or in small groups to pray, study scripture, worship, and fellowship together as they grow in Christ. Members seek out ways to serve and volunteer for service and ministry opportunities on committees and ministry groups.

Our church leaders are committed heart and soul to church growth, in which nearly every Christian is using his or her spiritual gifts to edify the church. Most members are living out their faith with power and contagious enthusiasm. Church structures are evaluated on whether they serve the growth of the church or not. Worship services are a high point of the week for the majority of members, and the loving and healing power of Christian fellowship can be experienced in small groups of many kinds. Nearly all members, according to their unique SHAPE, help fulfill the Great Commission, and the love of Christ permeates all church activities. God has created an environment in our church in which members and nonmembers, Christians and non-Christians, are drawn. Non-Christians are accepting Jesus Christ as their Lord and Savior on a regular basis.

Church Principles

We commit ourselves by God's grace to strive to uphold the Judeo-Christian principles outlined in God's Word, the Holy Bible.

God's principles are numerous; however
we view these three as core.
Love, faith, and hope.
—1 Corinthians 13:13

- **Love**—an act of worship demonstrating adoration, devotion, and service to God and others (Matthew 22:39).
- **Faith**—complete trust, confidence, and reliance on God and his promises in the Word (Romans 1:17).
- **Hope**—an optimistic expectation in God's promises for the future as clearly communicated in his Word, the Holy Bible. (Romans 15:13)

Church Standards

We acknowledge and accept all the standards, precepts and commands in God's Word as our guide and pledge to do our best, with God's help, to live according to them.

The Pillars

Quality

Creating a church environment characterized by empowering leadership, gift-oriented ministry, passionate spirituality, functional structures, inspiring worship services, holistic small groups, need-oriented evangelism, and loving relationships *(NCD Qualities for Church Growth)*

Service (Ministry)
Offering ourselves in selfless, God-inspired service to the Lord, each other, and our communities, and pledging to minister to the world around us as God leads

People (Worship, Discipleship, and Fellowship)
Making it a great place to serve by creating inspiring worship opportunities, spiritual growth, and meaningful fellowship for all our members

Growth (Evangelism)
Committing ourselves to share the gospel with others according to our unique SHAPE as God has designed us to love to do

Finance (Stewardship)
Pledging our time, talents, and treasures to building up the church and God's kingdom

Measurements
Areas for consideration by pillar

Quality

The Natural Church Development Survey, which measures the following eight quality characteristics of growing churches:

- empowering leadership
- gift-oriented ministry
- passionate spirituality
- functional structures
- inspiring worship services
- holistic small groups
- need-oriented evangelism
- loving relationships

Service (Ministry)
    ministry activities and number of members participating in them
    number of people in the community served by our church
    number of members completing SHAPE assessments

People (Worship, Discipleship, and Fellowship)
    worship service attendance
    tithing
    church membership and turnover
    participation of church fellowship activities
    participation in small group Bible study
    participation in other personal development activities

Growth (Evangelism)
    number of members active in church life (beyond attendance at the Sunday morning services)
    number of non-Christians we have shared Christ with
    number of confessed conversions or professions of faith

Finance (Stewardship)
    performance to budget
    tithes and offerings
    giving/member/year

The Crouch Family Blueprint

As for me and my house, we will serve the Lord!
—Joshua 24:15

Our Family Mission

To maintain an environment in our family and home that brings glory to God and is characterized by love, joy, peace, self-control, gentleness, goodness, and faith (Galatians 5:22).

Our Family Vision

Every member of the family is living out God's unique purpose for his or her life with fullness of joy, intense passion, and enthusiasm, adding value to the world (Romans 15:13).

Our Core Principles

Love, faith, and hope (1 Corinthians 13:13)

Intent

Our principles and standards are not rules we have to live by, but agreed-upon guidelines for daily behavior we strive to demonstrate them with one another, realizing that doing so enables us to accomplish our family mission and vision and maintain a better experience for everyone. For our family to be successful, each member must commit to try to behave according to these guidelines every day. If something doesn't work or make sense any more, we will discuss it as a family and make appropriate adjustments with consensus. Every family member's opinion is valid and valuable. If, after ample time and effort, a consensus is not possible, Dad will consider all opinions and viewpoints and make a decision. Once a decision is made, whether through consensus or parental decree, everyone in the family agrees to support it.

Our goal is to maintain a family and home environment based on the Judeo-Christian ethic as outlined in the Bible. Our first priority is to ensure that each family member is also in the family of God, having accepted Jesus Christ as Lord and Savior. In the Crouch home, the husband/father is the head of the household and the wife/mother is his right hand and helpmate, an equal partner in decisions and ways. The husband commits to love his wife as Christ loved the church, willing to give his life for her and the family if necessary. The wife commits to love her husband and submit to his authority as a Christian does to the Lord. Other family members actively participate in family matters and submit willingly to the parental authority. It is this wonderful and mysterious mix of love and respect for God and one another that enables the family to build and maintain a harmonious and joyous living experience.

Our Family's Core Principles
(1 Corinthians 13:13)

- **Love**—an act of worship demonstrating adoration, devotion and service to God and others (Matthew 22:39).
- **Faith**—complete trust, confidence, and reliance on God and his promises in the Word (Romans 1:17).
- **Hope**—an optimistic expectation in God's promises for the future as clearly communicated in his Word, the Holy Bible (Romans 15:13).

Our Standards of Behavior
(Sample noted here; see complete list in chapter 7)

Each member of the family pledges to strive to behave according to these standards, realizing that perfection is not possible, therefore relying on the forgiveness afforded us by faith, and making it a priority to ask for forgiveness from God and one another when we fall short.

1. **Love**—for God, each other, and others
    a. Treat others the way you would appreciate being treated.
    b. Consider family needs first, before friends, work, church or school.
2. **Joy**—deep, inner happiness; fun
    a. Laugh often.
    b. Make sure fun, sarcasm, and joking do not offend others.
3. **Peace**—a general state of order and calm

a. Clean up after yourself.
   b. Keep the home clean and orderly.
   c. Communicate with one another peacefully. If you can't converse peacefully in the moment, wait until you can.
4. **Temperance**—self-control, restraint, frugality
   a. Keep the home free from illegal activity and substances.
   b. Avoid behaviors that have negative impacts on you or others.
5. **Goodness**—kindness, fairness, and generosity toward one another
   a. Be kind and fair to one another.
   b. If a family member has wronged you and asked for forgiveness, offer it freely.
   c. Give cheerfully of your time and resources to others.

Measurements

1. **Quality**—striving for the highest quality of life
   a. Every family member will describe the quality of the family experience as excellent overall.
   b. Every family member will testify that the home experience is generally loving and harmonious.
   c. Disagreements are settled calmly and with an attitude of mutual benefit. Family members seek and generally achieve win-win outcomes.
   d. Instances where one family member hurts another are minimal.
   e. The home and grounds remain clean and in proper order.
2. **Service**—putting others above self in giving to one another and the community

     a. Other people impacted by our family will describe us as a close-knit, loving family committed to our family values and adding value to world around us.
3. **People**—working together to make it a great place to live
   a. Every family member will describe the relationship with other family members as loving and harmonious overall and would choose to live together even if they didn't have to.
4. **Growth**—always leaning forward
   a. The family and all of its members are moving in a positive direction.
5. **Stewardship** *(finance)*—responsible management of all resources entrusted to our care
   a. Every family member manages his or her time to no more than two hours per day of personal idle time.
   b. We are operating within our family budget.
   c. Material possessions endure as intended and instances of breaking or wasting are minimal.

My Individual Blueprint

My Personal Mission
To do the right thing in love to glorify God
and patiently trust him for the results

My Personal Vision
No regrets; to hear the words, "Well done, thou good and faithful servant," at heaven's door

My Core Principles

1. **Love**—an act of worship demonstrating adoration, devotion, and service to God and others (Matthew 22:39).
2. **Faith**—complete trust, confidence, and reliance on God and his promises in the Word (Romans 1:17).
3. **Hope**—an optimistic expectation in God's promises for the future as clearly communicated in his Word, the Holy Bible (Romans 15:13).

Supporting Principles Important to Me

1. **Marriage**—always put each other first; work to improve and deepen our relationship
2. **Family**—work together to be good parents, children, and siblings
3. **Health**—maintain good exercise and diet
4. **Service**—seek to fulfill God's purpose in ministry to others
5. **Humility**—stay away from the world's lure if it takes me away from God
6. **Fun**—make laughter a way of life
7. **Adventure**—look for ways to create mystery, excitement, and variance from routine

My Standards

I support and pledge to live according to the standards enumerated in the Holy Bible, my church's blueprint, and my family's blueprint. When I mess up, I pledge to acknowledge my error, apologize to those I've wronged, ask for their forgiveness, and strive to learn from and not repeat my error.

Areas of Measurement

1. Quality—I deliver a high-quality experience for everyone I serve.
    a. Competence: I am viewed as a content expert in my areas of expertise.
    b. Accuracy: I deliver safe, careful, precise delivery of my products and/or services.
2. Service—I deliver extraordinary service.
    a. Relationship: I build a strong, positive relationship with everyone I serve.
    b. Availability: I am fully present, fully aware, and fully available for those I serve.
3. People—I make it a great place for others to work, live, or be.
    a. Teamwork: I am a valuable, positive contributor to every team I serve.
4. Growth—I continually improve my services, facilities, equipment, and people.
    a. Resilience: I respond to change and adversity positively and productively.
    b. Innovation: I proactively initiate positive changes.
5. Finance—I responsibly manage my resources.
    a. Efficiency: I demonstrate wise use of my time, money, and materials.

For more resources to help you develop your own Blueprint for Excellence, visit my website.

Summary of Chapter 16

1. The house of excellence model is a strategic planning framework that can be applied to any environment and any endeavor with its focus on the human aspect of excellence.
2. When combined with the seven steps of a successful blueprint, you can create your own blueprint to guide you on your quest for excellence.

Take Action

1. Develop your strategic plan, your personal and specific blueprint, for whatever you are trying to do.
2. Use the information in this book and access my website for tools to help you.

CHAPTER 17

Leading Excellence

As for the best leaders, the people do not notice their existence. The next best, the people honor and praise. The next, the people fear. And the next, the people hate. When the best leader's work is done, the people say, "We did it ourselves."
—Chinese philosopher Lao-Tzu

Leadership is an active, living process. It is rooted in character, forged by experience, and communicated by example.
—John Baldoni

Leadership is a relationship.
—C. David Crouch

The story is told of a wise, old king who was searching for the wisdom of the ages. He tasked his team of counselors to search for the answer. After a year, the counselors returned with twelve volumes of information they claimed contained the wisdom of the ages.

Repulsed by the huge amount of information, the king instructed them to reduce it to a more manageable size. About three months later, the counselors returned. This time, they presented the king with one large volume of information.

Again the king exclaimed, "That's still too much! Go back and reduce it even further."

After a few more months, the counselors returned and presented the king with a fifty-page report.

Again, the king was not satisfied.

After two more attempts by the counselors to reduce the message, they finally returned with one sentence they said contained the essence of the wisdom of the ages for all to know. At last, the wise king was pleased. He was confident he had discovered the most important lesson of all that represented the wisdom of the ages.

"It's all about relationship!"

Regardless of your endeavor, it's all about *relationship*. You can replace the *it's* in that sentence with whatever it is you're dealing with. Life is all about relationship. Marriage is all about relationship. Family is all about relationship. Parenting is all about relationship. Church is all about relationship. School is all about relationship. Work is all about relationship. Sports are all about relationship. The civic club is all about relationship. The Girl Scouts are all about relationship. Your business is all about relationship. Service is all about relationship. Fulfillment is all about relationship. Success (or failure) is all about relationship. Excellence (or mediocrity) is all about relationship. Leadership is all about relationship.

> *70. Excellence is all about relationships.*
> *So is leadership.*

It's the leader's responsibility to build excellent relationships. Excellent relationships build excellent teams. Excellence requires you to cultivate the raw material of effective leadership. It's the leader's responsibility to create and sustain an environment that inspires excellence in everyone involved. The good news is that effective leadership is available to everyone—and so is excellence!

What is Effective Leadership?

Before we address the what, let's take a look at the *who*. Who do we consider to be some of the most effective leaders in history? I have a wonderful reference on my bookshelf entitled *Great Quotes from Great Leaders*, compiled by Peggy Anderson. Some of the individuals quoted in the book include Winston Churchill, Walt Disney, Albert Einstein, Henry Ford, Benjamin Franklin, Mahatma Gandhi, Thomas Jefferson, Helen Keller, John F. Kennedy, Martin Luther King, Abraham Lincoln, Vince Lombardi, Douglas MacArthur, Nelson Mandela, Golda Meir, Pope John Paul II, Ronald Reagan, Eleanor Roosevelt, Franklin Roosevelt, Margaret Thatcher, Mother Teresa, Sam Walton, Booker T. Washington, and John Wooden. Presidents, world leaders, army generals, titans of industry, social and religious leaders, all of whom have had a major impact on the world through their leadership. I'm sure you recognize most of the names on this list. It's wonderful to read the sage wisdom in the pages of the book as each leader shares his or her unique perspective on leadership effectiveness. We have certainly witnessed a plethora of effective leaders throughout history.

But be careful. There's a potential danger in this type of leadership reference. We may begin to think that effective leadership is only displayed on the national or world stage. Of course, that's not true. Some of the most effective leaders I know will never have their comments quoted in any book on leadership. They are everyday normal people like you and me. I've learned as much, if not more, about effective leadership from their daily examples than from the ones we read about in history.

Every encounter with another human being is an opportunity to learn and grow. Perhaps we can learn as much about effective leadership from those closer to us in life than those we study from afar. Perhaps they're both valuable teachers if we simply pay attention.

> *71. Every encounter with another human being is an opportunity to learn and grow.*

What is effective leadership? R. M. Stogdill, in his article in the *Journal of Psychology* in 1948 titled *Personal Factors Associated with Leadership: A Survey of the Literature*, asserts that there are almost as many different definitions of leadership as there are people who have tried to define it.

Let's try to simplify this a bit. Peter Northouse, in *Leadership Theory and Practice*, defines leadership as a process whereby an individual influences a group of individuals to achieve a common goal. The individual Northouse refers to is the *leader*. My simplest definition of a leader is anyone who has a follower. Effective means successful, useful, valuable, and efficient in the production of a desired result. *Effective leadership*, then, is a process in which an individual works efficiently with others who follow him or her in order to produce a successful, useful, and valuable desired result. Notice the *influencing* and *working with others* parts of these definitions. It's all about relationships—and that includes attaining desired results.

Let's deal with two common questions about leadership that have a tendency to sidetrack the discussion of effectiveness.

1. Are leaders made or born?
2. What's the difference between a leader and a manager?

Are Leaders Made or Born?

The quick answer is yes. Leaders are made *and* born. While there may be something in the DNA of an effective leader that makes her so, the qualities she demonstrates can also be learned. Even if there is a predisposition toward leadership effectiveness, those qualities must still be cultivated and developed.

Often when we think of a leader, we think of George Washington, Bill Gates, or Mother Teresa—someone who had a tremendous impact on an entire society. Certainly, those types of leaders are worth admiring. But what about the mother who works diligently to teach her children what's right, to raise them according to a set of values and behaviors to become a productive member of society? Isn't she just as effective? What about the Little League T-ball coach who works with seven- and eight-year-olds to teach them how to win and lose graciously on the baseball diamond? Is he an effective leader too? What about the one who is concerned about a friend going through a tough time and stands beside them with encouragement, presenting hope in the midst of trouble? Isn't she an effective leader?

The principles of leadership apply at any level and can be learned and put into action by anyone who has someone looking to them for guidance. All of us will be called upon at some point in our lives to demonstrate leadership in a situation that requires it. We all need to understand the principles of leadership effectiveness and be ready to serve when that time comes.

9/11 Leadership

On September 11, 2001, I was in Patterson, New Jersey, facilitating a sales training event with twenty-four salesmen and saleswomen from all across the country. Patterson is twenty miles due west of Manhattan. When we received word that morning of the planes crashing into the World Trade Center, we suspended the training and moved to the lounge area of the hotel to watch the events unfold on television. Like most Americans, we were stunned. Some of us decided to ride the elevator to the top level of the hotel to take a look. Off in the distance were two flumes of thick smoke streaming from the towers as they burned. We could actually see them burning from our hotel. The mood was somber and fearful. What would happen next? Was this the beginning of a major attack on America? *Are my kids okay? Is my family okay?* The parking lot was crowded with people needing to connect with family and loved ones. Cell phone signals were jammed. It was a scary feeling. Emotions were rampant and raw.

At some point that day, I realized someone needed to step forward to facilitate the activities, attitudes, and feelings of the group of salespeople assembled. What should we do about our training? Since flights had all been grounded, what should we do about getting home? We were stranded. What would our company expect from us? *If there was ever a time when a group of people needed to band together in a difficult and unexpected situation, this is it.* Since I was the facilitator, I decided the person who needed to step forward was me.

Some people who know me well may say I'm a natural born leader. But that's because they've observed me in action later in my life after I've invested thirty years learning how to become one. There may be something in my DNA that gives me a propensity to lead effectively, but I'm a reluctant leader. I'm just as content playing the follower role if I'm under the guidance of another effective leader. In this case, I reluctantly stepped forward to play the leader role. I realize there were probably others in the group who could have played that role just as effectively. Perhaps I was the first to realize we needed to begin formulating a plan. I'm not sure.

After we had all contacted our loved ones and watched the events unfold for a few hours, we spread the word to assemble back in the training room at six o'clock that evening. I facilitated a discussion about what to do. Together we developed a plan of action and divided up responsibilities. Everyone just wanted to go home. The end result of our collaboration was to cancel the training, coordinate the eight rental cars among us, and send everyone toward home the next day by car. Our eight cars spread out over the country as we all grouped together in them by geography. Our Hawaii participant made it to the West Coast in a few days and finally home a week later. I was more fortunate. Living only ten hours south in North

Carolina, I made it home on the evening of September 12 and was able to hug my kids that night.

You never know when you may be required to step up and lead the way. It's best to be prepared. Whether or not you have the DNA of effective leadership in you, you can learn what it takes to lead effectively. I hope you've realized by now that the information in this book is designed to help you do just that. No matter what you've done up to this point in your life, *you can* effectively lead others to excellence. Leadership does not have to be born into you; it can be developed into you. Anyone who can think and talk can develop into an effective leader. I find that truth incredibly exciting and hopeful. Leaders are both born and made.

A Leader or a Manager?

Is there a difference between a leader and a manager? Most of the sources I've read on this topic say yes. Leaders are typically visionaries who inspire and direct change toward a more desired future for everyone. Managers typically focus on the goals and objectives required to implement the mission and vision. They're more tactical in nature. Excellence needs both, and many times both exist in the same person. Great leaders can be great managers and vice versa. This question deals more with the functions of the two roles rather than the people who perform them.

Everyone has a combination of talents, strengths, and weaknesses. The key is to understand yours—and to complement yourself with others on the team who are strong where you're weak. If you're strong in leadership but weak in management, make sure you have a strong manager on the team. It's that simple. According to my definition of leadership, anyone who has a follower is a leader. My objective in this chapter is to distill the most critical elements of effective leadership that anyone can employ to improve the opportunity to develop into a great leader—regardless of the specific role you currently fulfill.

What Others Say About Leadership

Perhaps there's more written on the topic of leadership than any other subject in the world. Let's explore what some of my favorite authors and teachers have to say about leadership. Then, I'll boil it down to the three core areas of leadership that determine 80 percent of your effectiveness. If you study and perfect these three areas, you can become an effective leader. Remember that excellence doesn't require perfection. All you need is perseverance with a plan to get you there. This book is your plan. Develop your skill in the three core competencies in this chapter, partner with others who are good where you're not, and you *can* become an excellent leader.

I studied and catalogued the leadership lessons from hundreds of resources. Below is a summary of what I've learned from practitioners such as Ken Blanchard, Marcus Buckingham, Dale Carnegie, Daryl Conner, Jim Collins, Stephen Covey, Napoleon Hill, John Kotter, John Maxwell, Tom Peters, and Zig Ziglar; from sports legends including Tony Dungy, Mike Krzyzewski, Vince Lombardi, Don Shula, Dean Smith, Pat Summit, and John Wooden; and from academic resources such as the American Management Association, Blake and Mouton, R. L. Katz, Kirkpatrick and Locke, R. D. Mann, Peter Northouse, Roger Stogdill, and David Ulrich. These resources are noted in the bibliography, and a detailed study can be found on my website.

An effective leader is . . .

A learner, a reader, seeking training, taking classes, listening to others, service-oriented, sees life as a mission, radiates positive energy, cheerful, pleasant, happy, optimistic, upbeat, enthusiastic, hopeful, believing, balanced, socially, physically, emotionally and intellectually active, synergistic, trustworthy, empathetic, definite, decisive, responsible, resilient, passionate, courageous, discerning, disciplined, energetic, a change agent, humble, accountable, urgent, resonant, emotionally intelligent, self-aware, temperate, self-confident, transparent, adaptable, achievement-oriented, organizationally aware, inspirational, influential, a coach, a team player, motivational, creative, customer-focused, functionally skilled, intellectual, politically savvy, results-focused, strategic, visionary, honest, compassionate, friendly, approachable, kind, interdependent, understanding, balanced, dedicated, healthy, industrious, just, professional, technologically savvy, passionate, morally sound, fair, loyal, dependable, organized, reliable, expressive, keen-minded, resourceful, logical, planful, informative, efficient, cooperative, clean, courageous, a facilitator, aligned, competent, secure, conscientious, authentic, talented, ethical, sympathetic, imaginative, influential, convicted, vigorous, venturesome, flexible, directive, and supportive.

An effective leader also . . .

Challenges the process, changes, grows, innovates, improves, inspires a shared vision and enlists others in it, fosters collaboration, promotes cooperative goals, builds trust, gives power away, provides choices, develops competence, assigns tasks, offers support, sets examples, behaves according to values, achieves small wins, builds commitment, recognizes individual contributions, celebrates team accomplishments, deals with poor performances, initiates difficult but necessary conversations, takes initiative, uses good judgment, speaks with authority, strengthens others, never compromises on absolutes, focuses on objectives, empowers others, cultivates loyalty, faces brutal facts, keeps a clear conscience, knows when to change his mind, does not abuse authority, is sure of her calling, knows his limitations, knows how to delegate, moves with the cheese, focuses on the present, breaks all the rules, prioritizes, practices what he preaches, demands accountability in others, leads with love, has a positive attitude, develops others, manages conflict, builds effective teams, harnesses peer pressure, deals with ambiguity, has strong business acumen, is comfortable around higher management, possesses command skills, manages innovation, learns on the fly, solves problems, manages processes, manages vision and purpose, analyzes issues, sets goals, communicates powerfully, listens, builds good relationships, champions change, connects internal groups, begins with the end in mind, thinks win-win, seeks to understand, works hard, follows up, controls costs, eliminates waste, keeps good records, handles emergencies, trains others, builds bridges, manages risks, focuses on the big picture, empowers others, selects good talent, fosters a family environment, accepts the consequences of his actions, absorbs interpersonal stress, tolerates frustration and delay, and directs others.

We only looked at a small sample of what others have to say about leadership. Does this sound as ominous to you as it does to me? There's much more. Have you ever known anyone to possess all these characteristics and abilities? Is it even possible? To think this would describe any one person on the planet would be ridiculous. This sounds a lot like perfection, and we know no one is perfect. So where does this leave us? Is it even possible to become an effective leader if this is what it requires? I have some good news for you. We can simplify this tremendously. I've discovered the three things that will enable you to become an effective leader if you will simply do them. These three things will help you accomplish 80 percent of the list above—and that's all it takes to become effective. Are you ready?

The Pareto Principle Of Leadership Excellence

The *Pareto Principle*, also known as the 80/20 rule, states that roughly 80 percent of the effects of a thing come from 20 percent of the causes. For example, 80 percent of a business's sales come from 20 percent of its clients. In our context here, 80 percent of your effectiveness as a leader comes from 20 percent of the things you do to lead. *The Pareto Principle of Leadership Excellence* says you must *TAP* into three critical skills.

1. Build *Trust* in your relationships
2. Create *Accountability* around the work
3. Lead with *Passion*

> **Pareto Principle** *n.* also known as the 80/20 rule, states that roughly 80 percent of the effects of a thing come from 20 percent of the causes. It was named by business management consultant Dr. Joseph M. Juran in the late 1940s after Italian economist Vilfredo Pareto, who observed in 1906 that 80 percent of the land in Italy was owned by 20 percent of the population (*Wikipedia*). From his work with American business in the 1930s and 1940s, Dr. Juran observed a similar phenomenon on a broader scale he called the "vital few and the trivial many." However, Pareto Principle prevailed as the name, probably because it sounded better than Juran Principle. Its value is that it can remind us to focus on the 20 percent of the things that matter most (*About.com/management*).

Build Trust

> Trust is the one thing that changes everything.
> —Stephen M. R. Covey

An organization is simply a group of people working together toward a common objective. Since it involves many people working together, the need to forge relationships becomes obvious. Relationships are built or destroyed based upon the quality of our communications. Every time we interact with another human being, we're either improving our relationship with them or making it worse. Each interaction is a moment of truth.

Stephen R. Covey in *Principle-Centered Leadership* likens this concept to a bank account. Every time your interaction with someone is good, you make a deposit in the bank account of trust.

Every time it's bad, you make a withdrawal. Your objective is to keep a large balance of trust in your account—to make more deposits than withdrawals. You must maintain a high balance of trust in your bank account and build strong, positive relationships.

> *72. Communication determines the quality of trust.*
> *73. Trust builds hope.*
> *74. Hope anticipates excellence.*

Trust is instinctive, unquestioning belief in and reliance on the integrity, strength, ability, or surety of a person or thing. It is the confident expectation of something because of good reason, definite evidence, or past experience. It can be extended freely by choice or built over time. If extended freely, it must be validated over time or it will be lost. Trust builds hope, and hope anticipates excellence. Therefore, trust builds excellence. Furthermore, communication determines the quality of our trust. See the model below.

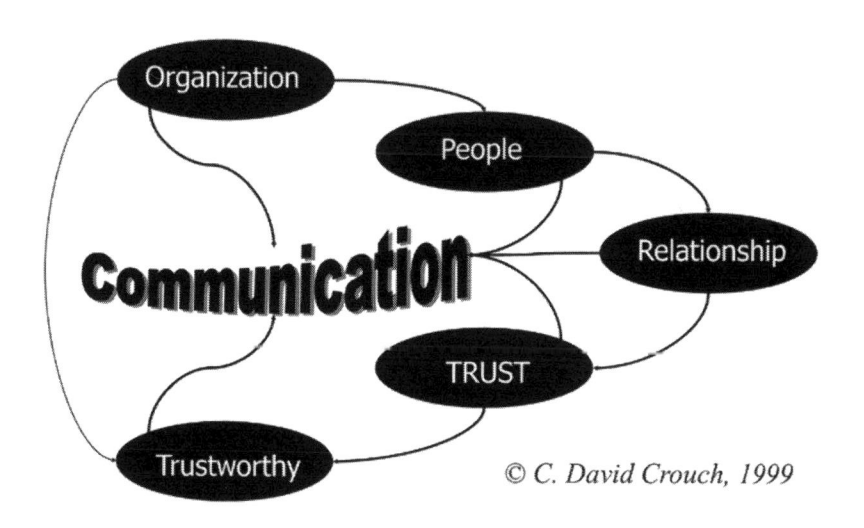

© C. David Crouch, 1999

At the core of excellence is *effective communication*. Through effective communication, I become trustworthy. By my trustworthiness, I build relationships of high trust. Since the organization is a group of people working together toward a common objective, and working together with others requires effective relationship building, my communication skills and ability to build trust become critical. If communication determines trust and trust drives excellence, how do we communicate with others in such a way as to build trust in our relationships?

Communication is arguably the most critical life skill to master. We assume human beings can communicate if they can simply speak and hear.

Charles F. Kettering said, "We can communicate an idea around the world almost instantaneously, but it sometimes takes years for an idea to get through one-quarter inch of human skull."

John Maxwell says, "Everyone communicates, few connect."

Communication is the golden thread that permeates every aspect of a culture of excellence. It determines the quality of trust in relationships. You must recognize its critical role and use it effectively to seek mutual understanding with others in every interaction.

Stephen M. R. Covey, in *The Speed of Trust*, identifies five waves of trust, four cores of credibility, and thirteen behaviors that build trust. The five waves are self-trust, relationship trust, organizational trust, market trust, and societal trust. Covey makes the case that all five waves of trust are accomplished through the four cores of credibility and the thirteen behaviors. The four cores are divided into two parts—character and competence. Integrity and intent determine character while capability and results determine competence. According to Covey, you must first be a person of integrity, honest and congruent, with a reputation for telling the truth. Next, you must have good intentions, not trying to deceive or protect anyone, without hidden motives or agendas. Third, you must demonstrate capability, expertise, knowledge, and skill in your area. Finally, you must produce good results over time so there is good reason for others to believe you can do so now.

According to Covey, building, maintaining, and restoring trust in relationships hinges on how effectively you develop the thirteen behaviors. Behavior is something that is totally within your control. You control the level of trust you build with others by how you behave. You can control the level of excellence you experience by controlling your behavior. The thirteen behaviors are talk straight, demonstrate respect, create transparency, right wrongs, show loyalty, deliver results, get better, confront reality, clarify expectations, practice accountability, listen first, keep commitments, and extend trust to others. I recommend Covey's book for developing these behaviors to the highest level in your life.

Can we simplify the concept of building trust even further? While working with a furniture manufacturer in North Carolina, we discovered three core behaviors. I call them the *DNA of Trust*.

The hundred-year-old organization had undertaken a major restructuring in its manufacturing process, transitioning from departmentalized production to cellular production. In departmental furniture manufacturing, the wood used to build furniture moves through a series of departments, each of which do something special and unique to the wood. The raw wood planks make an entry into the plant in the saw room to be cut to specific lengths for different uses. The cut wood leaves the saw room for either the glue room or the sanding room. In the glue room, it's glued together to make larger pieces for tabletops and desktops. The sanding room smooths the wood and prepares it for raw assembly. After it's assembled, it travels to the finishing room for stain and other protective finishes, then to the rub room for polishing and touch-up, and finally to packing and shipping. Of course, people work in each department to carry out these tasks.

After working this way for so long, employees had become accustomed to working independently. Once the employees finished the work of their departments, other employees called transporters moved the wood from one department to the next. The employees rarely, if ever, interacted or communicated with one another. They were separated by their departments and the unique work each department performed.

Cellular manufacturing required a different approach. Instead of moving the wood from one department to the next, the plant was restructured into cells with a member or two from each department becoming a team member in each cell. The cell would then be responsible for building a piece of furniture from start to finish. In the cell, each team member could see one another and communicate easily about any issues that would arise.

In the departmentalized structure, if issues arose, the transporter would have to move the wood back and forth or the supervisors would have a meeting to discuss the problem and solve the issue. The core idea of cellular manufacturing was to decrease the transport time and increase the efficiency of the production process. If problems could be solved at the point of creation, it would save a lot of time and produce a higher-quality product. This seemed to be a great idea, but there was one major problem. For one hundred years, employees had worked alone without any need to communicate with one another. In the new cellular environment, they would need to communicate all the time. This required a tremendous shift in the status quo. Management brought me in to help employees learn how to communicate with one another better, build strong teamwork, and thus produce higher-quality products more efficiently. Without strong teamwork and communication, cellular manufacturing would fail.

In the process of working with hundreds of manufacturing employees, we began to explore together the concept of building a great cellular team. We realized the importance of communication and building trust among team members. Together, we explored how to build high trust among team members within the cells. We brainstormed hundreds of ideas and pieces of input. Next, we categorized them into like groups and were able to identify three main things each individual must do to be trustworthy and build strong trust with others. We learned through experience that these three things done well build strong, trusting relationships.

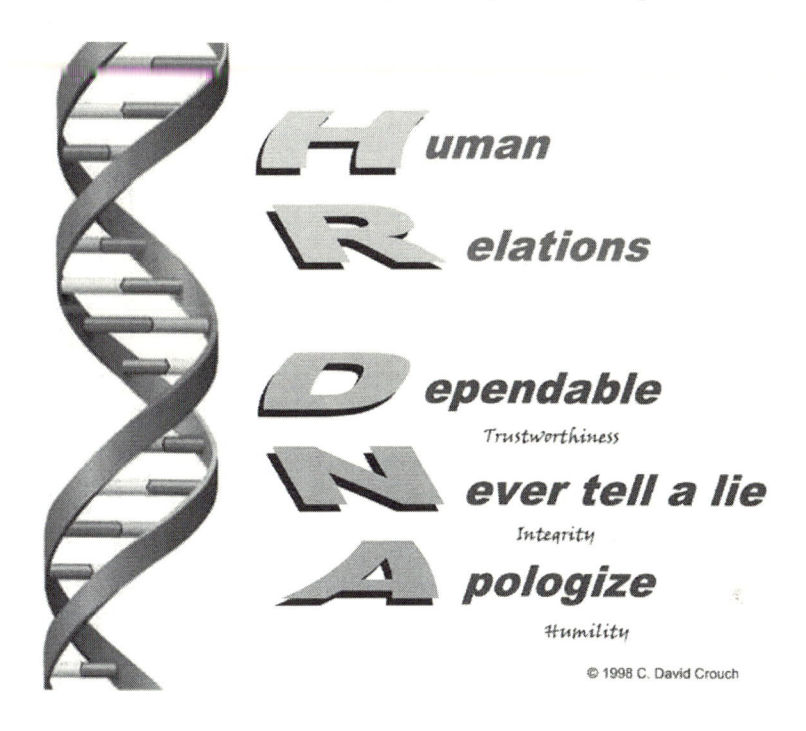

**Human
Relations
Dependable** Trustworthiness
Never tell a lie Integrity
Apologize Humility

© 1998 C. David Crouch

Just as DNA in the biological sense represents the fundamental building blocks of life, *HR DNA* captures the fundamental building blocks of building high-trust relationships. HR stands for human relations, and DNA is an acronym that describes the three critical behaviors that build trust—be dependable, never tell a lie, and apologize when you're wrong.

Dependability

A person who is dependable can be relied upon to keep and follow through with commitments. They are *trustworthy*, and their behavior is predictable because they consistently do what they commit to do. They show loyalty, practice accountability, and can be relied upon to do what's expected of them most of the time. Exceptions are rare and patterns of behavior are relatively constant. They are known for practicing what they preach—they do what they say. *Dependability* generates *loyalty* over time. There's nothing as valuable to a team or partnership as someone who has proven to be dependable. It brings peace of mind to the relationship and an assurance that things will get done properly and on time. Conversely, there's nothing more frustrating or destructive to a relationship than someone who is not dependable.

> *75. Dependability solidifies excellence.*

Do you know anyone who is frequently late for appointments, meetings, or commitments? Even worse, do you know anyone who just doesn't show up at all after telling you they would? How does that make you feel? This is my pet peeve. I can't stand it when people don't do what they said they were going to do. For goodness sake, can't they at least call to let me know they're going to be late?

Barring an accident that renders a person unconscious, there's no excuse for this type of disrespect. If your teammates can't count on you to follow through on your commitments, you can forget about any concept of excellence in your team. Never tolerate it on your team. Demand dependability by demonstrating it yourself and making it an expected team behavior in others. Dependability solidifies excellence!

Never Tell a Lie

Integrity means doing the right thing. A person of integrity lives according to sound moral principles. They are ethical, honorable, just, and fair. They are open and honest in their communications and take honesty very seriously. Using the language of Covey's thirteen behaviors of trust, they talk straight, demonstrate respect, create transparency, right wrongs, deliver results, confront reality tactfully, clarify expectations, listen first, and extend trust to others.

A person of integrity is also considered a person of honor. In these times when taking things that don't belong to you, stealing time by playing computer games at work, and other similar behaviors are commonplace, a real person of integrity stands out like a grasshopper in an ant farm. Integrity earns respect, admiration, and loyalty.

Earning a reputation of integrity takes time but can be lost in an instant. It can even be lost over something as simple as checking your e-mail on your iPad in a meeting. In one organization, one of the standards of behavior that everyone had agreed to uphold was to refrain from using electronic devices in meetings. It's disrespectful to the other team members who are distracted by it, to the meeting leader who's trying to facilitate effectively, and it demonstrates disrespect for the standard in general.

The senior team had made a big deal about the standards of behavior and pledged to demonstrate them at all times, requiring that subordinates do the same. They sealed the commitment by signing a declaration to that effect and publicized it vigorously throughout the organization. Not long after, a buzz was circulating around the company about one of the executives who was seen using his iPhone to surf the net and check e-mails at practically every meeting they attended. This continued for some time.

Many people mentioned it tactfully and discussed it with their own bosses. Some discussed it with the executive's boss as well, but nothing changed. The executive was allowed to persist. After several months of this, the focus of the buzz changed from the executive's behavior to his boss for allowing it to continue. It made a mockery of the standards of behavior, devaluing them to the entire organization. It made the executive team look like hypocrites as they allowed their teammate to persist in noncompliance with a very visible standard of behavior, and it degenerated into disrespect for executive leadership as they allowed it to continue. A simple thing can be a lesion in the organization that spreads a cancer of mediocrity and complacency. It will literally destroy a culture of excellence.

> ### 76. Integrity accelerates excellence.

Your reputation as a person of integrity should be so strong that even if someone tries to defame you or tell lies about you, others won't believe it. They'll give you the benefit of the doubt when rumors are spreading. But watch out! If too many rumors spread too far for too long, people may begin to believe some of them—and you could lose your good standing. When you have earned a reputation of integrity, you should protect it at all costs by remaining pure and honorable at all times. *Integrity accelerates excellence.*

I'd like to share something personal with you that I wrote for my dad when he turned eighty. I had attended several funerals and was moved by how so many of the loved ones would share what the deceased had meant to them in their lives. I realized I had never shared such a message with my dad, and I didn't want to wait until he died to do it.

I wrote him a letter, framed it with photos of us through the years, and gave it to him on his eightieth birthday. My dad is a man of honor, a man with a reputation of integrity. I'm proud to introduce you to Clarence Crouch Jr., my dad and my hero—a true man of integrity.

Dear Dad,

On this, your eightieth birthday, I want to take the opportunity to tell you what it's meant to me to have you as my father.

You've been such an inspiration to me these past forty-eight years. There's no question that I've become a better man because you have been my father, my example. I've benefited from your stability, your sense of commitment, your wisdom, your courage, and your strength. You've always been my safety net, and without you undergirding me with your support and presence, I know I would not be who I am or where I am today. You, with Mom, have instilled in me a litany of strong attributes, such as a drive for excellence, a commitment to virtues, values, and service, and a love for our God.

But perhaps more important than what you've done for me is who you are as a man. It's your daily living example that's taught me the most. I see in my father a real man of honor . . . a man who values God, family, love, and commitment . . . a man who has put his wife above all others at all times, remaining fully committed and faithful to that lifelong promise . . . a man who would rather invest an afternoon with his family than in life's many spoils . . . a man who has worked hard all his life so those who depend on him could have a better life . . . a man whose example of service to others knows no bounds . . . a man who always has a smile and a good word and the time to share them both . . . a man who always values relationships above things . . . a man always calm under pressure, stable and well balanced, with strength under control . . . a passionately honest and thrifty man who doesn't live for money or personal gain . . . a man admired by many, respected by all, and welcomed by any . . . and in a time when character, value, and virtue seem scarce, my dad is a man who, by this daily living godly example, has rightfully earned the title and reputation as a true man of honor!

Whatever else you think of yourself, Dad, please know this. There's no man on earth I would rather have to call my father than you. You are my hero, my role model, and my friend. I am and always will be proud to call you Dad. Happy birthday! I love you, Dad.

Forever grateful,
David

Dad passed away recently at the age of eighty-seven. Even as I write this today, I'm moved with immense emotion. I tell my own children that if I can be half the father to them that my dad is to me, then I'll consider myself a success as a parent.

These words are true. They accurately describe my father. His example has provided an extremely powerful and positive inspiration for me—and others. That's the power of integrity! It can change a person. It can change a team. It can change an organization. And it can change a world. Integrity builds trust and accelerates excellence. We need more men and women of integrity today more than ever.

Acknowledge, Apologize, and Ask

Acknowledge when you're wrong, *apologize* to the one you've wronged, and *ask* for their forgiveness. I'm talking about *humility*, the absence of pride or self-assertion. Another word for humility is modesty, demonstrating consciousness of one's own shortcomings and faults. It's the realization that you are far from perfect—and you remain thankful for the blessings you have. A humble person is meek, patient, and mild, not easily provoked to anger or resentment. The core behavior is to openly acknowledge when you've made a mistake, apologize to those affected by it, and ask for forgiveness. It sounds so simple, yet so few seem to practice it.

As mentioned earlier, this is your personal *service recovery plan*. You know it's going to happen. You're not perfect. No one is. You're going to mess up sooner or later. It's best to recognize that now and be prepared to follow these three simple steps when it happens. Covey said when you mess up, you make a withdrawal from the bank account of trust. The only way to redeposit is to acknowledge your mistake and apologize. No one is perfect. Everyone knows that. Sometimes, they just need to know you know it too. When you demonstrate humility in your relationships, you communicate to others that you know you're not perfect. They see clearly that you're human too.

77. Humility undergirds excellence.

If you blame others for your mistakes—or fail to acknowledge them to your team and colleagues—you'll lose their respect. You may even gain their utter disgust. Connors, Smith, and Hickman in *The Oz Principle: Getting Results Through Individual and Organizational Accountability* claim that most organizations fail due to leadership error, but that many leaders will never admit that fact. Someone who can authentically demonstrate humility and apologize when they're wrong earns deep respect. It knits relationships back together once wounded. *Humility undergirds excellence.*

To build strong relationships of high trust, employ the *DNA of Trust* in every encounter with others. Be dependable, never tell a lie, and acknowledge your mistakes. Others will respect you and want to follow you.

2. Create Accountability

> You must inspect what you expect.
> —Zig Ziglar

> Example is not the main thing in influencing others . . . it's the only thing!
> —Albert Schweitzer

Accountability begins with you. You can't expect anyone else to do the right thing if you don't set the example. Remember my story about checking e-mails in meetings? In that case, the CEO did not require his senior team to take accountability for demonstrating a standard of behavior. Consequently, the standards were mocked, others didn't comply with them, and the culture began to break down. *Accountability* means accepting responsibility for and providing satisfactory explanations of one's own actions and deeds. Accountability authenticates excellence. Lack of accountability thwarts it.

There are two basic approaches to accountability. Either we can *hold others accountable* for doing what they're supposed to do or we can require them to *take accountability* for doing what they're supposed to do. The difference is subtle, but it is distinctive. Holding others accountable places the responsibility for accountability on the leader. Requiring others to take accountability places the responsibility on the individual. Effective leaders are role models of personal accountability. They do what they're supposed to do as a matter of practice—and they expect everyone else on the team to do the same. Effective leaders create an environment of mutual respect in which others voluntarily give their best each day.

78. Accountability authenticates excellence.

The opposite of accountability is blame. Don't you utterly despise when people start making excuses for why they didn't do what they were supposed to do? Like me, you've probably heard them all before. "It's not my job." "I'm too busy." "I forgot!" "Nobody told me what to do." "That's the way we've always done it!" "I thought you were going to do that." "Don't blame me. It was her idea." "I was just about to get to that." "I didn't get the e-mail."

These are just a few of the excuses I've heard. In *The Oz Principle,* Connors et al state, "Instead of taking responsibility for shortfalls and failures, far too many of today's business leaders offer every conceivable excuse from shortage of resources to inept staff to competitor sabotage." If you don't believe that statement, just turn on the evening news. All you hear are politicians blaming others for the problems in America. No one will take accountability. It's difficult to discern if the buck actually stops anywhere anymore.

One of the executive teams I worked with had this problem as well. Every time a conversation emerged about how results were not being accomplished, someone in the senior team would say, "When are those managers and directors going to start doing their jobs?" (They blamed middle management.)

Each time I heard that statement, I would ask, "If the managers and directors are not doing their jobs, whose responsibility is it to make sure they do?"

A hush would fall over the room. After a few moments of awkward silence, someone would break the tension by changing the subject. I never witnessed the team's willingness to confront the issue. It became one of the main reasons that organization failed to reach its potential. Senior leaders would not take accountability for the unachieved results of their subordinates. The answer to the question is painfully obvious. It's the senior managers' job to make sure those in middle management who report to them do their jobs. If senior managers don't require middle managers to take accountability, the senior managers aren't doing their own jobs. If the CEO allows that to continue, a culture of no accountability is inevitable. Sadly, it happens far too often.

Research conducted by the Studer Group, a consulting firm in Pensacola, Florida, reveals that about 30 percent of the people in any organization will do what they're supposed to do regardless of what anyone else says or does. These are called high performers, and taking accountability for their own actions is one of their key attributes. It's what leaders really love about them. About 60 percent of the people will only do what they're supposed to do if someone is paying attention. That's why every team needs a leader and why peer-to-peer accountability is so important. Studer Group calls this group middle performers. High performers will generally help the leader require middle performers to take accountability. The remaining 10 percent aren't going to do what they're supposed to do no matter what. These are called low performers, the actively disengaged who are a thorn in your side.

I call these three groups drivers, doers, and draggers. The leader's responsibility is to recognize and support the *drivers*, coach the *doers* to higher performance, and move the *draggers* up or out. A strong culture of accountability will feed the human performance engine. It's the leader's job to create it.

Accountability is one of the most talked about issues among teams today yet perhaps the least understood and practiced. It is primarily a one-on-one activity between leader and team member. It's not a team sport. I've witnessed too many leaders trying to address the poor performance of an individual team member within a group meeting context. It just doesn't work. The dragger doesn't think the leader's talking to them, and the drivers and doers wonder why they're involved in the discussion. Leaders must create accountability one team member at a time.

The process of accountability is actually very simple. According to safety management expert Dr. Dan Petersen's *Authentic Involvement*, there are four steps in the accountability process. Define what's expected, train to enable performance, measure to ensure quality execution, and provide feedback for reinforcement of right performance and correction of wrong performance.

To complement the four steps of accountability, there are three particular *moments of truth* when the leader's behavior is critical—at the beginning of the relationship, in daily interactions, and at the periodic summary. Here are three tools to help you optimize each of the three moments of truth.

The Beginning of the Relationship

The tool for this critical first interaction is the *Ninety-Day Orientation Checklist*. I first mentioned this tool in chapter 15 under stage one of the P^4 Performance Process, creating perpetual understanding. In the appendix, you'll find a list of things to do in the first ninety days in order to set up your culture of accountability with your new team member, followed by an agenda for what to cover in each of the thirteen weekly meetings during the first ninety days.

While these tools are designed primarily for use inside a larger organization, the concept can be tailored to fit any environment. The idea is to clearly communicate what's expected and how it will be measured. This process will also enable you to begin equipping the new team member to take personal accountability for his or her role and self-manage effectively. If you take this process seriously, you'll be amazed by how your team members respond. They will learn to take accountability and self-manage their work—and they'll begin to tell others what a great team they've joined and what a wonderful leader they work with.

Daily Interactions

Once expectations are clearly set, your task is to reinforce and redirect behavior on a daily basis. As mentioned in chapter 15, the rule of thumb is *when you see it, say it*. Accountability means that the individual takes responsibility for doing his or her work. However, it's the leader's role to provide regular feedback to reinforce right behaviors and correct wrong ones.

To lead accountability on a daily basis, the leader must get out of their office and interact with staff. The old term for this is MBWA, managing by walking around. However, just walking around is not enough. It must have a purpose. Pay attention to the performance of others as it relates to the eight behavior outcomes and say something when you see it. It's best to be specific and immediate with your feedback.

Typically, the most important concerns for drivers are positive reinforcement and opportunities for development. Spend time with them to learn what they do well so you can pass it on to others. These high performers should become your mentors and trainers. You may want to create a think tank from your driver group to help you brainstorm continuous improvements to move the team forward.

For doers, the key is positive reinforcement and constructive coaching. Usually, doers perform well on a regular basis and just need encouragement to take it to the next level. Use the guide in chapter 15 to help you frame those discussions and interactions.

For draggers, the only options are immediate performance improvement or removal from the team. Don't play around with draggers. Deal with them swiftly and fairly. The sooner you do, the better you and your team will be. The conversation guide in chapter 15 will help you conduct those discussions appropriately.

Characteristics of Drivers, Doers, and Draggers

To properly address individual performance on a daily basis, you'll need to be able to quickly categorize the type of performance you're observing. These characterizations should help you determine whether you have a driver, a doer, or a dragger.

Drivers are self-starters. They require very little oversight or supervision, and you can count on them to do their work with consistent accuracy. They are highly competent, enabling you to hold them up as role models of excellence to other team members. If they possess the desire and potential to teach others, they can become your mentors and trainers. At the very least, they welcome other people observing their performances as demonstrations of excellence. They volunteer above and beyond the expectations of their roles and frequently serve on organizational change teams. They help the leader observe and reinforce behaviors of other team members and have learned how to appropriately address a peer who is performing poorly. They are role models of team principles and standards, and they encourage others to emulate them.

They build strong, high-trust relationships with other team members, are leaders in solving problems and resolving team conflicts, and aggressively initiate positive changes to make things better. That's why they're called drivers. When extra needs arise, they quickly offer help. They confront disrespectful behaviors in others and are role models of service excellence. They are extremely efficient and productive, yet humble and meek. When someone praises them for the great work they do, they typically say, "I was just doing my job." They're a joy to have on the team and a pleasure to be around. The more drivers you have, the better.

Doers are extremely valuable as well. They possess many of the characteristics of drivers, absent the teaching, role modeling, and going above and beyond. They are positive contributors to the team who consistently do what's expected of them. They are very reliable team members who prefer to do their work and be left alone. They usually do their work well, hence the name doer. They have no desire to teach others and are more reluctant than the drivers to volunteer for things outside of their own roles. They prefer to leave confronting disrespectful behaviors in others up to the leader or the drivers. They're pleasant to work with. These are the folks you rely on day in and day out to produce good work. They're the core of the team. They need you to provide positive encouragement for the things they do well and constructive coaching to improve their performances.

The more you encourage the good things they do, the less you'll have to deal with the bad.

> *79. The more you encourage the good things people do, the less you'll have to deal with the bad.*

Draggers are the troublemakers, the actively disengaged team members who make life miserable for everyone around them. Team leaders can usually identify draggers easily because they demand so much time and attention. They're painful and time consuming to deal with. Most people on the team view them as negative contributors. They may be rude, selfish, prone to gossip, and complain frequently. Sometimes, they can masquerade as highly competent in their work.

If I had a dime for every time I've heard, "They're a great worker—it's just that nobody wants to work with them," I'd be a wealthy man. For some reason, we've brainwashed ourselves into thinking that if someone is technically strong, it's okay for them to be interpersonally weak. The definition of a great team member must include both. That's such an important statement that I'm going to emphasize it.

> *In a culture of excellence, the definition of a great team member must include demonstrating strength in both the technical skills of the role and the interpersonal skills of team interaction.*

Draggers drag the team down. Someone who is good with customers but terrible with teammates is a dragger. Treat them as such, and you'll earn the respect of your drivers and doers in the process. Your team will become known as one that everyone wants to join.

In which category do you think your leaders and peers would place you? Are you a driver, a doer, or a dragger? How do you feel about your answer?

The Periodic Summary Discussion

A high-accountability culture requires regular summary performance discussions with each individual on the team. When you know you'll have to report the results of your activity to someone on a regular basis, you're much more likely to take it seriously and perform them better.

The *periodic summary discussion* provides the opportunity for drivers to have their contributions formally recognized, doers to have their contributions formally reinforced, and draggers to get formally noticed. The frequency of the periodic summary discussion will depend upon whether the individual is a leader or a rank-in-file team member. For leaders, there should be a monthly summary discussion. For team members, there should be at least a quarterly summary discussion.

In chapter 15, we discussed how to conduct the team member quarterly discussion. In the appendix, you'll find a tool to use when conducting a leader discussion. This pillar-based tool provides a guide to ensure that the boss leader and subordinate leader cover critical aspects that drive team and organizational results. That's accountability!

> 80. *Excellence requires consistency in accountability.*

Optimize your interaction when you begin the relationship, interact daily to provide feedback, and conduct your periodic summary discussions diligently. You'll create a culture of high accountability with a reputation for getting great results.

There's one more thing I need to cover on accountability before we move on—the *Achilles' heel*. None of this will work worth a hill of beans if it doesn't start at the top. As our example at the beginning of this section illustrates, the CEO must lead the way or the culture will begin to deteriorate. The top leader must use these tools with their senior teams, who must use them with their directors, who must use them with their managers, who must follow through by using the team member tools with their staff. If there's a break in the chain anywhere along that path, the system will begin to corrode.

It will start as a small cancer cell, infecting only the area it directly impacts. However, over time, the cancer will spread to other areas as others learn of the inconsistency in execution. If leaders at any level are allowed to continue without practicing accountability, you have no hope of sustaining excellence. Excellence requires consistency in accountability.

3. Lead with Passion

> No organization will rise above the passion
> of the leader.
> —Ken Blanchard

> A great leader's courage to fulfill his vision comes
> from passion, not position.
> —John Maxwell

Passion, defined as intense enthusiasm or devotion to a thing, has fueled history's worst atrocities and its greatest achievements. Its etymology has evolved from its original Latin meaning as the suffering of Christ on the cross to its old French meaning as strength of feeling, capable of suffering. A person of passion has intense devotion and enthusiasm for a cause and is willing to suffer for it. Passion serves as a contagion that inspires energy for the vision of excellence from followers. Conveyed with knowledge and high merit, passion will lead to great things. Excellence demands passion fueled by virtue and knowledge—knowledge of who you are and why you are here expressed with the best interests of those you lead in mind.

> It is fine to be passionate provided
> the purpose is good.
> —Galatians 4:18 (NIV)

> It is not good to have passion without knowledge.
> —Proverbs 19:2 (NIV)

What does passion look like in a leader? What does it take for you to be able to demonstrate passion with knowledge and virtue so you can inspire others to join you in your quest for excellence?

In the early 1980s, President Ronald Reagan delivered a speech on national television that demonstrated his passion for the idea of America. He was elected to office in 1980 at a time when the country was wounded from high inflation, soaring unemployment, and long gas lines. The nation had recently endured a crisis in Iran, in which Islamic students and militants had held fifty-two Americans hostage at the American embassy for 444 days. Their release immediately following Reagan's inauguration in January 1981 brought relief to the country, but citizens were still pessimistic and struggling.

Amidst this environment, Ronald Reagan spoke to the nation from the Oval Office. He appeared to speak from the heart with sincere compassion and concern for America. He expressed his optimism about America and its people, touting her as the greatest nation on the planet comprised of the most innovative and courageous people in the world. He made citizens feel good about being Americans again. It was obvious he loved his country and possessed an immense passion for all it had to offer. His passion and enthusiasm for America infected many citizens that night.

President Reagan is regarded as one of the greatest presidents in American history largely because of his ability to demonstrate his passion for his country and to make citizens feel good about being a part of it. He spoke with authenticity and conviction for a cause that was just and virtuous. His passion was contagious. America improved and entered a period of prosperity unequalled in her history. Passion in a leader is a powerful force for change.

81. Passion energizes excellence.

Thankfully, you don't have to be a superb orator like Ronald Reagan to demonstrate passion. Many strong leaders lack excellence in their oratory. So what exactly does passion look like?

No one would deny that Mahatma Gandhi, Mother Teresa, and Dr. Martin Luther King demonstrated intense passion for their respective causes. It could be observed as a fire in their eyes ignited by powerful determination. It burned with intense enthusiasm that was visible in their facial expressions. As passion is communicated, the heart begins to pump faster than normal, blood pressure rises, and body posture stretches tall and leans forward. Voice tone and pitch convey power. Words express strength and confidence in an almost uncontrollable energy from deep within. Passion is borne in the depths of the spirit from a belief in doing something right and good that will be of benefit to others (virtue). It is as though you're involved in something that you were specifically designed and created to do. The object of your passion is aligned with your purpose in life, generating the perseverance to see it through. You believe you've been called to a virtuous journey that is destined to succeed. It's exciting, adventurous, and right. You are committed to its fruition. You are sold out to the dream, and others can see it. Authenticity, truth, candor, virtue, honor, and knowledge are all demonstrated elements of passion. Those behaviors, attitudes, and expressions draw others to your vision.

Everyone has a seed of passion within. It must be discovered, not created. Passion emerges when you gain depth of insight into who you truly are. The key to leadership excellence is to discover your passion and deploy it fervently so that others are inspired to follow you.

Discovering Your Passion

When I was younger, I had a passion for acquiring wealth. My goal was to be a millionaire by age thirty. I was passionate and determined. By twenty-nine, though, I had made a mess of my life in passionate pursuit of that goal and was far from acquiring financial wealth. What happened? Why did my passion lead to destruction and despair rather than excellence and success? It was because the passion was not aligned with my life's purpose. I didn't even have a clue what my life's purpose was. All I knew was that I wanted to be rich, to be able to buy anything I wanted, to do anything I wanted, and to be anything I wanted any time I wanted. My passion was not based in knowledge and virtue. It was based in selfishness and greed. Now in my fifties, I know that my pursuit of wealth didn't align with who I am, why I'm here, or where I'm going. In my twenties, I was ignorant of those critical elements of passion. I didn't know myself well enough to be able to find my passion and target it in an honorable direction.

The key to discovering your passion lies in the quest to discover yourself. Who are you? Why are you here? Where are you headed in life? What have you been uniquely designed to love to do? If you can find the answer to those questions, you'll discover the source of your passion. Find your passion and apply it honorably. Only then will you experience true excellence and make a significant positive impact on the world around you.

The house of excellence model explained in this book is designed to help you find your passion and pursue it with honor. There are five basic steps to discovering your passion.
1. Lay a solid foundation for your life by determining your mission, vision, principles, and standards (chapters 3-7).

2. Assess your current state and compare it to your vision for the future (chapters 8-12 and chapter 16).
3. Set goals in the five pillars of performance and measure your progress (chapters 13-15).
4. Apply the lessons of effective leadership to inspire others to join you (chapter 17).
5. Understand your unique SHAPE.

SHAPE is an acronym coined by author Rick Warren in his bestseller *Purpose Driven Life*. Erik Rees explored Warren's process in further detail in his book *S.H.A.P.E.* The acronym stands for spiritual gifts, heart, abilities, personality, and experiences. When you analyze those five areas in yourself, you will have discovered your unique shape. You can then begin to better understand who you are and why you're here. Let's take the five areas one at a time as I paraphrase what Warren and Rees teach us about understanding our shapes.

Your Unique Shape

Spiritual Gifts

If that term offends you, remember that human beings are spiritual creatures. Your spirituality is one of the seven areas you must explore if you desire a high-quality life. Think of it as the special talents or gifts born into you. Everyone would agree that Michael Jordan was gifted as a basketball player. Frank Sinatra was gifted with a crooner's voice. Ronald Reagan was a gifted orator and communicator. Zig Ziglar was a gifted motivator and speaker. My wife is a gifted musician. Gallup defines a *talent* as any pattern of behavior that can be productively applied. We all have talents and gifts. You'll need to discover yours and begin developing them to their fullest potential.

If you Google the phrase *talent assessments,* you'll find many tools to help you discover your gifts. One of my favorites is Gallup's StrengthsFinder Survey. Through research, Gallup has discerned thirty-four talent themes in the human condition. This survey will show you how they rank in your life. You can find the survey at www.strengthsfinder.com and learn more about the process from *StrengthsFinder 2.0*. There is also a more in-depth insight into *spiritual gifts* for those who have experienced a spiritual conversion. Google *spiritual gifts inventory* for more resources. One of my favorites is the *Wagner Modified Houts Questionnaire*. You can learn more about it in Peter Wagner's *Your Spiritual Gifts*.

Heart

In Warren's model, heart is used to describe the combination of your hopes, interests, ambitions, dreams, and affections. It is the source of your motivation. What is it you feel in your heart you're designed to love to do? Your heart determines why you say the things you say, feel the things you feel, and do the things you do. Just as you have a physical heartbeat that sustains your body, you also have an emotional heartbeat that races when you think about the things that really turn you on. It's built in. You instinctively prefer some things to others. Some things radically excite you, and others bore you to tears. There are two indications that you're operating with heart—enthusiasm and effectiveness. If, while doing a thing, you have intense excitement and you're good at it, you're probably experiencing a heart desire.

Just last night, my wife and I were taking a golf cart ride through the community. I had just completed a survey of the quality of life in America as research for chapter 18 and e-mailed it to my research group. On the ride, the survey was still on my mind. I looked over at Debbie and said, "You know, honey, I just love doing surveys. They really float my boat." I continued to describe what had happened and how excited I was about it. That's an indication that I was operating with heart. Conducting surveys really turns me on. I know that probably sounds weird to many of you, but the survey process is one of the areas of my expertise that I really enjoy. It's built into who I am.

What are you truly interested in? What really turns you on so much that you would continue to do it even if you didn't get paid for it? What do you really love to do? What is your heart's desire?

Abilities

Only *you* can be you. There is no other *you* in this world. No one has the exact mix of skills and capabilities as you. You're unique, and no one else on earth will ever be able to play the role designed for you. Your *abilities* are your aptitude, your capacity to contribute.

While your heart is what you truly love to do, your abilities are the things you do well. Here are some examples of abilities people have: artistic ability, architectural ability, administering, baking, carpentry, coaching, debating, designing, embroidering, engineering, engraving, farming, fishing, gardening, inventing, leading, managing, masonry, making music, needlework, painting, planting, philosophizing, poetry, sailing, selling, tailoring, teaching, and writing. There's a place in this world where your specialties can shine and you can make a difference. It's up to you to find that place.

You are the only person on earth who can use your abilities. No one else can play your role because they don't have the unique shape that has been designed into you. To discover your passion, you must seriously examine your strengths and weaknesses. Whatever you're good at, you should be doing. Are you?

Personality

Your *personality* or disposition affects how and where you use your gifts and abilities. Two people may have the ability to encourage others, but if one is an introvert and the other an extrovert, they will express themselves in different ways. Similarly, when you're forced to serve in a manner that is out of character for you, it creates tension and discomfort, requires extra energy and effort, and produces marginal results.

Psychologists have perfected several tools to help you gain understanding of your unique personality characteristics. One such tool is the Myers-Briggs Type Indicator (MBTI). First published in 1962 by Katharine Cook Briggs and her daughter Isabel Briggs Myers, it is a psychometric questionnaire designed to measure psychological preferences in how you perceive the world and make decisions. It is arguably considered to be the world's most widely used personality assessments. After completing the survey, the assessment scores your results and places you into one of sixteen personality types based on four combinations of opposing variables called dichotomies—introvert/extrovert, intuitive/sensing, thinking/feeling, and judging/perceiving. Once you've determined your profile, you can explore what the psychologists have to say about it in many different ways. You can access a modified free version online by googling *myers briggs test free*. Follow the instructions online to learn about yourself. You can also google your four-letter profile and continue to explore. *Please Understand Me* by David Keirsey and Marilyn Bates can also help you.

Another very popular personality assessment tool in called DISC, a quadrant behavior model based on the work of Dr. William Moulton Marston. The DISC instrument examines the behavior of individuals in their environments, focusing on the styles and preferences of such behaviors. It classifies four aspects of behavior by testing a person's preferences in word associations. DISC is an acronym for the four aspects of behavior—dominance, influence, steadiness, and compliance. These four dimensions are grouped in a matrix, identifying characteristics such as introvert or extrovert, task or social focus, assertive or passive, and open or guarded.

These are only two popular examples. There are many others. All are designed to help you better understand your own personality tendencies so you can better target them toward a more productive and meaningful experience. Once you have a solid personal understanding, you can begin to understand others and work toward building strong, productive relationships of high trust.

Experiences

Your *experiences* in life help to shape and mold you into the person you are. Everyone's experiences are different. Warren suggests exploring your experiences in six main areas.

1. What did you learn growing up in your family?
2. What were your favorite subjects in school?
3. What jobs have you been most effective in and enjoyed the most?
4. What have been your most meaningful experiences?
5. How have you served others in your past?
6. What problems, hurts, thorns, and trials have you learned from?

Some of our most valuable learning comes through the difficult and painful experiences we endure. Some of my most powerful lessons have come through the pain of divorce, bankruptcy, abortion, failure, sudden loss of a job, and the death of loved ones. If you keep a right attitude about your difficulties, you can learn to appreciate them for the personal growth they can provide.

The good news is that life can be excellent, even through the painful experiences. If you're feeling pressure and resistance in your life today, if things are tough right now, remember that this is necessary for you to develop to your full potential. Persist and overcome through the pain, and you will eventually experience your increase. Remember that life is a journey of constant development. Learn to persist through the pain caused by pressure and resistance. It's the only path to true development. If you can learn to enjoy the process and express thankfulness for the pain, life will become an exciting daily adventure that brings you deep lasting peace and the fullness of joy. Regardless of the circumstances, your life can be excellent every day, even through the pain. Use your painful experiences to help you understand your shape and lead with passion.

> *82. Excellence needs passion fueled by knowledge and virtue.*

Passion must be based in the knowledge of who you are, why you're here, and where you're going. Gaining that knowledge may take some time, but it will be time well invested. View it as a constant journey of self-discovery that eventually leads to a life of joy and fulfillment. When you find your passion and express it in virtuous ways, you find your life groove. Operating in your personal and unique life groove is like soaring effortlessly to greater heights on the wings of eagles. It's a wonderful way to experience the fullness of life, and others will be inspired to join you. A person with passion is a powerful force.

Leadership is the critical raw material undergirding a foundation of excellence. Effective leadership can be learned. You can become an excellent leader who inspires others to voluntarily and passionately give their best every day when you build trust, create accountability, and lead with passion. Put the principles and practices from this chapter in place in your life, and you will be equipped to lead others to excellence as well. Now get busy—and enjoy the journey!

Summary of Chapter 17

1. Leadership is the key raw material for excellence.
2. Anyone can become an effective leader if they can learn to TAP into the Pareto Principle of Leadership Excellence—build trust, create accountability, and lead with passion.
3. Trust is the one thing that changes everything. Communication determines the quality of trust in relationships. Trust builds hope, and hope drives excellence.

4. The Pareto Principle of trust is captured in the acronym HRDNA, which stands for human relations, dependability (trustworthiness), never tell a lie (integrity), and apologizing when you're wrong (humility). Focus on these three areas, and you will build high-trust relationships.
5. There are four steps to accountability—define what's expected, train to enable performance, measure to ensure quality, and provide feedback for reinforcement and correction.
6. The three moments of truth where accountability is created are at the beginning of the relationship, during daily interactions, and during the periodic summary discussion.
7. Teams are comprised of three types of performers—drivers, doers, and draggers. Learn how to communicate with each type to create a culture of accountability.
8. Consistency in execution is required for accountability to be created and sustained. It must begin at the top and cascade through the entire organization. As the leader goes, so goes the team!
9. Passion must be based in virtue and knowledge—knowledge of who you are, why you're here, and where you're going. To create excellence, discover your passion and pursue it honorably.

Take Action

1. Make a list of all the people in your life who have taught you something about leadership. Set a goal to send them a thank-you note sometime over the next year for the impact they've had on your life.
2. Get a copy of Stephen M. R. Covey's *The Speed of Trust* and make sure you're demonstrating the four cores of credibility and the thirteen behaviors that build trust.

3. SWOT your current effectiveness at building trust, creating accountability, and leading with passion. Make a plan to develop from where you are to where you'd like to go.
4. Determine your leadership SHAPE.
5. Use the tools mentioned in this chapter to help you build stronger trust, create better accountability, and lead with more intense passion.

CHAPTER 18

America the Excellent!

Truth will ultimately prevail where there is pains to bring it to light.
—George Washington

Words may show a man's wit but actions his meaning.
—Benjamin Franklin

The government is the strongest of which every man feels a part.
—Thomas Jefferson

Those who deny freedom to others, deserve it not for themselves; and, under a just God, cannot long retain it.
—Abraham Lincoln

The above quotes are from four of the most revered men of American history. We hang onto their words of justice and truth. The American experiment, led by such men as these, had become a beacon of light for the world to admire. She had stood tall against the world's tyrants for more than two hundred years. Her language and monetary systems were adopted as the world's standard. Her capitalistic economic system and representative democratic republic has influenced other countries and peoples in many ways. Lately, however, many have begun to doubt the sustenance of this great experiment of personal liberty and opulence.

By late 2011, America had amassed over $15 trillion in debt. Gas prices had surpassed four dollars per gallon several times. Unemployment was above 8 percent, and the housing market had collapsed. Much of her manufacturing had moved overseas, and the stock market was struggling to recover. Corporate greed was running rampant, and the country had become politically polarized. Her people seemed to be losing faith in the government's ability to lead and govern effectively; 82 percent were saying America was headed in the wrong direction (Rasmussen Reports, Nov 2011).

Nearly two-thirds of Americans felt the government had lost touch, and 49 percent thought neither party in Congress represented the people anymore. Gallup surveys confirmed the condition too; only 9 percent viewed the economic condition as excellent or good, and 72 percent thought the economy would get worse. Only 13 percent approved of the performance of Congress. Some were saying America's fall, like that of the Roman Empire, appeared imminent.

> *I think our basic fundamentals and values as individuals and as a family have deteriorated significantly in the past twenty-five years. Collectively, we are no longer committed to a God-respecting, freedom-protecting, everyone-looks-out-for-each-other nation. No common mission or value system is in place. The political arena is loaded with professional politicians who are only interested in getting reelected. As individuals, they are more inclined to follow surveys and polls rather than making the right decision, hanging tough, and processing accordingly. They only make decisions for the short run, not the long haul. This is why there will be no change. Democrats and Republicans will continue to dig in to their own ideals. The divide in political philosophy will get bigger. No common mission, no commitment to a value based foundation—a stalemate for sure.*

There is far too little regulation of banks and financial markets. The income gap between the top 20 percent and everyone else has gotten too wide, at least in part because of a sense of selfishness that has affected those at the top. Our country will continue to struggle until we get religion and corporate influences out of our politics. Policies and laws must be based on science, facts, and research, not faith and beliefs. Too many people have forgotten that our government has to do what's right for all, not just the loudest, nuttiest, or most religious.

—Anonymous opinions from my *Quality of Life in America* survey, Nov. 2011

Why had so many come to feel as though America had seen her better days? How is it that what many had come to call the greatest human experiment of all time seemed to have lost her luster? In an effort to answer those questions, I decided to apply my house of excellence model to the country I love so much. A thorough examination of America through the lens of the house of excellence should shed some light on these questions. Come with me while we use the concepts in this book to assess the organization we call America.

Intent

I'm sure you've discovered in the pages of this book many of my personal biases and perspectives on the issues of life, politics, and religion. My purpose in this chapter, however, is not to persuade you to any particular political or spiritual bent, but to attempt to accurately assess America against the principles of excellence we've discussed. I've tried to approach these questions from my perspective as an organizational development professional absent any personal bias.

To conduct my assessment, I'll access documents in the public domain, including the Constitution, the Declaration of Independence, the Articles of Confederation, the Federalist Papers, and Thomas Paine's *Common Sense*. If I were to actually be commissioned by the president of the United States to do such a work, I would hold personal interviews with him, his cabinet, and key leaders of Congress and the government. I would survey all employees of the federal government to understand their perceptions of the organization in which they work and serve. I would survey a statistically valid cross-section of the citizenry to understand their perceptions of quality of life in America, service provided by government, and citizen engagement in the process of America. I would also conduct representative citizen and federal employee focus groups around the country to gain greater insight into the information provided from the surveys.

Of course, I'm not able to personally access the president, his cabinet, congressional leaders, other government leaders, or federal employees. Therefore, I'll have to conduct my assessment from information publicly available. Given that reality, please understand that we're conducting our assessment through less than optimal means. Nonetheless, I'll do my best.

Here's what I'll attempt to accomplish in this chapter.

1. Discern the founder's original intent on mission, vision, principles, and standards.
2. Determine how to measure progress under each of the five pillars of performance.
3. Assess the current state of America against those measures.
4. Assess gaps between current and future state.
5. Make recommendations to move her toward the desired future state.

Assessment of Original Intent

The Foundation of America

America's Mission

According to the Preamble of the Constitution, America exists "in order to form a more perfect Union, establish justice, insure domestic tranquility, provide for the common defense, promote the general welfare, and secure the blessings of liberty to ourselves and our posterity."

Adopted on September 17, 1787 by the Constitutional Convention in Philadelphia, Pennsylvania, and finally ratified on May 29, 1790, by the last of the thirteen original colonies, the Constitution of the United States describes the reason the thirteen states decided to unite. It provides the framework for the establishment of a federal government designed to work with the states, the citizens, and all the people within its borders and is the oldest written national constitution in the world still in use today.

Interestingly, the early exploration of America was motivated by other purposes. Christopher Columbus, reaching the Caribbean Islands in 1492, was sailing for the crown of Spain and searching for the riches of the New World. Spanish conquistador Ponce de León's purpose was similar as he came ashore in Florida in 1513. Most of the early visitors also explored the New World with similar purposes. The French, Dutch, and Spanish all sent explorers to claim new lands for their homelands. The first English settlers arrived at Jamestown in 1607, followed by the pilgrimage to Plymouth, Massachusetts, in 1620.

Some of the early settlers pursued riches, and others sought freedom from religious persecution in their home territories. Britain even used the New World to rid itself of some fifty thousand convicts. But it wasn't until the mid-1700s that the American colonies began to unite. According to the colonists, repeated injustices imposed by the English crown had reached intolerable peaks. By 1775, their patience had run out, the American Revolution against Britain had begun, and the new nation known as America emerged. America's evolution to national status was motivated mostly by perceived British injustices culminating in taxation without representation. The Preamble of the Constitution seems to capture best the intent of her founders and the reason she came into existence.

America's Vision

I did not find an explicit vision statement like you could find in most businesses and organizations today. However, from a study of the founding documents and a detailed word study of the principles and values they espouse, we can postulate what the founders may have envisioned with the establishment of the United States of America. They envisioned a place that would one day become *the greatest nation in the world.*

To understand the meaning of those words, we need a descriptive paragraph to create a clear word picture. Here's my speculation of what the founders may have had in mind:

> *For the future of America, we see a strong nation demonstrating freedom, justice, and equal opportunity for all of her people. All states, entities, government officials, and citizens are dedicated to preserving the nation's principles and values. Most of her citizens experience lives full of joy, peace, and security, largely due to the preservation of their independence, the reliance on their Creator as the supreme source of natural law, and the certainty of the ability to defend herself against any who would come against her. Her citizens are actively engaged in her sustainability, behaving out of a strong sense of duty to preserve her ideals and perpetuate her promises. Her government is just and*

> *efficient, a pure representation of those it serves and enjoying the enthusiastic consent of the governed. She is a world leader in commerce, education, and the pursuit of knowledge and is a model of justice, liberty, and prosperity for all people everywhere. She keeps her fiscal house in order and is considered to be the best place on earth in which to live. She is respected the world over and considered a model of communal excellence for all peoples and nations.*

America's Core Principles

To discern her core principles, let's review some of her most fundamental documents to see what we can find.

The Declaration of Independence

Authored primarily by Thomas Jefferson with help from John Adams, Benjamin Franklin, Robert Livingston, and Roger Sherman, and ratified by the Continental Congress on July 4, 1776, this document declares America's assertion of independence from the British Crown and establishment as a sovereign nation.

> We hold these truths to be self-evident, that all men are created equal, that they are endowed by their Creator with certain unalienable Rights, that among these are Life, Liberty, and the pursuit of Happiness. That to secure these rights, Governments are instituted among Men, deriving their just powers from the consent of the governed. That whenever any Form of Government becomes destructive of these ends, it is the Right of the People to alter or to abolish it; and to institute new Government, laying its foundation on such principles and organizing its

powers in such form, as to them shall seem most likely to affect their Safety and Happiness. Prudence, indeed, will dictate that Governments long established should not be changed for light and transient causes; and accordingly all experience hath shown, that mankind are more disposed to suffer, while evils are sufferable, than to right themselves by abolishing the forms to which they are accustomed. But when a long train of abuses and usurpations, pursuing invariably the same Object, evinces a design to reduce them under absolute Despotism, it is their right, it is their duty, to throw off such Government, and to provide new Guards for their future security.

The next section of the document contains a list of charges against King George III of England, demonstrating injustices and injuries experienced by the colonists. It notes the disappointment that their appeals to the Crown to relax the unjust policies had been unsuccessful. Many of the colonists had been very patient and sought to cooperate with the Crown, to remain connected, but the level of injustice became intolerable.

"Such has been the patient sufferance of these Colonies; and such is now the necessity which constrains them to alter their former Systems of Government."

"They [the Crown of England] have been deaf to the voice of justice and of consanguinity."

In the final section, the signers declare their separation from the British Crown. They state,

"That these United Colonies are, and of Right ought to be Free and Independent States ... and that as [such] they have the full Power to levy War, conclude Peace, contract Alliances, establish Commerce, and to do all other Acts and Things which Independent States may of right do."

Let's take a close look at the principles revealed and see what we can learn. I've listed them here in the order in which they appear in the document along with some of their more common synonyms and definitions to help us search for clarity and understanding.

- **truth**—fact, certainty, genuineness, reality, accuracy, exactness, legitimacy
- **self-evident**—manifest, undeniable, indisputable, obvious
- **equality** (created equal)—created the same, identical, alike, equivalent, comparable
- **creator**—maker, originator, designer, architect, author, initiator
- **rights**—civil liberties and privileges reasonably understood of the human condition
- **government**—administration, rule, supervision, management, direction, control
- **life**—existence, being, survival
- **liberty**—freedom, independence, autonomy, emancipation, self-government
- **happiness**—contentment, joy, bliss, pleasure, delight
- **justice**—fairness, impartiality, integrity, honesty, righteousness, virtue, morality, ethics, lack of prejudice, objectivity, neutrality
- **consent**—permission, approval, blessing, authority of the governed
- **safety**—security, protection, well-being

- **prudence**—carefulness, caution, discretion, good judgment, forethought
- **duty**—responsibility, obligation, what you have to do or should do
- **guard**—protector, sentinel, safeguard, watch, security
- **security**—safety, refuge, sanctuary, defense, protection
- **cooperation**—collaboration, support, assistance, teamwork
- **patience**—endurance, tolerance, fortitude, stamina
- **sufferance**—the power or capacity to endure or tolerate pain and distress; consent, permission, or sanction implied by failure to interfere or prohibit
- **consanguinity**—relationship by descent from the same ancestor; blood relationship; close association; connection
- **unity**—agreement, harmony, concord, together
- **freedom**—liberty, autonomy, independence, self-determination, sovereignty, free will
- **independence**—autonomy, sovereignty, self-government, freedom, liberty, self-determination, self-rule
- **peace**—calm, quiet, tranquility, harmony, serenity
- **alliance**—coalition, union, agreement, association
- **commerce**—trade, business, buy/sell, import/export, exchange

The Preamble to the Constitution

Perhaps another look at the Preamble would be prudent in consideration of our search for principles and values. I see several insightful words. Here are the new ones I'm adding to our list.

- **united**—joint, combined, unified, cohesive, integrated, amalgamated
- **union**—amalgamation, combination, blending, coming together

- **tranquility**—quiet, calm, harmony, serenity
- **defense**—protection, guard, security, cover, resistance
- **welfare**—well-being, happiness, goodness, safety
- **posterity**—all of a person's descendants; all succeeding generations. This alludes to the principles of longevity, permanence, or durability and of being able to sustain the union over time. The founders wanted America to last and her liberty and justice to be available to everyone for a very long time. I like the principle of durability for this concept.
- **durability**—the ability to continue to exist for a long time in spite of tough times; toughness, robustness, sturdiness, strength, resilience, stability, permanence, hardiness, endurance, stamina, strength, vigor, potency

Analyzing the Principles and Values

Let's now explore the principles in more detail to see what we can discern. Here's the whole list in alphabetical order for us to consider.

alliance	liberty
commerce	life
consanguinity	patience
consent	peace
cooperation	prudence
creator	rights
defense	safety
devotion	security
durability	sufferance
duty	tranquility
equal opportunity	truth
government	union
guard	united
happiness	unity
independence	welfare
justice	

First, let's combine those that have similar meanings. This will help us create a more manageable list.

1. Alliance means union. Union, united, unity, and one nation all mean blending together in harmony and agreement, integrated in one accord. Consanguinity means close association or connection. The authors of the Declaration of Independence used it to describe how the Crown of England had become deaf to their desire to remain connected to England. Consanguinity is a cousin of unity. Plus, it's a word not many people are familiar with that could create confusion. Cooperation means collaboration and support. That too, sounds like unity. Indivisible also means unified. I'm going to choose the word *unity* to represent the meaning of all of these words.
2. Consent is used in the definition of sufferance. Let's use *sufferance* to encompass both.
3. Creator and self-evident seem related. It's evident that the founders valued faith in a supreme being. Let's use the principle of *faith*, belief in and reliance upon a supreme being, to represent this concept. For the founders who didn't believe in God, faith might still have served as a guiding principle—faith in the self-evident goodness of people striving for the best life has to offer.
4. Defense, guard, safety, and security all have each other in their definitions. Let's use *security* for all of these since it seems to be the broader context.
5. Equal opportunity means a chance for everyone to experience liberty, justice, and the pursuit of happiness. America's opportunities should be made available to everyone. The founders viewed this as just and fair. Justice also means fairness. Nobility means goodness. It seems to me if we are just, equal opportunity and nobility will result. I'm going to combine them for now and use *justice* to encompass them all.

6. Independence and liberty are synonyms. Rights are civil liberties. I'll use *liberty* for all three due to its beautiful use and position at the beginning of the Declaration of Independence.
7. Happiness is in the synonym list for welfare, which means well-being, goodness, and safety. The framers used the word welfare in the Preamble, yet they used the pursuit of happiness in the first paragraph of the Declaration as one of the three unalienable rights. Additionally, the term welfare has taken on different meaning in modern times. For those reasons, I'm choosing *happiness* to mean both.
8. Peace and tranquility are synonyms. I like the simplicity of the word *peace*.

That's my first pass at the principles. Let's take a look at what's left.

commerce	life
dedication	patience
durability	peace
duty	prudence
faith	security
government	sufferance
happiness	truth
justice	unity
liberty	

We started with thirty-one principles and now we have seventeen. It's important to note that all of these principles are important. As we reduce the list to gain a sense of priority and core, we have to make decisions and judgments. Our goal is to discern the three to six principles the founders may have considered core to the formation of the nation.

5. Commerce and patience are only mentioned once and are deep within the document. For that reason, I'm taking them out of consideration as core.
6. Durability seems to be a very important principle. The founders obviously wanted to establish a strong nation that would endure the tests of time. That seems clear. But is it core? It's only mentioned twice in the documents we studied with the words "posterity" and "shall not perish." However, posterity was used in the Preamble. It seems logical that anyone establishing a new nation would intend for it to last. Surely any nation not durable would be destined to fail. Does it remain in the list or do we take it out? I'm struggling with this one.
7. Government is the method to be used to ensure the principles are kept. It's mentioned several times in the Declaration, but it is not a principle in and of itself. Governments can change; principles cannot. It's out.
8. Prudence means good judgment, discretion, and forethought. I contend it can be included in the concept of justice. It's out.
9. Sufferance and consent of the governed are important but I believe can also be included in the concept of justice and fairness. I'm taking them out.
10. Truth may be considered a synonym for principle. The way it's used in the Declaration gives insight to this. "We hold these truths [principles] to be self-evident." For this reason, I'm taking it out.

We're now left with ten principles to consider for the core.

durability	liberty
duty	life
faith	peace
happiness	security
justice	unity

This is a very strong list of principles. It's apparent that all of these were important to the founders. Remember that our task here is to discern the few most important core values. Jim Collins, in *Built to Last*, suggests that ten is still too many to be considered core; the core list is only three to six things. Core values are piercingly simple and provide substantial guidance that will rarely, if ever, be compromised. This is where our task becomes very difficult.

Life, liberty, and the pursuit of happiness were the first three truths to be listed in the Declaration. Liberty, freedom, and independence appear to be so core that the founders were not willing to ever compromise on them. Happiness was reinforced in the Preamble when they said, "to promote the general welfare" of the people. I struggle slightly with life because I don't find it used in any other documents. It seems so fundamental that our very existence is a basic truth we would hold dear that we may be able to consider its elimination as core.

Duty appears fundamental to the very reason the founders were willing to fight and die for liberty and justice. They felt it was their duty to throw off such government when it becomes oppressive and lacks the consent of the governed. Justice, unity, and security are included in both the Declaration and the Preamble in various forms. The Preamble also includes peace (tranquility) and liberty. Faith played such a significant role it was referenced in every document I studied and in the writings of most of the founders in some form. Unity, or some form of it, is also found everywhere. It even made its way into the nation's name, *The United States of America*, and in its original motto *E Pluribus Unum*.

All ten principles above seem core. Can we eliminate any of them? Would the founders be willing to preserve these principles regardless of the consequences that may come to them personally (including death) or regardless of changes in the environment? Are there any of them on the list the founders would have been willing to discard, even temporarily, if it became expedient to do so?

Using those questions as a guide, I might consider eliminating happiness. Many times, we've been willing to sacrifice happiness in the moment for the freedom to pursue happiness later. One might argue that preserving our tranquility, peace, and happiness has been at the root of many of our wars. The Declaration states that the pursuit of happiness is the unalienable right of man, not necessarily happiness in the moment. I think life is very similar. Our founders were willing to sacrifice their lives for freedom, justice, and the pursuit of happiness. We can say the same for peace. While our goal is to ensure domestic tranquility, we would be willing to sacrifice peace in the moment to preserve our hope for it in the future. We may discard peace, life, and happiness for a time in order to preserve our liberty and security. For this reason, I recommend we eliminate peace, life, and happiness as core—but preserve their important meaning and intent by including them in the vision statement description.

Would the founders be willing to compromise their faith or the concepts of justice, liberty, or security for expediency in the moment? I don't think so. At this point, I'm satisfied that we've embarked upon a set of core values our founders held and intended for America to never compromise upon.

Let's review. We've combed through the founding documents and discovered thirty-one principles to consider. We combined the ones that had similar meanings and eliminated ones that appeared to be of a smaller stature. Finally, we used Jim Collins's litmus test of questions to eliminate a few more. That left us with seven principles. I know our objective is three to six, but I don't see how we can eliminate any more. I believe the founders would have fought and died to preserve all seven of these. Ladies and gentlemen, may I present to you what I believe to be the seven core principles our founders intended for America.

The Core Principles for America
durability, duty, faith, justice, liberty, security, and unity

America's Standards

Standards represent specific critical behaviors we want every member of our organizations to strive to emulate. They demonstrate our principles and propel us toward the realization of our missions and visions. Leaders will model them, and citizens will strive to uphold them. There will be rewards for those who demonstrate them well and consequences for those who don't. *Are there standards of behavior the founders intended for everyone to emulate as we go about our daily lives in America? If so, what are they—and where can we find them?*

One might suggest we look within the text of the Constitution of the United States and in the laws and statutes within our legal system. That's where I decided to start.

The Constitution outlines the framework of the government and its relationship with the states, citizens, and all the people within its borders. It primarily enumerates the structure and powers of the federal government. The seven articles address the legislative branch (Article One), the executive branch (Article Two), the judicial branch (Article Three), relationship with the states (Article Four), how to amend the document (Article Five), the establishment of the Constitution as the supreme law of the land (Article Six), and the requirements for ratification (Article Seven). The Constitution has been amended twenty-seven times. The amendments deal with citizens' rights, provide more specific instruction about federal court processes, provide more guidance on the relationship between the federal government and the states, abolish slavery, and provide clarity for the operation of the three branches of government. What the Constitution does not do is identify specific behavioral expectations of the citizens that demonstrate the values.

What about the laws and statutes created by our legislative branch? Since 1789, Congress has enacted some twenty thousand federal statutes. I reviewed many of them and realized they do not address specific behavioral guidelines for individuals. They generally address areas of commerce and government and deal more with what people can't do than what they should do. That analysis also holds true for state and local laws. Today, there are far too many laws on the books for any one person to ever be aware of. Besides, most of them have been enacted long after the founders set up the framework for America. That's not a bad thing, but my interest at this point is more about understanding the founders' intents than the rules and laws put into place sometime after.

Then where do we look? I decided to approach this question the same way I have approached it in the other environments I've presented in this book. Let's look at our core principles and the documents from which they emerged to see if we can discern what the founders might have intended as specific behavioral expectations for all of the nation's citizens. To do this, let's clearly define each core principle.

What specific critical behaviors are necessary from every member of this organization in order to demonstrate the values and principles every day? Our goal will be to identify one or two critical behaviors for each core principle that we think our founders would like to have seen in every citizen of America. These standards of behavior then would better enable the citizens of America to do what is necessary on a daily basis to enable the mission and vision to be realized. In other words, the standards provide guidance for each American on how to behave in order to help build and sustain the greatest nation in the world.

Core Principles Defined and Standards of Behavior Recommended

1. **Durability** *n.* the ability to continue to exist for a long time in spite of tough times. *Syn.* sustainability, toughness, strength, resilience, endurance.

a. Always place the needs of the many above the needs of the few or the one when preservation of the union is at risk.
   b. Obey and comply with the laws of the land unless they require you to compromise on one or more of the principles.
2. **Duty** *n.* conduct based on moral or legal obligation; a sense or feeling of obligation. *Syn.* responsibility.
   a. Do that which you should or need to do in order to preserve the other principles and help accomplish the mission and vision, even if it means putting your own life in danger.
3. **Faith** *n.* unquestioning belief, trust, confidence in, reliance on, and allegiance to a Creator or God that does not require proof or evidence (*Webster's 4th Edition*); the assurance of things hoped for. *Syn.* confidence, trust, reliance, assurance, conviction, belief, devotion, loyalty.
   a. Trust the Creator for the wisdom, strength, and guidance to do what's right and needed to fulfill our mission and vision.
   b. Recognize that basic human rights are endowed by our Creator rather than man. Treat all human beings with respect and seek mutual understanding in all endeavors.
4. **Justice** *n.* the quality of being righteous; impartiality or fairness, sound reason. *Syn.* parity, integrity, honesty, virtue, morality, ethics, lack of prejudice, objectivity, neutrality, equal opportunity, egalitarianism (social equality).
   a. Treat others equally and impartially without regard to personal differences or bias.
   b. Respect and honor the political, social, and economic differences of opinion and differences in status.
   c. Demonstrate honesty and integrity in all interactions.

5. **Liberty** *n.* the sum of rights and exemptions possessed in common by the people of a community, state, or nation. *Syn.* freedom, independence, autonomy, emancipation, self-government.
    a. Exercise your free will as you see fit while respecting and refraining from imposing on the free will of others.
    b. Respect the rights of others and behave in such a way as to honor and protect them.
6. **Security** *n.* freedom from fear, anxiety, danger, or doubt; a sense of safety or certainty; the preservation of domestic tranquility. *Syn.* refuge, sanctuary, defense, protection.
    a. Never harm another citizen unless it is required to defend yourself, your property, your loved ones, or your country's principles.
    b. When safety or security is threatened, join with others in whatever way possible and reasonable to defend our collective rights, privileges, and principles.
7. **Unity** *n.* the state of being united, oneness; continuity of purpose. *Syn.* agreement, harmony, together, combined, cohesive, integrated, indivisible, consanguinity, cooperation.
    a. Always seek mutual understanding.
    b. In areas of disagreement, treat others with respect and tact.
    c. Once a decision has been made, agree to support it.
    d. Share grievances with someone who can help you solve the problem. Refrain from gossip and slander that destroys the unity of the group. Talk *to* the person, not about them.
    e. Consider the needs of others and the group above your own.

I'm not suggesting that these are the only standards there are or should ever be. I am suggesting that they may be a good place to start. Standards of behavior should be discerned and developed by a group of high performers who are capable of placing the interests of the organization above their own. My purpose here is to begin to understand the standards of behavior our founders may have developed should they have used the house of excellence model as a guide. I'm also suggesting that it may be worth consideration to identify, teach, and reinforce a simple set of behavioral standards for all citizens of the nation.

Pillar Measurements

Next, let's consider how we should measure America's progress toward the accomplishment of her mission and vision. *What are the things we need to measure in order to know how we're doing at any point in time? Are we moving toward our vision or away from it—and how do we know?* We'll consider them one pillar at a time.

The Quality Pillar

Attempting to measure the quality of the American experience has been an intriguing journey for me. Quality is always the most challenging and complex outcome to measure. Our goal is to provide excellent quality of life to all citizens. To help gain insight into current state, I studied the information available from government agencies and many nonprofit organizations. A list of those agencies and resources is included at the end of this chapter. I also conducted a survey of my own in November 2011 and consulted survey data from organizations such as Gallup and Rasmussen. Detailed information from the study is also available on my website.

From this extensive study, I identified thirty-five measures of quality for consideration as shown in the chart below. I scored each measure on a one-to-five rating scale, with one being poor and five being excellent, and generated an overall score for the quality pillar we can insert into our organizational scorecard. In a real situation, we would debate the rating scale until we achieved a methodology we could all agree upon. Here's how the rating scale works.

(1) Poor = < 50th percentile (worse than average)
(2) Fair = 50th-64th percentile (better than average)
(3) Good = 65th-75th percentile (roughly top half of the 2nd quartile)
(4) Very Good = 75th-89th percentile (the top quartile)
(5) Excellent = 90th percentile or greater (the top decile)

I scored each metric according to the scale above and weighted the more important ones higher. For example, on the unemployment metric, America is eleventh of eighteen countries measured. Since the metric is ranked highest unemployment to lowest unemployment, America places at the sixty-first percentile in that metric, (eleven divided by eighteen). A performance at the sixty-first percentile falls in the *fair* range of our measurement scale so that metric would receive a score of two. Applying this logic to each metric, we can calculate an overall score for the quality pillar.

Quality Metric	Weight	Result	Rank	%tile	Rating	Score
Quality of Life Index	10.0%	7.615	13/111	88th	4	0.4
Well-Being Index	0.0%	65.6	?	?	?	
Human Development Index	10.0%	0.91	4/187	98th	5	0.5
Net Happiness Measure	5.0%	84%	13/50	74th	3	0.15
Crime	6.0%	11 mil	1/82	2nd	1	0.06
Civil Liberties	9.0%	6	1/15	100th	5	0.45
Inflation Rate	1.0%	1.40%	35/223	84th	4	0.04
Standard of Living	9.0%	$31,111	2/34	94th	5	0.45
Tax Rates	1.0%	15.91%	112/141	79th	4	0.04
Unemployment	4.0%	8.60%	11/18	61st	2	0.08
Poverty	3.0%	12%	23/153	85th	4	0.12
GDP/capita	3.0%	$41,889	2/169	99th	5	0.15
Home Ownership	1.0%	67.40%	8/14	43rd	1	0.01
Homelessness	1.0%	1%	?	?	?	
Education: Tertiary	3.0%	37%	2/18	89th	4	0.12
Education Duration	3.0%	16.7 yrs	14/30	53rd	2	0.06
Literacy Rate	4.0%	99%	1/146	100th	5	0.2
Energy Usage per Person	0.3%	8.16 toe	1/18	100th	5	0.0125
Energy Production (coal)	0.3%	531 mil	2/65	97th	5	0.0125
Energy Production (electric)	0.3%	71.40%	116/223	48th	1	0.0025
Energy Production (nuclear)	0.3%	20.70%	19/223	84th	4	0.01
Oil Imports	0.3%	10.4	1/21	100th	5	0.0125
Oil Reserves	0.3%	22.45	14/97	86th	4	0.01
Environment	2.0%	44%	---	44th	1	0.02
Divorce Rate	1.0%	4.95/t	1/34	1st	1	0.01
Marriage Rate	1.0%	9.8/t	1/27	100th	5	0.05
Abortion	0.5%	6 mil	2/19	10th	1	0.005
Life Expectancy	5.0%	78.37	49/227	79th	4	0.2
Death Rate	1.0%	8.38/t	94/192	51st	2	0.02
Obesity	1.0%	30.60%	1/28	3rd	1	0.01
Heath Care Spending/capita	5.0%	$6,567	1/18	100th	5	0.25
Terrorist Incidents	6.0%	548	14/165	8th	1	0.06
Total Highways	1.0%	6.4 mil	1/118	100th	5	0.05
Motor Vehicles	1.0%	765/t	1/134	100th	5	0.05
Aircraft Departures	1.0%	8.5 mil	1/155	100th	5	0.05
	100.0%			**Total Score**		**3.67**

To determine the weights, I used the priority from my Quality of Life survey and tried to allocate heavier weights based upon it. To the items that did not make the top fifteen, I gave 1 percent or less weight. I also awarded higher weights to the general overall metrics (total of 25 percent), believing them to be strong measures of quality of life in America. I allocated the remaining 75 percent of the weight according to the priority feedback.

Using this logic, it's interesting to note how close the weighted objective composite metric of 3.67 is to the perceived quality score of 3.32 from my nonscientific survey. While the logic behind my numbers may be subject to debate, I'll use the 3.67 score for this exercise. For this to be a metric supported by the organization, we would need to debate the logic and come to consensus on the rating scale, weights, and actual components of the metric.

The Service Pillar

The service pillar measures the quality of the service provided as perceived by the customer. In this case, we'll consider the customer to be all citizens of America. The provider of the service is the federal government and all its entities. The objective is for the federal government to provide excellent service to the citizens of America. To assess this pillar, I want to know how the citizens of America perceive the service provided by the federal government. If we had generally accepted global definitions of high-quality governmental service, we could measure America against them and compare her globally. Absent those metrics, I'll use the available perception data.

I've chosen two methods to understand citizen perception—my own survey and the data provided by professional survey companies. In my nonscientific survey, I asked participants to rate the service provided by the federal government in each of the following areas: all agencies of the federal bureaucracy, the executive branch, the legislative branch, the judicial branch, and their overall perception. I used the same five-point scale defined under quality. The overall rating was a 1.97, which represents a perception rating close to *fair*. All agencies of the federal government received a 2.04 rating; the executive branch a 1.97; the legislative branch a 1.58; and the judicial branch a 2.28.

According to Rasmussen Reports, 80 percent of likely voters say the federal government does not have the consent of the governed. (As you recall, consent of the governed was one of the founder's key values). Forty-nine percent think neither party in Congress represents the people. Only 6 percent think most politicians keep their promises. Only 34 percent have a favorable opinion of the Federal Reserve.

Gallup reports that only 13 percent of Americans approve of the performance of Congress. Seventeen percent have confidence in the US Supreme Court, 15 percent in the institution of the presidency, 13 percent in the criminal justice system, and 6 percent in Congress. However you slice it, Americans hold a low opinion of the service provided by the federal government and its institutions.

Since the survey I conducted provides a measure on the one-to-five rating scale, I've chosen to use the 1.97 overall perception rating from that survey for the key metric in the service pillar.

The People Pillar

In this pillar, we want to assess the level of engagement of the employees of the federal government and of the citizens of America. Federal employees can tell us how to measure the federal government as a great place to work, and the citizens can tell us how engaged they are in the process of America. I also want some sense of how desirable America is as a place to live for others. How many people are trying to come here compared to other places in the world?

To begin assessing this, I asked my survey participants to rate their personal engagement levels and their perceptions of the engagement level of most Americans. They rated their own as good to fair (2.86) and others as fair to poor (1.89).

When I asked them about engagement activities, 83 percent said they vote most of the time, and 69 percent said they have volunteered to help out in their community. Nineteen percent said they have served in public office or have supported someone who served.

According to data collected and reported by Nation Master, Americans rank first out of seventeen countries with 77 percent saying they are very proud of their nationality. Twelve percent report being volunteers of political organizations. Although citizens report being very proud of their country, *citizen engagement* remains low.

Voter turnout is certainly an indication of citizen engagement. According to the Statistical Abstract of the United States and Federal Election Commission, 55.5 percent of voting-age Americans voted in the 2004 presidential election and 56.8 percent in 2008. Off-year elections generally turn out a lower percentage with 37.1 percent in 2006 and 37.8 percent in 2010. In the 1800s, voter turnout reached was high; it was 81 percent in 1860 and remained in the seventies or eighties until 1904. From a historically comparative perspective, *voter turnout* is a negative metric that needs to improve.

Immigration rates can give us an indication of America as a desirable place to be. Nation Master reports America as first in the world in new citizenships, total number of immigrants, and inflow of refugees; 20 percent of the total number of immigrants in the world live in America.

The US Merit Systems Protection Board issued a report to the president of the United States in September of 2008 concerning *federal employee engagement* issues. The report states that a survey of the federal workforce conducted in 2005 revealed that 35.3 percent of federal employees are engaged, 17.5 percent are not engaged, and 47.2 percent are somewhat engaged.

For our scorecard metrics on the people pillar, we'll consider using the perception of citizen engagement number from my survey, federal employee engagement, voter turnout, and immigration rates.

The Growth Pillar

In the growth pillar, we assess the amount of forward progress the organization is experiencing. The goal is to grow at a reasonable pace in a positive direction. For America, we'll consider population growth, GDP growth, growth competitiveness, and innovation.

The Finance Pillar

In this pillar, the goal is responsible stewardship of all resources entrusted to our care. We need to assess financial prudence and care and use of our resources. We'll consider budget performance, debt, and GDP per capita for the financial measure. (Note: If we were conducting this exercise in reality, we would need to include a measure of *sustainability* in the finance pillar. Since such a measure is quite complex, I've chosen not to tackle it in the framework of this text.)

Summary of Pillar Scorecard Measures

To simplify our scorecard and remain within the guidelines of six to eight goals total, I've italicized the ones I intend to include on the final scorecard. The other measures are important, as are many more, but our goal is to create focus and align action around key outcomes that will propel us toward the realization of our vision.

- quality: *composite score* of thirty-five measures of quality of life in America.
- service: *citizen perception of service* by the federal government
- people: perception of citizen engagement, *federal employee engagement*, *voter turnout*, and immigration rates
- growth: population growth, *GDP growth*, *growth competitiveness*, and innovation
- finance: budget performance, *debt*, and *GDP per capita*

Let's now assemble all the information we've gathered into a blueprint document for the organization of America.

America's Blueprint For Excellence

Mission

To form a more perfect union, establish justice, ensure domestic tranquility, provide for the common defense, promote the general welfare, and secure the blessings of liberty to ourselves and our posterity

Vision

To become the greatest nation in the world

Core Principles

Durability

Committed to the sustainability of our nation and its core ideology

Duty

Acting from a sense of obligation to preserve our union

Faith

Acknowledging our Creator as the source of human dignity and equality

Justice

Preserving equal opportunity for all and treating all citizens fairly and honorably

Liberty

Ensuring enduring freedom and self-government

Security

Protecting liberty and justice for all

Unity

Joining together with the interest of the whole above the self

Standards of Behavior
(for all citizens)

Durability
1. Always place the needs of the many above the needs of the few or the one when preservation of the union is at risk.

Duty
2. Do that which you should or need to do in order to preserve the other principles and help accomplish the mission and vision, even if it means putting your own life in danger.

Faith
3. Trust the Creator for the wisdom, strength, and guidance to do what's right and needed to fulfill our mission and vision.

Justice
4. Treat others equally and impartially without regard to personal differences or bias.
5. Respect and honor the political, social, and economic differences of opinion and status.
6. Demonstrate honesty and integrity in all interactions.

Liberty
7. Exercise your free will as you see fit while respecting and refraining from imposing on the free will of others.
8. Respect the rights of others and behave in such a way as to honor and protect them.

Security
9. Never harm another citizen unless it is required to defend yourself, your property, your loved ones, or your country's ideals.

10. When safety or security is threatened, join with others in whatever way possible and reasonable to defend our collective rights, privileges, and principles.

Unity
11. Always seek mutual understanding.
12. In areas of disagreement, treat others with respect and tact.
13. Once a decision has been made, agree to support it.
14. Share grievances with someone who can help you solve the problem. Refrain from gossip and slander that destroys the unity of the group. Talk *to* the person, not about them.
15. Consider the needs of others and the group above your own.

Pillar Measurements to Consider

Quality
- economics
- education
- environment
- family life
- health
- safety/security
- social issues

Service
- citizen perception of service

People
- citizen engagement
- federal employee engagement
- voter turnout
- immigration rates

Growth
- population
- GDP
- competitiveness
- innovation

Finance
- budget performance
- gross public debt
- GDP per capita
- sustainability

Assessment of Current State

America's Current Scorecard

Based on the measures we identified above, here is my numerical assessment of America's current performance in all five pillars. I weighted each pillar equally and made some judgments about rating scales that would need to be questioned and tested. If this were a real exercise, I would recommend a mastermind team of subject matter experts be commissioned to ardently deliberate the variables of this measurement system—which goals to include, how to determine the rating scales, and what weights to assign to each—just as I recommended earlier for other organizations. In my opinion, no one person (including me) is capable of accurately determining these things on his or her own.

Pillar	Goal	Wt.	Rating Scale 1	2	3	4	5	Result	Rating	Score Wt x rating
Quality	Increase the composite score of 35 quality metrics to 4.0 or higher	20%	<3.0	3.00	3.50	4.00	4.25	3.67	3	0.60
Service	Increase citizen perception of service to 4.0 or higher	20%	<3.0	3.00	3.50	4.00	4.25	1.97	1	0.20
People	Increase federal employee engagement to 50% or higher	10%	<30%	30%	40%	50%	60%	35.3%	2	0.20
People	Increase voter turnout to 75% or higher during presidential elections	10%	<40%	40%	60%	75%	80%	56.8%	2	0.20
Growth	Increase GDP growth to 5% or higher	5%	<3.0%	3.0%	4.0%	5.0%	5.5%	3.2%	2	0.10
Growth	Maintain growth competitiveness at the 95th percentile or higher	15%	<70%	70%	80%	90%	95%	98%	5	0.75
Finance	Reduce the gross public debt to 50% of GDP or lower	15%	>100%	100%	90%	50%	40%	101%	1	0.15
Finance	Maintain GDP per capita at 90th percentile or higher	5%	<70%	70%	80%	90%	95%	94%	4	0.20
	Total of all weights	100%							Total score	2.40

The scorecard communicates the following interpretations about America's current performance.

- Performance in perception of service provided by the federal government and the level of national debt she has acquired is unacceptable.
- America is doing okay in overall quality of life and is superior in gross domestic product per capita.
- America needs to improve her results in federal employee engagement, voter turnout, and GDP growth.
- America is performing at distinguished levels in growth competitiveness compared to other countries.

Weighting each pillar equally at 20 percent communicates that they are equally important. The weights noted within the pillars communicate that federal employee engagement and voter turnouts are equally important measures under the people pillar (both are weighted at 10 percent). They also say that growth competitiveness is three times more important than GDP growth and that reducing the national debt is three times more important than increasing GDP per capita. In this exercise, I used my own personal judgment for determining the weights. In a real scenario, they would need to be heavily debated and agreed upon by the mastermind group.

A SWOT Analysis of America

Based on all the information we've gathered thus far, we'll now conduct a SWOT analysis to discern America's strengths, weaknesses, opportunities, and threats. This understanding will help us craft a plan for improvement toward the desired future state—the vision for America.

America's Strengths

1. The foundation—mission, vision, and principles
2. Overall quality of life in America
3. Numerous civil and political liberties
4. Low inflation rate
5. Comparable tax rates
6. High standard of living
7. Low poverty
8. High GDP per capita
9. Strong tertiary education attainment
10. High literacy rate
11. Energy usage and production
12. High rate of marriage
13. Strong life expectancy
14. High healthcare spending per capita
15. Transportation system
16. National pride
17. Immigration—lots of people want to come to America
18. Growth competitiveness
19. Innovation
20. The American spirit

America's Weaknesses

1. High crime
2. High unemployment
3. Low percentage of homeownership
4. Homelessness
5. Low education duration
6. High oil imports
7. Environmental sustainability
8. High divorce rate
9. High abortion rate
10. High death rate
11. High obesity rate
12. Terrorist attacks
13. Low perception of service provided by federal government
14. Low confidence in the government
15. Low level of citizen engagement in the process
16. Mediocre voter turnout
17. High illegal immigration (11 million)
18. Low population growth (debatable)
19. Low GDP growth
20. High deficits
21. High debt
22. Complacency of the citizenry

America's Opportunities

1. Reconnect to the foundation
2. Assess criminal justice system
3. Assess tax structure
4. Assess education system
5. Evaluate oil import/export situation
6. Improve environmental sustainability
7. Assess perspective of family issues

8. Address obesity problem
9. Assess and improve security
10. Improve perception of service by federal government
11. Improve federal employee engagement
12. Improve citizen engagement and voter turnout
13. Operate within budget
14. Reduce the national debt

America's Threats

1. Lack of understanding and adherence to her founding principles
2. Weak sustainability
3. Confusing, complicated tax system
4. High unemployment
5. Inconsistent quality of education
6. Reliance on energy imports
7. Degradation of the family unit
8. Prevalent obesity and poor health
9. Political, social, and economic polarization of citizens
10. Racial tensions
11. Terrorism
12. Weak border control
13. Lack of confidence in government
14. Perception of governmental ruling class in Washington
15. Low citizen engagement
16. Citizen complacency
17. Expanding entitlements
18. Population growth
19. Expanding debt and deficits
20. Power of big business
21. Global economic instability

Summary Comments about America's Current State

As the surveys noted, many have claimed America is still the strongest nation in the world. Also noted at the beginning of the chapter, many Americans feel the country has lost her way and abandoned her foundation as expressed by the founding fathers. Others express that she is embarking on a new dawn of political, social, and environmental enlightenment—and needs to do so. The country appears intensely polarized around these two perspectives. Such division, if not navigated effectively, could become her downfall. Many great societies have suffered similar fates. Conversely, such division, if harnessed appropriately, could propel America forward. If becoming and remaining the world's greatest nation was the vision of the founders, its sustainability is indeed in jeopardy.

The *more perfect union* mentioned in her mission is sharply divided around several of her core founding principles. This separation at the core is perhaps her most critical issue to be resolved. Many presidential candidates proclaim their support of a return to original intent; however, based on this assessment, there is a sharp gap in clarity of understanding about what that original intent really is. This is due to the lack of specificity around these elements in the core documents. As you've noticed here, I've had to discern them. Once clearly discerned, several inconsistencies become evident.

From input provided in the surveys cited, we can discern some ideas about the principles being demonstrated today. Duty to support the preservation of the union may be affected by a growing sense of entitlement. Faith may have been compromised in the name of religious tolerance. Justice, virtue, morality, and ethics may have been eroded for selfish political or economic expediency. The liberties of the individual or the few too often receive priority favor at the expense of the rights of others.

Unity of purpose and intent has become sharply divided. Service to others too often takes a back seat to individual preference and self-preservation. The ideal of individual liberty has overpowered the concept of unity and self-sacrifice. Too many citizens are concerned primarily about what they personally desire or need as opposed to what's best for the whole country. Too many good citizens have become complacent, disengaged from the process. America's unity is in danger of dissolution and may be the greatest current threat to her sustainability.

America's current level of performance overall is fair to good, with a score of 2.40 out of a possible 5.0 on the balanced pillar scorecard. Quality of life in America today is a mixed bag. Overall, America is still considered by the majority of her citizens as the best place in the world to live. Most of her citizens experience a standard of living far above the rest of the world. Poverty and homelessness are relatively low. Individuals experience a level of liberty unsurpassed globally. Tax rates are higher than some countries, but they are lower than many others. Opportunities for advanced education are limitless in spite of rising costs. Life expectancy is long, and people feel relatively safe and secure in their homes and neighborhoods in most areas of the country. Her national defense is strong, and the faith of the citizenry to ward off attacks against her remains stable. In America, people are free to go wherever they desire, and her government has provided the best transportation system in the world to ensure ample freedom of mobility. Inflation is low, and gross domestic product is strong. That's the good stuff.

On the flipside, several aspects of quality of life present concerns. Incidents of reported crime are the highest in the world. Some personal liberties have come under attack, such as expression of religious views, the right to bear arms, and the right to be born once conceived (legal abortion). These issues serve to polarize and inflame emotions on both sides.

Unemployment is comparatively high. Although the literacy rate is high, American children are falling behind other nations in scholastic achievement. The war over traditional energy sources versus renewable ones is intense, and the issue of environmental sustainability is highly contested. In many ways, the concept of family is also a source of contention. Differences of opinion around issues of homosexuality, same-sex marriage, and civil unions divide the country. The divorce rate is the highest in the world, and more children are aborted in America than in any other country except Russia. America is the most obese nation in the world, causing tremendous pressure on the healthcare system. Terrorism threatens the security of many Americans, and the issue of stronger border security is divisive, but real.

Service and people pillar results also give some cause for concern. Perceptions of the level of service provided by the federal government are extremely low and the confidence that Congress truly represents the people and governs at their consent are at all-time lows. From the people pillar perspective, only one-third of federal employees are engaged in their work, and one-half of the eligible citizenry are voting in presidential elections. Citizen engagement in the process of America is low, and illegal immigration is a political hot potato.

Growth pillar results are mixed. Population growth and GDP growth are only fair, which may not be a bad thing in some respects, each being potentially a double-edged sword. Population growth is good for the tax base but bad for use of resources. GDP growth is good for prosperity but potentially bad for the environment. Growth competitiveness and innovation are strong, which bode well for future growth strategies.

Financially, America is teetering on disaster. Annual deficits run around 10 percent each year. Borrowing uncontrollably to fund industries, political preferences, and world causes has amassed a debt equal to above 100 percent of GDP at $15 trillion. Approaching $4 billion per day, interest on the debt alone has become astronomical, and many wonder if America will ever be able to turn the fiscal tide. GDP per capita remains strong, but unless borrowing and spending are better controlled, a financial meltdown appears likely. The great recession following the economic collapse of 2008 has undoubtedly impacted these results at least to some degree.

From this assessment, there certainly appears to be cause for concern about the current state of America. Americans, however, possess an uncanny ability to rally to the cause. The strength of the American spirit and the fortitude of her ideals and principles have the power to bring hope and future stability to this ostensibly bleak outlook. If she decides to do so, America can overcome her current weaknesses and threats to emerge once again as the strongest nation in the world. It's up to her people to unify toward a particular direction.

Strategies and Recommendations for Action

I want to compare the current state to the desired future state and make recommendations for forward progress. However, I have a problem. I'm not sure that the vision of the founders is the vision for today. There appears to be two perspectives on America's future as I identified in the political, social, and economic polarization postures. One of my recommendations will address this observation. For my purposes here—and so that I can continue with strategies and recommendations for action—I'm going to assume that America's vision hasn't changed from the one apparent in 1776 and that she still desires to be the greatest nation in the world.

To improve America, I recommend ten major strategies for consideration:

1. Gain clarity and unity on America's foundation, her mission, vision, principles, and standards.
2. Effectively address areas of concern in quality of life.
3. Improve citizen perception of service by the federal government.
4. Improve citizen engagement in the process of America.
5. Improve federal employee engagement in the government as a great place to work.
6. Improve gross domestic product per capita.
7. Maintain high growth competitiveness.

8. Balance the budget and reduce the debt.
9. Assess and improve performance management strategies.
10. Build a culture of leadership excellence.

Strategies for the Foundation
1. Gain clarity and unity on the foundation. Due to the polarization issues, reassess and gain unified clarity on the foundational elements of America—her mission, vision, principles, and standards.
    a. **Convene a Constitutional Convention**, similar to the one convened in the late 1770s that produced the Declaration of Independence and the Constitution, to reconsider and come to agreement on America's core ideals. I recommend two representatives per state be selected by the people of that state to convene for however long it takes to reach consensus. The congress should be facilitated by a team of organizational development professionals who have the capability of presiding impartially over the discussions, debates, and decisions. Emerging documents and decisions would require ratification of at least three-quarters of the states to become law. Current members of the three branches of government or the federal workforce would be ineligible to participate due to obvious potential of bias but could serve in advisory capacities as needed. Representatives should be qualified, capable, average citizens who care deeply about the future state of America evidenced by their acts of patriotism and involvement in the past. They must have the capacity to put aside personal desires and be able to represent the people of their state and the concerns of the whole nation. This could be a full-time effort for those involved so their economic needs while serving would

need to be met by private donations of the citizenry. Their jobs and careers should be preserved and made available to them upon their return, similar to the way members of the National Guard are treated.
b. **Run a pure *original intent* candidate for president.** In the presidential campaign underway at this writing, several candidates are presenting themselves as *Constitutionalists,* but I don't see anyone speaking to the seven core principles we've discerned from the founding documents. The polarization around those principles is where the battle for the conscience of the country is being waged.
c. **Integrate the principles and standards into the formal education system.** Once agreed upon, teach them in the public school system and in the immigration process to ensure that all citizens understand America's principles and their responsibilities as citizens to uphold them.
d. **Develop reward and recognition strategies** to acknowledge and reinforce excellence in the demonstration of the principles and standards.

Strategies for Quality
2. Effectively address areas of the quality of life in America that currently perform in the poor to fair range and develop action to improve them. Aspects of quality can be segregated into the following major group headings:
    - economics—inflation, tax rates and structures, unemployment, poverty, GDP, deficits, debt, classlessness, trade deficit
    - education—quality of education, literacy rate, availability, costs, secondary and tertiary attainment, equal access, mean duration

- environment—sustainability, conservation, preservation, waste management, climate, geography, natural resources, food supply, energy, pollution, emissions, water
- family—marriage, divorce, retirement, homeownership, standard of living
- health—quality of care, costs, structure of the healthcare system, preventive health, disease control, life expectancy, disparity reduction, obesity, mortality, respect for life
- safety and security—crime, defense, terrorism, immigration control, transportation
- social issues—drugs, alcohol, sexual abuse, child abuse, homelessness, abortion, homosexuality, pornography, runaways, battered women, child support, happiness, population, religion, civil liberties, class warfare, racial tensions

Note: this list is not intended to be comprehensive in nature but to provide an idea of how the quality issues can be organized and addressed.

a. **Appoint a team of no more than twelve experts** from the citizenry for each category and charge them with the responsibility to assess each quality criteria. Develop improvement plans for all those that score in the poor to fair range. Due to the current low opinion of Congress, current members of the federal bureaucracy could serve in an advisory capacity but not be allowed as voting members of the teams. Plans must include source of funding and strategies for execution.

Strategies for Service
3. Improve citizen perception of service by the federal government and restore confidence in all federal institutions.
    a. **Survey the citizenry every election cycle** to collect perception of service data. Use the data to develop action to improve citizen perception. Voting only serves to provide input on elected officials. We need a mechanism to assess the service provided by the paid members of the federal workforce. I would also recommend that state and local municipalities consider a similar strategy.
    b. To improve confidence and gain consent of the governed, **eliminate the concept of the career politician and the ruling elite** in Washington. Limit terms of congressmen and congresswomen to a level similar to the limitations on the office of the president. Elect members of Congress on an alternating election cycle to ensure consistency of thought and leadership. Require Congress to abide by all the laws they enact upon the people. Eliminate pork barrel projects and lobbyists and the ability of Congress to vote themselves pay raises and benefits enhancements. *(Note: the new Constitutional Convention should consider these issues.)*
    c. **Reevaluate federal employment policies** and bring them in line with generally accepted employment practices in private industry (i.e. pay scales, benefits, etc.)

Strategies for People
4. Improve citizen engagement.
    a. **Make it easier to vote**. Employ all available technologies to simplify the voting process. Eliminate the need for a citizen to physically get to a specific

place and time to vote. Ensure integrity in the process by requiring proof of citizenship.
   b. **Survey the citizenry** every election cycle to collect engagement data. Develop plans for improvement based on the data.
   c. **Equalize funding and media coverage for political candidates** to reduce the perception that holding political office requires a person to amass a fortune to be able to participate and endure excessive unfair scrutiny in the process.
5. Improve federal employee engagement.
   a. **Survey the federal workforce** at least every two years to collect data and develop improvement plans. Use a third party vendor to conduct the survey and strive for ninety-fifth percentile engagement levels.

Strategies for Growth

6. Improve GDP per capita.
   a. Since I am not an economic expert, I'll leave the specifics of this strategy to those who are. My recommendation would be to assemble such a group of experts and commission them with nonpolitical authority to recommend adjustments to the way the economy is currently being managed and influenced by federal systems.
7. Maintain high growth competitiveness.
   a. Eliminate barriers to innovation and technological exploration.
   b. Assess the state of the country's public institutions at least every other year to develop and execute improvement plans.
   c. Improve environmental sustainability. Ensure this objective is included in the sphere of focus of the quality team responsible for environmental concerns.

Strategies for Finance
8. Balance the budget and reduce the debt.
   (Again, I am not a financial expert, so my specific recommendations may fall prey to my personal bias. A similar strategy here as I mentioned above under growth may be more appropriate. However, I am a business major, have managed several businesses, and have worked as an executive in several businesses over my thirty-five-year career. Based on that experience, I would recommend we consider at least some of the following tactics.)
   a. Balance the budget.
   b. Eliminate pet pork barrel projects and personal favors from the economic decision-making process.
   c. Implement lean management strategies in all governmental agencies.
   d. Reevaluate federal employment policies to bring them in line with generally accepted business practices.
   e. Simplify the tax code.
   f. Implement meaningful consequences for leaders in the executive and legislative branches of government if spending does not match revenue.

Strategies for Performance
9. **Assess and improve performance management strategies** at all levels. Ensure differentiation of excellent versus mediocre or poor performance. Reward and recognize high performance appropriately. Deal with poor performance fairly and swiftly.
10. **Build a culture of leadership excellence.**
    a. Clearly define and communicate the qualities of effective leadership.
    b. Build and execute training programs for anyone elected or appointed to leadership positions.
    c. Assess actual performance of those in leadership positions against the qualities of effective leadership

on a regular basis and require them to take accountability for the engagement level of those who serve under their leadership and the citizenry they represent.
d. Reward and recognize excellence in leadership in many appropriate ways.

Application at the Community and Citizen Levels of Measurement

To complete our exercise, we need to understand how the organizational (federal) level of performance relates to the community and individual citizen levels.

Community Level

The task of each community would be to gain full understanding of all the pillar measurements at the federal level and select areas of measurement for the community that they can or need to impact. The idea here is that strong states and communities will build a strong America. It would be advisable for states and communities to develop their own blueprints, but they must align with and complement the Blueprint for America. As the Constitution states, anything not specifically enumerated in it is left up to the states and communities to determine. The Blueprint for America would be used as a guideline.

Individual Citizen Level

To measure individual citizen performance, we can use the eight behavior outcomes identified in chapter 15. The objective for each citizen should be to become a high-performing American citizen. We need to clearly identify what that looks like, create rewards and recognition for those who achieve high levels of performance, and institute appropriate consequences for those who exhibit low levels of performance. Accountability should be managed at the lowest level, probably the community level. To aid consistency across the nation, we could prepare a generic citizen performance assessment based on the eight behavior outcomes and encourage the states and communities to add specific performance measures relevant to their interests. We could then build education programs around the eight behavior outcomes to ensure every citizen understands the responsibilities of citizenry and how personal performance would be measured. As mentioned before, these should be integrated into the public school system and the immigration process and reinforced at certification checkpoints along life's path, such as driver's license renewals, voter registrations, etc. The generic tool might look something like this.

Quality Pillar
1. **Competence**—Do your neighbors and fellow citizens view you as a content expert on the understanding of your role as a citizen of the United States of America?
2. **Accuracy**—Do you perform your role as a citizen safely, accurately, and timely?

Service Pillar
3. **Relationship** –Do you build strong, positive partnerships with other citizens you serve and work diligently to meet or exceed their needs?
4. **Availability**—Are you fully present and fully available when others need you?

People Pillar
5. **Teamwork**—Do your fellow neighbors and citizens view you as a positive contributor to the American experience? Do you uphold the American principles and standards and encourage others to do the same?

Growth Pillar
6. **Resilience**—When things change, are you a part of the solution or a part of the problem? Do you positively and productively respond to change and adversity?
7. **Innovation**—Do you work toward continuous improvement, offering and implementing new ideas and methods to improve the American experience?

Finance Pillar
8. **Efficiency**—How well do you manage the resources of time, money, materials, and the environment entrusted to your care?

If this sounds ridiculous, think about the last time anyone ever asked you questions like these:

- What is the mission and vision of America?
- What are America's core principles and standards and their relevance to you as a citizen?
- What is your role and responsibility as a citizen of America—and how is it measured?

Would it be a bad thing or a good thing if we regularly reinforced these core concepts in the citizenry and built rewards and recognition efforts to reinforce them on a regular basis? I think you know my answer.

Remember that the more we encourage the good behavior in others, the less we have to deal with the bad. Perhaps thinking about citizenship in this way could bring new insights and strategies that would encourage excellence in individual citizen behavior.

Final Thoughts

The kind of America I want is an America where respect for others and self-sacrifice is highly valued; where the good of the many outweighs the selfish desires of the few or the one; where durability, duty, faith, justice, liberty, security, and unity are cherished by all people; where all citizens have confidence in their government and the ideals it espouses; and where the unique American spirit of innovation, courage, and resolve are enabled to thrive. I imagine your desire for America is similar. Perhaps if we really set our minds to do so, we can come together and restore America to her once-realized level of greatness.

> *83. Continual renewed commitment to the virtuous principles of excellence ensures sustainability.*

I hope this exercise has been as interesting for you to read as it has been for me to conduct. It's inspired me to further engage myself in my country and to do whatever I can to help ensure her sustainability. I realize we may not have addressed all the issues we would need to should we embark upon this journey in reality. My hope, however, is that this chapter has provoked your thinking around our concepts of excellence and perhaps inspired you to consider different action to make things better—to strive to be a positive contributor to the world around you in your neighborhood, your community, your state, and your country.

America is experiencing many challenges today, but she is also doing many things right! I believe she is still the best place to live and work on this planet. A continual renewed commitment to the virtuous principles of excellence shared in this book by all of us who call her home would do her good. I pray that the majority of decent, hardworking Americans will join me in reengaging in the American process so we can work together to make America great once again. With us all working in unity and common purpose, I believe she can once again become *America the Excellent!* I certainly hope so anyway for my grandkids' sake!

Summary of Chapter 18

1. The house of excellence model can be applied to countries as well.
2. America's mission is captured in the words of the Preamble of the Constitution of the United States—*in order to form a more perfect union, establish justice, insure domestic tranquility, provide for the common defense, promote the general welfare, and secure the blessings of liberty to ourselves and our posterity.*
3. The founder's vision for America, while not explicit, may have been for her to become *the greatest nation in the world.*
4. America's core principles are *durability, duty, faith, justice, liberty, security,* and *unity.*

5. Key outcomes of America's performance might include a composite score of thirty-five quality of life metrics, citizen perception of service by the federal government, federal employee engagement, voter turnout, GDP growth, growth competitiveness, the national debt, and GDP per capita.
6. America's current overall score on the criteria listed above is 2.40 on a five-point scale, representing an overall performance in the fair-to-good range.
7. Restoring the hope of *America the Excellent* is possible if we all purpose to join together in unity and common purpose.

Take Action

1. Study the founding documents to find out for yourself what the original intentions of the Founding Fathers were in creating the American system.
2. If you're a citizen of America, consider your personal level of engagement in the American system. Are you satisfied with it? If not, what will you do to improve it?
3. Use the individual metric in this chapter to assess your personal performance as a citizen. How are you doing? What do you need or want to do to improve? Are you part of the solution to America's concerns or are you a part of the problem?
4. If you're a citizen of another country, how can this way of thinking influence your country and you toward improving the overall performance and experience where you live?

Resources for Measurements

1. OECD via Wikipedia
    a. Healthcare spending per capita
    b. Standard of living
2. www.economist.com—Quality of Life Index

3. www.measureofamerica.org—Human Development Index
4. www.nationalhomeless.org—Homelessness
5. www.nationmaster.com
    a. Civil and political liberties
    b. Crime
    c. GDP (gross domestic product)—total
    d. GDP per capita
    e. Education
        i. Duration
        ii. Literacy rate
        iii. Tertiary attainment
    f. Energy
        i. Usage per person
        ii. Energy Production (Coal
        iii. Energy Production (Electricity by fossil fuel)
        iv. Energy Production (Nuclear)
        v. Oil Imports
        vi. Oil Reserves
    g. Environment
    h. Family
        i. Abortion
        ii. Divorce rate
        iii. Marriage rate
    i. Growth competitiveness
    j. Health
        i. Life expectancy at birth
        ii. Obesity
    k. Immigration rates
    l. Innovation
    m. Net happiness measure
    n. Population growth
    o. Poverty
    p. Tax rates
    q. Terrorism

   r. Transportation
     i. Total highways
     ii. Motor vehicles
     iii. Aircraft departures
   s. Unemployment
6. www.governmentdebt.us—gross public debt
7. www.usgovernmentspending.com—budget performance
8. www.well-beingindex.com—Well-Being Index
9. US Census Bureau via Wikipedia
  a. Homeownership
10. World Factbook via Wikipedia
  a. Crude death rate
  b. Inflation rate

CONCLUSION

Everyone can be excellent at something! Do you believe that now? In this work, I've taken you on a journey toward excellence to help you build it in any environment or endeavor you choose. During that journey, we've learned that building excellence in life is a lot like building a house. We explored starting with a strong foundation that included developing an inspiring mission and vision undergirded by strong principles and standards.

We built pillars of performance around quality, service, people, growth, and finance that helped us create a balanced approach to strategy and action. We added a three-layer roof that enabled us to measure our progress at the individual, team, and organizational levels and create a culture of accountability, alignment, and focus. We added the seven steps of strategy that enabled us to create a customized Blueprint for Excellence. And we explored how to build trust, create accountability, and discover and deploy our passions so that we can effectively lead and inspire others to join us in our quests.

It's been an exciting journey for me. I hope it has been for you too. Whatever you decide to do with this information is, of course, up to you. But I guarantee you this—if you seriously commit yourself to a life of excellence, you'll never regret it! Your life will be forever altered toward greatness; you will impact others in ways you may have never imagined; and you'll find joy, peace, and fulfillment for your soul in the process.

Excellence really does create a life that matters. Become an *excellentologist* today. Don't procrastinate any longer. Start building your house of excellence now!

With sincere encouragement,
C. David Crouch

For more information, visit my website:
www.excellentexperiencebook.com.

APPENDICES

A. Identifying Your Principles Exercise
B. Guidelines for Individual Performance Measurement
C. MVP Self-Assessment
D. Periodic Summary Discussion Worksheet
E. Ninety-Day Orientation Checklist
F. Orientation Weekly Meeting Guide
G. The Leader's Monthly Meeting Guide

Appendix A
Identifying Your Principles Exercise
(from chapter 6)

accountability	goodness
achievement	growth
accuracy	health
authority	honesty
availability	humility
balance	independence
change	innovation
cleanliness	integrity
commitment	joy
communication	justice
community	knowledge
competence	learning
continuous improvement	legacy
cooperation	love
courage	loyalty
creativity	money
customer satisfaction	optimism
decency	order
dignity	passion
diversity	peace
duty	perfection
effectiveness	quality
efficiency	recognition
fairness	relationships
faith/religion	resilience
family	respect
fitness	security
freedom	self-control
fun	service

simplicity	trust
status	unity
stewardship	urgency
storytelling	volunteerism
structure	wealth
teamwork	wisdom

Instructions:

1. First, circle the words above that mean the most to you.
2. Next, identify your top twelve.
3. Next, narrow the twelve down to your top six.
4. And finally, identify the two most important principles you value the most.

This exercise helps you begin to identify what you value the most. It's important to understand those principles in life upon which you are not willing to compromise. Your principles will help to guide your behavior along your journey toward excellence. Never compromise on your principles—no matter how tempting it may sometimes be.

Appendix B
Guidelines for Individual Performance Measurement
(from chapter 15)

These guidelines provide definitions and explanations to help you use the eight behavior outcomes to drive individual excellence in each of the five pillars of performance. The following guidelines apply to all eight behavior outcomes:

- Unacceptable—if even one area of this behavior outcome is unacceptable, the category must be rated unacceptable (Level 1) and a developmental plan is required. If performance does not improve immediately, the job is in jeopardy.
- Fully successful—if even one area of performance related to this category is not considered fully successful, this area must be rated needs improvement (Level 2) and a developmental plan is required. If fully successful (Level 3) status in all areas of this category is not achieved in a reasonable amount of time, a job role change may need to be considered.
- Distinguished—all aspects of performance in this behavior outcome are at perceptible distinguished levels; is a teacher, mentor and role model to others in his or her area of expertise.

Quality

1. **Competence**—Qualified and capable, exhibiting sufficient skill and knowledge to effectively complete assigned tasks. Do your customers and teammates view you as a content expert in your area of expertise?
    a. Unacceptable—Considered unacceptably weak in one or more areas of competence listed for this job role;

keeping certifications, credentials, mandatory learning up to date is problematic and noncompliant.
   b. Fully successful—Considered a content expert in all areas of competence listed for this job role. Self-manages certifications, credentialing, and mandatory learning requirements and keeps them up to date.
   c. Distinguished—Is a teacher, mentor, and role model to others.

2. **Accuracy**—Safe, careful, precise delivery of products and services that lacks errors and conforms exactly to standards and targets. Do you deliver your products and services safely, accurately, and timely?
   a. Unacceptable—Too many noticeable unsafe acts, errors and/or complaints; careless about quality of work.
   b. Fully successful—Involved in no preventable accidents or unsafe behaviors; errors and/or complaints are unnoticeable or insignificant; careful execution of consistent high-quality work.
   c. Distinguished—Makes valid safety suggestions and voluntarily implements improvements; helps monitor and improve the quality of others.

Service

3. **Relationship**—Connectivity created through service to others. Do you build a strong, positive relationship with every guest you serve, both internal and external, and work diligently to meet his or her needs?
   a. Unacceptable—Ignores or repeatedly violates standards of behavior; builds poor relationships with guests; poor execution of the CARE model of service; treats guests as an inconvenience; rude or inattentive;

receives noticeable complaints; demonstrates little or no empathy for the guest; sloppy and unprofessional; no compliments during the period; improper use of keywords and follow-up phone calls; ignores service recovery.
  b. Fully successful—Demonstrates standards of behavior on CARE and service with every guest; respectful, friendly, smiles when appropriate, makes good eye contact, is tactful and polite; listens and pays attention to develop empathy for the guest situation; is fully present and fully aware in the presence of guests; projects a professional image in dress, posture, and manner; practices immediate service recovery when needed; receives compliments from guests at a reasonable level relative to the job role.
  c. Distinguished—Receives frequent impressive compliments from guests; role model of compassionate, attentive service, dress, posture, and manner; helps others deliver effective service recovery that leads to strengthened loyalty from guests.

4. **Availability**—Within one's reach, accessible; able to be contacted. Are you fully present, fully aware, and fully available when your guests or teammates need you?
   a. Unacceptable—Frequently not available to meet guest and team needs; attendance issues are noticeable.
   b. Fully successful—Always available to meet guest and team needs; attendance issues are negligible.
   c. Distinguished—Always available and helps to ensure the availability of others; attendance is never an issue. No unscheduled absences or attendance occurrences during the performance period

People

5. **Teamwork**—Collaborating effectively with others to deliver the highest-quality products and services on a continuous basis. Do your teammates view you as valuable, positive contributor to your team?
    a. Unacceptable—Frequently demonstrates disregard for company principles and values; overlooks trash and spills; avoids communication; is involved in frequent unproductive conflict or personal attacks with others or avoids conflict; cannot be counted on to follow-up on commitments; is considered a negative contributor to the team; demonstrates low initiative and must frequently be told what to do; team loyalty is questionable; participates in less than 50 percent of all team and organization activities; is selfish and self-absorbed; shortcuts policy and procedure; is rude to others; blames others; overconfident about own abilities and brags about them; gossips, speaks negatively about others and the team.
    b. Fully successful—Honors and emulates company principles and values; picks up trash and cleans up spills when noticed; asks questions, listens and seeks mutual understanding with others; resolves conflicts and remedies problems with tactful confronting; word is bond, is reliable to follow through with commitments and responsibilities; considered a go-to person and positive contributor to the team; values and practices doing the right thing, is honest and trustworthy; little or no supervision of work is required; team loyalty is unquestioned; participates in 80 percent of all team and organization activities; remains team and guest focused, is part of the solution; results oriented; follows policy except when safety or quality are at risk; exercises sound judgment;

proactive problem solver; respectful of others; accepts full responsibility for own behaviors and outcomes; strong performer but humble about it; resists gossip; speaks positively about others and the team.

c. **Distinguished**—Role model on company standards and principles and encourages others to emulate them; role model of integrity, honesty, and trustworthiness; encourages others to pick up trash and clean up spills; builds strong, high-trust relationships; aggressively helps resolve team conflicts; helps the leader hold others accountable for their work; demonstrates positive organizational impact; frequently volunteers outside the job role; performance is so strong that the leader learns from them; role model of team loyalty; participates in 95 percent of team and organization activities; helps and encourages other team members to adhere to policies; solves team problems and is an aggressive troubleshooter; confronts disrespectful behavior in others; accepts responsibility for team behaviors and outcomes; always puts the needs of others ahead of their own; actively resists and discourages gossip.

Growth

6. **Resilience**—The ability to positively and productively respond to change and adversity. When faced with change, are you a part of the solution or part of the problem? How well do you handle change and represent the team?
    a. **Unacceptable**—Complains about changes and is slow to respond to change; a resister.
    b. **Fully successful**—Remains positive, focused, flexible, organized, and proactive through change; adjusts to

change quickly and quickly bounces back to a state of readiness and productivity.
   c. Distinguished—A teacher, mentor, and role model to others on managing up and handling change; aggressively initiates change and helps others manage through it.

7. **Innovation**—Continuous improvement, offering and implementing new ideas and methods to improve product and service delivery; initiating positive change to make things better. How well do you learn, grow, and improve?
   a. Unacceptable—Demonstrates little or no interest in learning new things or new ways of work; offers no new ideas to improve their work. Fails to complete performance improvement goals from previous period.
   b. Fully successful—Actively seeks personal growth and improvement; frequently finds new ways to do their work better; completes all continuing education expectations for the job role; completes all performance goals from previous period.
   c. Distinguished—Passionate, constant learner; helps others learn and grow; frequently finds new ways to help the team improve service and quality delivery; completes more continuing education than expected.

Finance

8. **Efficiency**—The ability to accomplish tasks with a minimum expenditure of time, materials, and money while preserving safety, courtesy, progress, and the positive memorable experience for the guest. How well do you manage the resources entrusted to you?

a. Unacceptable—Wastes or steals time while on the clock; wastes or steals money, and/or materials and supplies; slothful, lazy; offers no valid cost-saving ideas during the period.
b. Fully successful—Works productively while on the clock; handles company money, materials, and supplies wisely and with proper respect; recycles when possible; offers valid cost-saving ideas and improvements reasonable and relative to the job role; performs within the team's specific productivity guidelines.
c. Distinguished—A teacher, mentor, and role model to others on proper respect of company time, materials, and money; helps leader monitor the efficiency and productivity of others on the team and helps team implement more efficient, cost-effective ways to work.

Appendix C
MVP Self-Assessment
(from chapter 15)

Use this assessment to evaluate your personal performance. Rate yourself on each statement by providing the most accurate response according to the following scale:

Almost always	Most of the time	Sometimes	Hardly ever

Quality Pillar—Competence

1. I am viewed as a content expert in my area of expertise.
2. My guests come to me for advice.
3. I self-manage my certifications, credentialing, and mandatory learning requirements on time.
4. I am considered a teacher, mentor, and role model in my area of expertise.

Quality Pillar—Accuracy

1. I practice safe behaviors and prevent accidents and incidents from occurring.
2. I provide valid suggestions to improve safety and voluntarily implement safety solutions.
3. I protect confidential information and obey all regulations.
4. I am above reproach and encourage others to comply when it comes to the protection of confidential information.
5. I carefully execute high-quality work.
6. I help my leader monitor the quality of the work of others on my team.

7. My errors and/or complaints have no impact on team outcomes.

Service Pillar—Relationship

8. I demonstrate my organization and team service standards of behavior.
9. I am friendly, polite, and respectful with guests, smile when appropriate, and make eye contact.
10. I am considered by others as a role model on guest service and teach/mentor others to deliver excellent service.
11. I regularly look for and execute ways to wow my guests.
12. I listen, focus, and pay attention to my guests in order to develop empathy for their situations.
13. I exhibit a professional image with dress, posture, and manner.
14. I am considered a role model on our appearance standards.
15. When I become aware of an opportunity for service recovery, I own the problem and see it through to successful resolution.
16. I am considered a role model for our service recovery program and mentor others so they can deliver effective service recovery also.

Service Pillar—Availability

17. I am available for guests when I am on the clock.
18. My attendance behaviors have a positive impact on guest service.
19. I report to work and leave work when scheduled or expected.
20. I volunteer to cover others when a teammate can't make it to work.
21. I help my leader monitor and improve the attendance behaviors of others on my team.

22. When I become aware of a guest need, I respond within expected or appropriate time frames.
23. When I see others failing to respond to guest needs timely or appropriately, I bring it to their attention and tactfully encourage them to improve.

People Pillar—Teamwork

24. I honor and emulate our organizational principles and standards of behavior.
25. I am considered a role model for our principles and standards and encourage others to emulate them.
26. I am considered a go-to person and a positive contributor to my team.
27. I serve on organization-wide teams.
28. When I serve on organization-wide teams, I am a strong, positive contributor.
29. I am results-oriented and considered a part of the solution for my team.
30. I ask questions and listen to seek mutual understanding with my teammates.
31. I build strong, high-trust relationships with my teammates.
32. I am honest and trustworthy; I do the right thing.
33. I am considered a role model of honesty, trustworthiness, and integrity.
34. I am respectful of others.
35. I tactfully and appropriately confront disrespectful behavior when I see it in others.
36. I accept full responsibility and accountability for my behaviors and outcomes.
37. I accept responsibility for my team's behaviors and outcomes and initiate action with others to improve them.
38. I am very good at my job, but I remain humble before others.

39. My teammates would say I put the needs of the team ahead of my own.
40. I pick up trash and clean up spills whenever and wherever I see them.
41. When I see someone else pass by trash or a spill, I tactfully and appropriately encourage him or her to clean it up.
42. I work to solve my problems and resolve my conflicts with others in a positive and productive way.
43. I aggressively help others on my team solve problems and resolve conflicts in positive and productive ways.
44. Others can rely and depend on me to follow through on my promises and commitments.
45. I pull my own weight on the team, and I help my leader hold other teammates accountable for their contributions as well.
46. I do my work right without having to be told or reminded.
47. I volunteer to do work outside of my own job role.
48. I volunteer to do work outside of my own team.
49. I do my work so well that my leader doesn't have to check up on me.
50. I do my work so well that my leader and others learn from me.
51. I am loyal to my team and stand with my teammates when challenged by others as long as I don't have to compromise our principles.
52. I attend and participate actively and positively in team and organizational activities.
53. I attend and participate actively and positively in team meetings.
54. I attend and actively listen to organizational messages delivered by our leadership team.
55. I follow company policies and procedures.
56. I tactfully and appropriately help my leader monitor the compliance of others relative to company policies and procedures.

57. I have been trained on my organization's peer interview process and help my leader select new team members when needed.
58. I speak positively to others about my teammates, our leadership, and our organization.
59. When I encounter others gossiping, I ignore them and walk away.
60. When I encounter others gossiping, I approach them and politely and tactfully ask them to stop.

Growth Pillar—Resilience

61. I remain positive, focused, flexible, organized, and proactive through change.
62. I aggressively initiate positive changes.
63. I help others be successful and effective through team and organizational changes.
64. I am an active, positive contributor on organizational change teams.
65. I effectively lead organizational change teams.

Growth Pillar—Innovation

66. I actively and aggressively initiate action to personally improve my performance and grow in my career.
67. I am a passionate, constant learner.
68. I help others learn and grow in their performances and careers.
69. I complete the expected amount of continual learning requirements for my job role.
70. I find new and better ways to do my work.
71. I present and implement ideas to help others on my team improve their quality of work and service to our guests.

72. I am an active, positive contributor on continuous improvement teams.
73. I effectively lead continuous improvement teams.

Finance Pillar—Efficiency

74. I am productive and efficient in my work.
75. I help others become more productive and efficient in their work.
76. When I am on the clock, I work.
77. When I see others wasting time on the job, I approach them and tactfully encourage them to get back to work.
78. I am a good steward of the materials, supplies, and equipment entrusted to me.
79. When I see others wasting materials and supplies, I approach them and tactfully encourage them to be more responsible.
80. I handle company money and property with integrity and accuracy.
81. When I become aware that someone has mishandled company money or property, I notify my leader or corporate compliance department.

Appendix D
Periodic Summary Discussion Worksheet
(from chapter 15)

Use this worksheet as a guide for your periodic summary discussion. The gold standard is to conduct a periodic summary review at least once per quarter with each individual who reports to you. Leaders of leaders should use this worksheet quarterly in conjunction with the Leader's Monthly Meeting Guide (Appendix G).

Let's Look Back

1. How do you feel about your performance for the past period?
2. What do you feel are your greatest accomplishments this past performance period?
3. What do you feel is your greatest opportunity for improvement in your performance?
4. What have you learned during this past performance period?
5. Please prepare your responses to the following questions and be prepared to discuss any areas of concern you have (from the Gallup Q12, www.gallup.com).

    a. Do I know what's expected of me at work?
    b. Do I have the materials and equipment I need to do my work right?
    c. At work, do I have the opportunity to do what I do best every day?
    d. In the last seven days, have I received recognition or praise for doing good work?
    e. Does my supervisor, or someone at work, seem to care about me as a person?
    f. Is there someone at work who encourages my development?

g. At work, do my opinions seem to count?
h. Does the mission/purpose of my organization and team make me feel my job is important?
i. Are my coworkers committed to doing quality work?
j. Do I have a best friend at work I can confide in?
k. In the last six months, has someone at work talked to me about my progress?
l. This last year, have I had opportunities at work to learn, grow, and improve?

General Comments:

Let's Assess

At this point, we'll discuss your performance on the eight behavior outcomes and come to agreement on the measurements.
- Be prepared to discuss your measurements using your self-assessment form with the eight behavior outcomes supported by evidence of performance for anything rated other than Level 3, fully successful.
    - What, if anything, has changed in your performance since the last periodic summary discussion? If nothing has changed, the assessment will be the same as last time. If anything has changed, be prepared to support the change with evidence from the standards and guidelines.
- How would you summarize your performance for the past period?
- Do you fully understand what you're doing well and what you need to improve upon?
- Do you have any other questions about your performance this past period?

Let's Look Forward

1. What changes would you like to see in your role over the coming period?
2. Is there anything you would like to do at work that you don't currently have the opportunity to do?
3. What do you need from me, as your supervisor, that you're not currently getting?
4. What can I, as your supervisor, do over the next period to help you succeed at work?
5. What contributions, accomplishments, or improvements are you planning for the coming performance period? Please be specific, stating the action and the target completion date.
6. Is there anything else you'd like to discuss about your performance before we adjourn?

Our next summary discussion will occur on _____ (enter target date).

Appendix E
Ninety-Day Orientation Checklist
(from chapter 17)

1. **Before the new team member starts:**
   a. Prepare the team for their arrival.
   b. Assign and prepare the mentor.
   c. Send a welcome note to the new team member's home signed by all team members.
   d. Send a letter from the leader welcoming them to the team and reviewing key first day information, such as what to wear, where to park, what time to arrive, where to go, and who will be there to greet them. If budget allows, send a nice bouquet of flowers or a nice houseplant with the letter.
   e. Have the leader or mentor call them on the business day before their start date to welcome them, review the information in the leader letter, and ask if they have any questions.
   f. Prepare their workspace with all supplies, equipment, and resources required, such as phone, computer, and office furniture.

2. **During the first week:**
   a. Make sure a team member is present prior to their arrival on the morning of their first day to greet them. This should be someone from the team they've already met and whose face they will recognize.
   b. If they will be attending a formal orientation process, arrange for a team member to have lunch with them one day during the orientation. It would be best if this is the team leader or mentor, but any key team member who is a strong, positive role model will do.

c. Send a short, handwritten note to their home, letting them know you're excited about them joining the team. (A note to the home is a powerful communication tool that communicates care for the new team member and makes a strong, positive impression on all family members in the household.)
d. Schedule and conduct a meeting with the team leader and mentor. This is the first meeting of the thirteen-week meeting format referenced in chapter 15. This should be an informal get-to-know-you type interaction to create a plan for the thirteen weekly meetings to follow. During the session, be sure to say something like this:
   i. "Tom, as team leader, it's my responsibility to help you understand what's expected of you and how it is to be measured, and to provide you feedback on a regular basis about your performance. I'm sure most of that feedback will be positive, but as you know, there may come a time when I'll have to talk to you about performance that may not be exactly what is needed. Sometimes, that type of conversation can be uncomfortable for us both. To help prepare for that, would you please let me know how you'd like me to approach you in a situation like that?"
   ii. At this point, Tom is probably speechless because the likelihood is that no one has ever asked him this question before. If that happens, give him a few minutes of silence to think about it and then say:
      1. "I understand if that's a difficult question to answer. Let me tell you how I'd like you to approach me if

you notice me doing anything contrary to what I'm committed to do. Maybe that will help. If you see me behaving in a way that doesn't make sense to you or appears to be contradictory to our agreed-upon principles and standards, I would appreciate it if you would give me a sentence of preparation before you dive in to the comments. Remind me about this conversation we're having right now and let me know that you've observed something you need to share with me. That will give me a chance to prepare myself for what's coming and then I'll be in a better place to receive it."

    iii. Note: This is a critical accountability conversation that will set you up for the daily encounters you will have in which you need to address incorrect behaviors or coach to higher performance. It paves the way for that potentially difficult and uncomfortable conversation and creates the expectation that it's bound to occur sooner or later.

  e. Have the mentor ensure the new team member gets settled in, meets all the other team members, and completes the orientation checklist for week one.

3. **During the first ninety days:**
   a. Have the mentor meet with the new team member once per week to assess progress and answer questions.

b. Have the leader meet with the mentor and new team member once per month for the same reason.
   c. Have different team members have lunch with them at different times to begin building relationships.
   d. Rotate them through the different areas of the team to familiarize them with each function, role, and the people of each area.
   e. Introduce them to different shifts (if applicable).
   f. Introduce them to each team member so they can understand what they do and how they need to interact with them.
   g. Reinforce good behaviors noticed with positive affirmations and encouragement and address areas of concern when observed.
   h. Manage up other team members, their mentor, the team leader, other teams, and the organization as a whole with the goal of positively reinforcing their decision to join this team and organization.

4. **At the end of ninety days:**
   a. Conduct the first periodic summary discussion. Have the new team member assess themselves against the eight behavior outcomes. Use this as an opportunity to improve mutual understanding of what's expected and how it is to be measured.
   b. Set up a schedule for continued communication—once per week, once per month, once per quarter, etc. Be flexible to do what's needed for both of you to continue building a strong working relationship.
   c. Celebrate the completion of the first ninety days in an appropriate way. Take them to lunch, celebrate with the team, welcome them officially to the team, etc.

Appendix F
Orientation Weekly Meeting Guide
(from chapter 17)

Team Leader/Mentor: Meet separately with the new team member once per week during the first ninety days to effectively prepare them for their role on the team. The leader's focus is connection to the team, and the mentor's focus is connection to the job. The leader will oversee the orientation process, and the mentor will coordinate on-the-job training activities, ensuring competency and skill development. Use the questions below to guide your weekly discussions. Meet with the leader, mentor, and new team member at weeks four, eight, and thirteen.

1. How are you doing so far?
    - Review the schedule and any key concerns
2. What issues exist that I can help you with?
    - Capture any actions planned forward
3. Review key orientation material from the orientation checklist and guide.
    - Recap what was learned in the previous week
    - Recap planned activity for the coming week
4. What else do you need from me to be successful in your role?
5. Review and prepare for next week's meeting.

Week 1: The setup; mentor present. Create a plan for the first ninety days, establish goals, and clarify the mentor relationship. Review the expectations of the new team member for the orientation period.

> *Suggestion*: Have the new team member complete a Team Member Profile (see website) and share it at the next team meeting. Have all team members share

their profiles as well and use it as a team-building exercise with the new team member.

Week 2: Review and discuss the *organization* history, mission, vision, principles, standards, a general overview of the team member's role on the team, and key team safety issues.

Week 3: Review and discuss the *team's* history, mission, vision, values, standards, and the specific duties of the team member.

Week 4: Mentor present. Review progress on job specific competencies and issues. Review and discuss nonnegotiable principles and standards of behavior for the organization and the team. Conduct and process the thirty-day evaluation (see website).

Week 5: Review and discuss an overview of the evaluation process (how the team member's performance will be measured against organization and team standards) Discuss the eight behavior outcomes, how they are rated, how often you will have performance discussions, and what you expect from the new team member in the assessment process.

Week 6: Review and discuss quality pillar behavior outcomes of competence and accuracy. Ask the team member to provide evidence of behaviors observed in themselves or others recently that demonstrate these behavior outcomes. Connect specific aspects of their job role to these behavior outcomes and discuss how they are measured in your team.

Week 7: Review and discuss service pillar behavior outcomes of relationship and availability. Ask the team member to provide evidence of behaviors observed in themselves or others recently that demonstrate these behavior outcomes. Connect specific aspects of their job role to these behavior outcomes and discuss how they are measured in your team.

Week 8: Mentor present. Review progress on competencies and orientation checklist.

Week 9: Review and discuss the people pillar behavior outcome of teamwork. Ask the team member to provide evidence of behaviors observed in themselves or others recently that demonstrate these behavior outcomes. Connect specific aspects of their job roles to these behavior outcomes and discuss how they are measured for your team.

Week 10: Review and discuss growth pillar outcomes of resilience and innovation. Ask the team member to provide evidence of behaviors observed in themselves or others recently that demonstrate these behavior outcomes. Connect specific aspects of their job roles to these behavior outcomes and discuss how they are measured for your team.

Week 11: Review and discuss the finance pillar outcome of efficiency. Ask the team member to provide evidence of behaviors observed in themselves or others recently that demonstrate these behavior outcomes. Connect specific aspects of their job roles to these behavior outcomes and discuss how they are measured for your team. Ask the team member to prepare a self-assessment of their performance for the first twelve weeks over the next week and for discussion at the next meeting.

Week 12: Use the team member's self-evaluation for discussion about his or her performance and how it's measured (see website for example). Review the entire performance evaluation process and clear up any questions, misconceptions, or concerns the team member has about what's expected and how it will be measured. Prepare and process all ninety-day items.

Week 13: Conduct and process the ninety-day evaluation. (This is the first periodic summary discussion of the P^4 Performance Process.)

Appendix G
The Leader's Monthly Meeting Guide
(from chapter 17)

Purpose: To build trust, maintain focus, ensure alignment, and develop accountability

Method: Meet one-on-one with each direct report once per month

(At our one-on-one meeting, bring information and be prepared to address the following items.)

Personal: How are you doing?

Quality: Wins and challenges, goal progress (monthly report card, ninety-day action plan), safety record

Service: Wins and challenges, goal progress (monthly report card, ninety-day action plan), guest satisfaction measures/feedback

People: Wins and challenges, goal progress (monthly report card, ninety-day action plan), turnover rate, driver/doer/dragger status, rounding logs, thank-you notes, engagement results/issues

Growth: Wins and challenges, goal progress (monthly report card, ninety-day action plan), volumes, new services, markets, products, etc.

Finance: Wins and challenges, goal progress (monthly report card, ninety-day action plan), overtime, labor stats actual versus budget, revenue, and expenses

Feedback: What's going well in your team?
Is there anyone I need to recognize?
Do you have the tools you need to do your job?
What systems or processes can work better?
Is there anything you're aware of that would prevent our customers/guests from receiving excellent products or services?
What do you need my help with to meet your goals?

Development: Review learning requirements and progress from leadership development sessions

Schedule: Review upcoming month's schedule and support needs, if any. Agree on the date of the next monthly meeting.

BIBLIOGRAPHY

American Management Association Study. *Leading into the Future.* New York: American Management Association, 2005.

Anderson, Peggy. *Great Quotes from Great Leaders.* Naperville, IL: Simple Truths, LLC, 2007.

Bacon, Terry R. *Balanced Leaders Balance To Be Effective.* Baptist Health Care Leadership Institute Publication, April, 2006 issue, p 17, 2006.

Barrett, David A. *Leadership Perspective: Cultivate Both Character And Competence.* Baptist Health Care Leadership Institute Publication, April, 2006 issue, p 10, 2006.

Beck, Glenn. *Broke: The Plan to Restore Our Trust, Truth, and Treasure.* New York: Simon and Schuster, Inc., 2010.

Bell, Chip R. and Patterson, John R. *Leaders as Bridge Builders.* Baptist Health Care Leadership Institute Publication, April, 2006 issue, p 14, 2006.

Blanchard, Ken. *The Simple Truths of Service.* Blanchard Family Partnership, 2005.

Blanchard, Ken and Barrett, Colleen. *Lead with Luv.* Saddle River, NJ: FT Press, 2011.

Blanchard, Ken et al. *Leadership by the Book.* New York: William Morrow and Company., 1999.

Blanchard, Ken and Hodges, Phil. *Lead Like Jesus.* Nashville, TN: Thomas Nelson, 2005.

Blanchard, Ken and Hodges, Phil. *The Servant Leader.* Nashville, TN: J. Countryman, 2003.

Blue Ridge HealthCare. *Standards of Behavior.* Self published, 2004.

Boone, Louis E. and Kurtz, David L. *Contemporary Business.* Mason, OH: Thomas South-Western, 2006.

Buckingham, Marcus and Coffman, Curt. *First, Break All the Rules.* New York: Simon and Schuster, 1999.

Carnegie, Dale. *How to Win Friends and Influence People.* New York: Simon and Schuster, 1981.

Caterpillar Safety Services. *Recognize It!* Caterpillar Inc.: Peoria, IL, 2006.

Chadwick, David. *The 12 Leadership Principles of Dean Smith.* New York: Total/Sports Illustrated, 1999.

Chambers, Oswald. *My Utmost for His Highest.* Westwood, NJ: Barbour and Company, Inc., 1935.

Child abuse, http://www.acf.hhs.gov

Cocklereece, Dr. Tim. *Simple Discipleship.* St. Charles, IL: ChurchSmart Resources, 2009.

Collins, Jim. *Good to Great.* New York: HarperCollins, 2001.

Collins, Jim. *Aligning with Vision and Values.* Baptist Health Care Leadership Institute Publication, April, 2006 issue, p 6, 2006.

Collins, Jim and Porras, Jerry. *Built to Last: Successful Habits of Visionary Companies.* New York: HarperCollins, 1994.

Conner, Daryl R. *Managing at the Speed of Change.* New York: Random House, 1992.

Connors, Roger et al. *The Oz Principle.* New York: Penguin Group, 2004.

Constitution of the United States, the 9th Edition. New York: Harper and Row, 1996.

Covey, Stephen M.R. *The Speed of Trust.* New York: Free Press, 2006.

Covey, Stephen R. *The 7 Habits of Highly Effective People.* New York: Simon and Schuster, 1989.

Covey, Stephen R. *Principle-Centered Leadership.* New York: Simon and Schuster, 1991.

Covey, Stephen R. et al. *First Things First.* New York: Simon and Schuster, 1994.

Crisis counseling, http://www.crisiscounseling.com

Crouch, C. David. *Quality of Life in America Survey.* www.letsbuildexcellence.com, 2011.

Crown Ministries. *Money Map.* www.CrownMoneyMap.org

Disney. *Values Make Our Brands Stand Out.* www.corporate.disney.do.com. Retrieved November 4, 2010.

Divorce statistics, http://www.aboutdivorce.org/

Economist Intelligence Unit. *2005 Quality of life index.* http://www.economist.com/media/pdf/quality_of_life.pdf . Retrived November, 2011.

Employee engagement, http://en.wikipedia.org/wiki/Employee_engagement. Retrieved November, 2011.

Folkman, Joe. *Top 9 Leadership Behaviors That Drive Commitment.* www.zengerfolkman.com, 2010.

Fortune 100 best places to work, www.greatplacetowork.com

Gallup Surveys. www.gallup.com, Retrieved November, 2011.

Gallup-Heathway (2010). *Well-Being Index.* www.well-beingindex.com, 2010.

Goldsmith, Marshall. *Team Building or Time Wasting?* Baptist Health Care Leadership Institute Publication, April, 2006 issue, p 3, 2006.

Goleman, Daniel et al. *Primal Leadership.* Boston, MA: Harvard Business Press, 2002.

Gross, T. Scott. *Positively Outrageous Service.* New York: MasterMedia Limited, 1991.

Harvey, Eric and Lucia, Alexander. *Walk the Talk.* Dallas, TX: Performance Publishing, 2003.

Henning, Joel. *The Power of Conversations at Work.* Phoenix, AZ: Henning Showkeir and Associates, 2000.

Hamilton, Madison, and Jay. *The Federalist Papers.* New York: Penguin Group, 1961.

Hill, Napoleon. *Think and Grow Rich.* New York: Fawcett Crest, 1960.

Johnson, Spencer M.D. *The Present.* New York: Doubleday, 2003.

Johnson, Spencer M.D. *Who Moved My Cheese?* New York: G.P. Putnam's Sons, 1998.

Kabachnick, Terry. *I Quit But Forgot to Tell You.* Dallas, TX: Cornerstone Leadership Institute, 2006.

Keirsey, David and Bates, Marilyn. *Please Understand Me.* Del Mar, CA: Gnoseology Books Ltd. (*Keirsey Temperament Sorter II*), 1984.

Ken Blanchard Companies. *Critical Leadership Skills in a New Business Reality.* Escondido, CA: The Ken Blanchard Companies, 2010.

Kirkpatrick, Donald. *Model for Learning Measurement.* http://www.kirkpatrickpartners.com. Retrieved November, 2011.

Kotter, John P. *A Sense of Urgency.* Boston, MA: Harvard Business Press, 2008.

Kotter, John P. and Cohen, Dan S. *The Heart of Change.* Boston, MA: Harvard Business Press, 2002.

Kouzes, James M. and Posner, Barry Z. *The Leadership Challenge.* San Francisco, CA: Jossey-Bass Publishers, 1995.

Lencioni, Patrick. *The Five Dysfunctions of a Team.* San Francisco, CA: Jossey-Bass, 2002.

Lencioni, Patrick. *Profiles in Humility.* Baptist Health Care Leadership Institute Publication, April, 2006 issue, p 7, 2006.

Lewis, Robert. *The Church of Irresistible Influence.* Grand Rapids, MI: Zondervan, 2001.

Lominger International. *The Leadership Architect Suite.* www.kornferry.com, 2011.

Maxwell, John. *Everyone Communicates, Few Connect.* Nashville, TN: Thomas Nelson, 2010.

Maxwell, John C. *The 17 Indisputable Laws of Teamwork.* Nashville, TN: Thomas Nelson Publishers, 2001.

Maxwell, John C. *The 21 Irrefutable Laws of Leadership.* Nashville, TN: Thomas Nelson Publishers, 1998.

Maxwell, John C. *Today Matters*. New York: Warner Faith, 2004.
MacArthur, John. *The Master's Plan for the Church*. Chicago: Moody Press, 1991.
MacArthur, John. *The Book on Leadership*. Nashville, TN: Thomas Nelson, Inc., 2004.
Miller, John G. *QBQ, The Question Behind the Question. Practicing Personal Accountability in Work and in Life*. New York: G.P. Putnam's Sons, 1997.
National Coalition for the Homeless. Retrieved Nov. 2011 from www.nationalhomeless.org/factsheets/How_Many.pdf, 2009.
Nation Master. *As referenced in the text*. www.nationmaster.com. Retrieved November, 2011.
NIV Study Bible. Grand Rapids, MI: Zondervan, 2002.
Northouse, Peter G. *Leadership Theory and Practice*. Thousand Oaks, CA: Sage Publications, 2004.
Patterson, Kerry et al. *Crucial Conversations*. New York: McGraw Hill, 2002.
Patterson, Kerry et al. *Influencer*. New York: McGraw-Hill, 2008.
Payne, Thomas. *Common Sense*. New York: Penguin Group, 1969.
Peters, Thomas J. *In Search of Excellence*. New York: Harper and Row, 1982.
Petersen, Dr. Dan. *Authentic Involvement*. National Safety Council, 2001.
Pink, Daniel H. *Drive: The Surprising Truth about What Motivates Us*. New York: The Penguin Group, 2009.
Ramsey, Dave. *Financial Peace*. www.daveramsey.com.
Ritz-Carlton. *Service Values*. www.corporate.ritzcarlton.com. Retrieved November 4, 2010.
Rasmussen Reports. www.rasmussenreports.com. Retrieved November, 2011.
Rath, Tom. *StrengthsFinder 2.0*. New York: Gallup Press, 2007.
Rees, Erik. *S.H.A.P.E., Finding and Fulfilling Your Unique Purpose for Life*. Grand Rapids, MI: Zondervan, 2006.

Salary.com. *Performance Review Survey.* www.salary.com, 2006.

Sanborn, Mark. *The Fred Factor.* New York: Doubleday, 2004.

Savage, Candace. *Eagles of North America.* Minocqua, WI: NorthWord Press, 1987.

Scholtes, Peter R. *The Leader's Handbook.* New York: McGraw-Hill, 1998.

Schwarz, Christian A. *Natural Church Development: A Guide to Eight Essential Qualities Of Healthy Churches.* St. Charles, IL: ChurchSmart Resources, 2003.

Shula, Don And Blanchard, Ken. *Everyone's a Coach.* New York: Harper Business, 1995.

Social Science Research Council. The Human Development Report. www.measureofamerica.org, 2011.

Stogdill, R. M. "*Personal Factors Associated With Leadership: A Survey of the Literature.*" Journal Of Psychology. 25: 35—71, 1948.

Studer, Quint. *Hardwiring Excellence.* Gulf Breeze, FL: Firestarter Publishing, 2003.

Studer, Quint. *Results That Last.* Hoboken, NJ: John Wiley And Sons, 2008.

Switzler, Al. *Leader-Led Training.* Baptist Health Care Leadership Institute Publication, April, 2006 Issue, p. 12, 2006.

Wagner, C. Peter. *Your Spiritual Gifts.* Ventura, CA: Regal Books, 2005.

Walton, Mary. *The Deming Management Method.* New York: Dodd, Mead, 1986.

Warren, Rick. *The Purpose Driven Church.* Grand Rapids, MI: Zondervan, 1995.

Warren, Rick. *The Purpose Driven Life.* Grand Rapids, MI: Zondervan, 2002.

Webster's New World College Dictionary, 4th Edition. Cleveland, OH: Wiley Publishing, 2004.

Wikipedia. *As referenced in the text.* www.wikipedia.com

Zenger, John H. And Folkman, Joseph. *The Extraordinary Leader.* New York: McGraw-Hill, 2002.

Ziglar, Zig. *See You At The Top.* Carrollton, TX: Pelican Publishing, 1977.

For more resources on creating the excellent experience, visit my website: www.excellentexperiencebook.com.

INDEX

accountability, 33, 250, 358
  Achilles heel, 365
  drivers, doers, and draggers, 361
  the four steps of, 360
  the three moments of truth, 361
accuracy, 283, 438
Adams, John, 384
Aflac, 185
algorithmic work, 274
alignment, 39, 235, 241, 248
Amazon.com, 140
American Bankruptcy Institute, 212
American Express, 185
American Management Association, 343
American Revolution, 383
Anderson, Peggy, 338
Aristotle, 9
Articles of Confederation, 380
Atlanta, Georgia, 153, 207
attitude, 54
availability, 285, 439
Avery, Ellen, 167
Bailey, Kathy, 212
balanced clarity of focus, 230
bald eagle, North American, 82
Baldoni, John, 336
bankruptcy, 212
Baptist Health South Florida, 186
Barker, Joel, 82

Barnes and Noble, 140
Bates, Marilyn, 373
Beck, Glenn, 228
Bedford Falls, 85
Belton, Ben, 154, 160
Benjamin's Clothing Store, 153
Bennigan's Restaurant, 207
Best Buy, 227
Blake and Mouton, 343
Blanchard, Ken, 12, 68, 78, 111, 130, 287, 343, 366
Blue Ridge HealthCare, 51, 70, 84, 101, 117, 143, 162, 165, 166, 315
blueprint for excellence, 41, 312
  church, 324
  country, 404
  family, 328
  individual, 332
  organization, 315
  team, 321
Boone & Kurtz, 312
Boston Consulting Group, 185
Boy Scouts, 217
Briggs, Katherine Cook, 373
Buckingham, Marcus, 12, 175, 187, 277, 343
budget, 225
Bush, George W., 212
Camden Property Trust, 185
capitalism, 212
Caribbean Islands, 382
Carlyle, Thomas, 64
CarMax, 185

Carnegie, Dale, 206, 343
Cary, North Carolina, 186
Caterpillar Safety Services, 299
Chambers, Oswald, 12, 79
change, 73, 194
Chevrolet, 139
Chrysler, 139
Churchill, Winston, 338
citizen engagement, 403
Cocklereece, Dr. Tom, 125
Coffman, Curt, 277
Colgate Palmolive, 185
Collins and Porras, 99
Collins, Jim, 12, 29, 47, 85, 220, 343, 392
   Collins & Porras, 84
Columbus, Christopher, 382
commitment
   continuum, 184
   team member, 182
communication, 49, 182, 281, 299, 347
   difficult conversations, 300
   trust model, 348
competence, 283, 437
Connecticut, 186
Conner, Daryl, 12, 73, 194, 197, 290, 343
Connors, Smith and Hickman, 357
Constitutional Convention, 382, 417
Continental Congress, 384
Coral Gables, Florida, 186
core ideology, 47
Covey, Stephen, 12, 31, 78, 209, 343, 346

Covey, Stephen M.R., 9, 12, 39, 287, 346, 348
Crane, Tim, 185
Crim, Dan, 182
Crouch, Callie, 12, 172
Crouch, Debbie, 11, 172, 226
Crouch, Isaac, 12, 172, 203
Crouch, Jane, 11
Crouch, Jr., Clarence, 7, 11, 207, 354
Crouch, Ron, 12
Crouch, Samuel, 12, 172
Crown Ministries Money Map, 224
Culbert, Samuel, 279
culture, 181, 364
CVS Pharmacy, 220
Darwin, Charles, 194
debt financing, 223
Declaration of Independence, 380, 384
Deming, W. Edwards, 137, 279, 284
dependability, 351
development, 195
DISC personality profile instrument, 281, 373
Disney, 25, 50, 64, 101, 112, 119, 137, 143, 159, 163, 165, 207, 217
Disney, Walt, 338
divorce rate, 190
DNA of Trust model, 351
DreamWorks Animation, 185
drivers, doers and draggers, 360
   characteristics of, 362
Dungy, Tony, 343

Edward Jones, 185
efficiency, 216, 290, 442
eight behavior outcomes, 282
Einstein, Albert, 25, 338
Embassy Suites, 159
employee engagement, 185
  federal government, 403
employee turnover, 181, 186
encouragement, 302
environment
  airline. *See* Southwest Airlines
  banking, 156, 217
  church, 72, 89, 106, 122, 146, 170, 188, 201, 221, 324
  country, 367, 378
  entertainment. *See* Disney
  family, 52, 75, 92, 106, 126, 148, 171, 189, 203, 223, 328, 354
  government, Chapter 18, 381
  healthcare, 28, 70, 84, 101, 117, 138, 143, 158, 162, 167, 176, 244, 251, 315
  hospitality. *See* Ritz-Carlton, Embassy Suites
  individual, 78, 93, 108, 130, 149, 173, 191, 205, 227, 332
  manufacturing, 245, 252, 256, 261, 264, 266, 349
  nonprofit. *See* Boy Scouts, Girl Scouts, Red Cross, United Way
  organization, 69, 84, 100, 117, 139, 165, 185, 198, 217, 315

retail. *See* Benjamin's Clothing Store, Best Buy, Men's Warehouse, Walmart
  software. *See* Google, SAS
  team, 71, 86, 104, 121, 144, 168, 175, 187, 199, 219, 321
excellence, 56
  definition of, 56
  synonyms for, 56
excellent teen model, 203
excellentology, 23, 26
  excellentologist, 15, 24, 26, 41, 432
  principles of, 40
federal government, 401
Federalist Papers, 380
FedEx, 185
feedback, five characteristics of, 299
flywheel effect, 85
Ford Motor Company, 139, 220
Ford, Henry, 338
foundation of excellence, 33, 47, 132
Fox News, 205
Franklin, Benjamin, 338, 378, 384
frugality, 216
Gallup, 187, 277, 304, 370, 379, 402
  StrengthsFinder, 281, 370, 371
Gandhi, 269, 338, 368
Gates, Bill, 340
GDP, 404, 421
General Mills, 185

Girl Scouts, 337
goal setting, 40
    annual planning, 240, 249
    bhag goal, 84
    guidelines, 238
    SMART goals, 236, 241
    tactics, 246
Godspell, 21
Goodnight, Jim, 186
Google, 185, 370
Grace Hospital, 167
Grady, Ed, 7, 21
Great Place to Work Institute, 185
Greenville, South Carolina, 207
Griffith, Andy, 85
Gross, T. Scott, 287
H.E.A.R.T. service recovery, 162
hedgehog principle, 220
Henning, Joel, 49, 55
heuristic work, 274
high performer, 288
Hill, Napoleon, 12, 69, 88, 206, 343
Hodges, Phil, 68, 111, 130
Hollywood, Florida, 32
Honda, 139, 141
House of Excellence, 25, 39, 136, 235, 312, 369, 426
Houston, Texas, 186
HR DNA. *See* DNA of Trust
humility, 30, 356
Huntsville, Alabama, 207
Hybels, Bill, 68, 111
hypocrisy, 37, 100, 112, 116, 218, 250, 353
immigration rates, 403

innovation, 196, 290, 442
integrity, 352
intrinsic motivation, 275
Jamestown, Virginia, 382
Jefferson, Thomas, 338, 378, 384
Jesus Christ, 13, 74, 90, 94, 107, 122, 130, 170, 262, 324, 366
Johnson, M.D., Spencer, 94, 286
Johnson, Tim, 72, 89
Journal of Psychology, 339
Juran, Dr. Joseph M., 346
Kabachnick, Terri, 113
Katz, R.L., 343
Keirsey, David, 373
Keller, Helen, 21, 338
Kennedy, John F., 338
Kettering, Charles F., 348
Keynes, John Maynard, 215
Keynesian Economics, 214
King George III of England, 385
King, Dr. Martin Luther, 338, 368
Kirkpatrick and Locke, 343
Kotter, John, 343
Kouzes and Posner, 37
Krzyzewski, Mike, 343
Laing, Kathy, 12
Lane, Ralph, 153
language
    of excellence, 33, 49, 55
    of mediocrity, 60
Lao-Tzu, Chinese philosopher, 336
Lawrence, Jackie, 12
LC3 corporation, 214
leader vs. manager, 342

leader's role, 35, 68, 99, 112, 278, 280, 337
leadership, 189, 339
Lencioni, Patrick, 12, 287
Lewis, Robert, 72
Lincoln, Abraham, 338, 378
Lindsey, Hal, 97
Livingston, Robert, 384
Lombardi, Vince, 338, 343
loyalty, 155, 352
Lyons, Beverly, 12
Lyons, Dr. David, 12, 76
MacArthur, Douglas, 338
MacArthur, John, 72
Machiavelli, 194
Malcolm-Baldridge National Quality Award, 51, 113
managing up, 54, 61
Mandela, Nelson, 338
Mandino, Og, 206
Mann, R.D., 343
Marriott, 185
Marston, Dr. William Moulton, 373
mastermind group, 69, 73, 86, 100
Matel, 185
Maxwell, John, 12, 36, 97, 112, 287, 343, 348, 366
Mayberry, 85
Mayo Clinic, 185
McGimsey, Rick, 12
measurements, 235
   finance, 219
   growth, 198
   individual scorecard, 269
   organization scorecard, 241

   people, 181
   quality, 142
   rating scale, 237
   scorecard, 236
   service, 166
   team scorecard, 240
   weights, 238
Meir, Golda, 338
Men's Warehouse, 185
Mercedes Benz, 218
Meyer, Joyce, 13
Microsoft, 185
mission, 34, 64
money, 213, 217, 221
Morganton, North Carolina, 167, 208, 315, 324
Mother Theresa, 338, 340, 368
MSN Money, 215
Mull, Carrie, 12, 175
MVP Self-Assessment, 445
MVP'S (*most valuable players*), 34, 192
Myers, Isabel Briggs, 373
Myers-Briggs personality profile instrument (MBTI), 66, 281, 373
Nation Master, 403
Natural Church Development, 146
   eight quality characteristics, 146
NetApp, 185
new employee orientation, 175
   leader's monthly meeting guide, 463
   ninety day checklist, 361, 455
   weekly meeting guide, 459

Nissan, 139
Nixon, Richard, 217
Nordstrom, 185
North Carolina State Employees Credit Union, 157
Northouse, Peter, 339, 343
Nugget Market, 185
O'Reilly, Bill, 205
Oak Hill United Methodist Church, 202, 324
Optimist Club, 217
Orlando, Florida, 163
P⁴ Performance Process, 279
   stage 1—perpetual shared understanding, 280
   stage 2—pay attention daily, 298, 362
   stage 3—periodic summary discussion, 303, 365, 451
   stage 4—performance alignment, 304
Paine, Thomas, 381
Pareto Principle of Leadership Excellence, 345
Pareto, Vilfredo, 346
passion, 366
Patterson, Kerry et al, 288, 303
Patterson, New Jersey, 340
Pensacola, Florida, 360
performance evaluation, 269
   behavior outcomes, 277, 282
   five levels of, 296
   general guidelines, 298
   guidelines for individual measurement, 437
Performance Review Survey, Salary.com 2006, 270

Peter Principle, 32
Peters, Tom, 343
Petersen, Dr. Dan, 360
Pfizer, 137
Philadelphia, Pennsylvania, 382
pillar team process, 242
pillars of performance, 39, 135
   finance, 212, 263
   growth, 194, 260
   people, 175, 258
   quality, 137, 251
   service, 153, 255
Pink, Daniel, 213, 274, 276, 279
Plymouth, Massachusetts, 382
Ponce de León, 382
Poore, Jake, 153
Pope John Paul II, 338
principles, 36, 97, 384
priority for action, 230
productivity. *See* efficiency
profit, 219
Qualcomm, 185
Quality of Life Survey 2011, 270, 380, 400
Ramsey, Dave, 228
Rasmussen Reports, 379, 402
Reagan, Ronald, 64, 338, 367
Red Cross, 217
relationship, 285, 337, 438
resilience, 197, 289, 441
   continuum, 197
Ritz-Carlton, 25, 51, 103, 120, 137, 143, 165
Roman Empire, 379
Roosevelt, Eleanor, 338
Roosevelt, Franklin D., 135, 215, 338

Roosevelt, Theodore, 21
Sacco, Frank, 32
Sanborn, Mark, 157, 287
SAS Software Company, 185
Satey, Phil, 75
Scholtes, Peter, 270, 273, 279
Schwartz, Charles, 73
Schwarz, Christian A., 146
Schweitzer, Albert, 358
Seijts, Gerard, 182
September 11, 2001, 212, 340
service
    AIDET, 165
    CARE model of service excellence, 161
    four types of guests, 160
    good service, 158, 159
    indifferent service, 157
    service failure, 156
    service recovery, 162, 357
    terrible service, 156
    The Ellen Avery Effect, 167
    The Fred Factor, 157
    the navy blue blazer, 153
    the WOW factor, 163
SHAPE, 262, 370
Sherman, Roger, 384
Shula, Don, 343
Smith, Dean, 343
socialism, 213
Southwest Airlines, 25, 137, 217
standards of behavior, 37, 111, 394
Starbucks Coffee, 185
Statistical Abstract of the United States and Federal Election Commission, 403

Stew Leonard's, 185
stewardship, 216, 221
Stogdill, R.M., 339, 343
strategic plan. *See* House of Excellence
strategic planning, 312
Studer Group, 165, 360
Studer, Quint, 37, 235, 248
Summit, Pat, 343
SWOT, 314
teamwork, 287, 440
Thatcher, Margaret, 338
Thompson, Robb, 287
Thoreau, Henry David, 28
tithing, 221
topping out ceremony, 311
Toyota, 25, 137, 217, 271
trust, 33, 228, 346
U.S. Congress, 196, 217, 379, 402
U.S. Constitution, 380, 394
    Preamble, 382, 387
U.S. Department of Health & Human Services, 191
U.S. Merit Systems Protection Board, 403
U.S. Supreme Court, 402
UCLA Bruins, 250
Ulrich, David, 279, 343
United States of America
    blueprint for excellence, 405
    current state summary, 413
    mission, 382
    pillar measurements, 398
    principles, 384
    recommendations, 416

resources for measurements, 429
standards, 394
SWOT, 410
vision, 383
United Way, 199, 217
University of North Carolina at Chapel Hill, 206
vision, 35, 83
Wagner Modified Houts Questionnaire, 371
Wagner, Peter, 371
Wall Street, 217
Walmart, 138, 217, 220
Walt Disney World, 163
Walton, Sam, 338
Warren, Rick, 13, 72, 74, 79, 170, 202, 248, 370
Washington, Booker T., 338
Washington, George, 340, 378
Wegmans, 185
Welch, Jack, 175
Wesley, John, 212
Weston, Liz Pulliam, 215
Wood, Kenneth W., 95, 194
Wooden, John, 250, 338, 343
World Trade Center, 212, 340
Ziglar, Zig, 12, 78, 82, 94, 100, 195, 206, 221, 241, 312, 343, 358, 370
quality of life areas, 149
Zimmer, George, 186